MW00576297

THE QUOTABLE JUNG

THE QUOTABLE

JUNG

COLLECTED AND EDITED BY
JUDITH R. HARRIS

WITH THE COLLABORATION OF
TONY WOOLFSON

PRINCETON UNIVERSITY PRESS
PRINCETON, NEW JERSEY

Copyright © 2016 by Princeton University Press
Published by Princeton University Press,
41 William Street, Princeton, New Jersey 08540

press.princeton.edu

Jacket photograph © Douglas Glass/Paul Popper/Popperfoto/Getty Images

Library of Congress Cataloging-in-Publication Data

The quotable Jung / collected and edited by Judith R. Harris with
the collaboration of Tony Woolfson. — Hardcover Edition.
pages cm
Includes bibliographical references and index.
ISBN 978-0-691-15559-3 (hardback)
1. Jung, C. G. (Carl Gustav), 1875–1961. 2. Jungian psychology.
I. Harris, Judith, editor. II. Woolfson, Tony, editor.
III. Jung, C. G. (Carl Gustav), 1875–1961.
BF315.Q86 2015
150.19′54—dc23
2015008350

This book has been composed in Minion Pro text with ITC Kabel Std. display.

Printed on acid-free paper. ∞

Printed in the United States of America

1 3 5 7 9 10 8 6 4 2

I dedicate this book to the spirit of C. G. Jung

Contents

Preface

In the early 1970s in Boston, Massachusetts, I met up with a friend for lunch, as we often did between practice sessions. We were both studying and preparing for careers in piano performance, and we had many a conversation about the true nature of the creative process. On this particular cold and rainy day, which has stuck in my memory for more than forty years, my friend appeared with a gift for me, a book he had found in a secondhand bookstore and which he insisted I read immediately—*Memories, Dreams, Reflections* by Carl Gustav Jung.

I was twenty years old at the time, and, like many of us who have entered the world of the unconscious as Jung had done, this was my first encounter with his work. In my teens I had avidly read many of Freud's works, as well as Horney, Rogers, Erickson, and others, but nothing compared to the impact of Jung's memoirs given to me on that fateful day in Boston all those years ago.

Not long afterward, I read Jung's Commentary to *The Secret of the Golden Flower*, which sparked my interest in yoga and the psyche-body connection. Almost twenty years later, I moved to Zürich and began my training at the C. G. Jung Institute in Küsnacht, where I graduated as a Jungian analyst in 1999.

Like many of us, I had long been searching for a spiritual dimension through which to find a deeper meaning in my life. Having lived in the artistic world, I had been trying to understand how men and women like J. S. Bach, Vincent Van Gogh, and Virginia Woolf had been able to enter into seemingly mysterious places. All I could come up with was the realization that something bigger and greater lay behind and within these creative geniuses. I remained bewildered until I read *Memories, Dreams, Reflections* and then I began to find my way.

Jung was addressing the same questions I had been wrestling with all my life. Is there a God? And. if so, what about the apparently tragic events that occur in the course of a lifetime? Is it possible to find meaning in suffering?

From the very beginning of my discovery of Jung, I began to record my dreams and note down certain passages in Jung's works that held a special meaning for me and to which I felt I might want to return at different points in my life. Slowly, over the years, my own concordance of quotes from various volumes of Jung began to emerge, and later on this evolved further into an extensive compendium of quotes from the collected works, the seminars, the letters, his memoirs, and other smaller works. This compendium not only provided a never-ending source of material for my own teaching and writing, but it also enriched many an analytic hour in my own practice. Most important of all, keeping a record of these significant passages brought a much greater depth to my understanding of the wisdom of C. G. Jung. By the time the idea for *The Quotable Jung* emerged, I had already compiled well over five hundred computer files on different topics, all of which could be found in Jung's works.

Fred Appel of Princeton University Press came down to *The Red Book Symposium* in Washington, D.C., in June 2010 and approached The Philemon Foundation[1] with the idea of doing a *Quotable Jung* to follow *The Quotable Jefferson, The Quotable Einstein, The Quotable Thoreau,* and *The Quotable Kierdegaard.*

Jolande Jacobi[2] had already compiled an anthology for the Bollingen Foundation, that was first published in 1945, a second edition of which was published by Princeton University Press in 1970, some years after Jung's death. Many more works of Jung had been published between 1945 and 1970, including six books of major importance, among them Jung's last seminal work, *Mysterium Coniunctionis*, his magnum opus concerning the fundamental problem of the opposites.

Jolande Jacobi's compilation, *Psychological Reflections*, was the single most comprehensive work of its kind for nearly half a century, and many are the readers that are indebted to her for the depth of her scholarship.

Forty-four years later, *The Quotable Jung* draws on even more newly published material, in particular, the *Visions Seminars* (two volumes), the *Nietzsche Seminars* (two volumes), *The Psychology of Kundalini Yoga*, and the *Letters* (two volumes), which all bring us much closer to the man Jung himself, especially because in those seminars and letters, Jung speaks freely and in a language that a layperson can easily understand.

To this list, we can now add *The Red Book*, published in 2009 after many years shrouded in secrecy and mystery. We are now able to follow in much greater detail Jung's own "confrontation with the unconscious" and appreciate his unequalled efforts in self-exploration, a task many of us strive to undertake for ourselves.

This volume will introduce the reader to the ideas of Carl Gustav Jung. I am sure that only a few readers will know that although for many years Sigmund Freud has been a household name for most people, a century ago Jung was by far the better known of the two, especially in the United States. This was mainly due to Jung's pioneering work on the Association Experiment, a test devised by Jung to demonstrate the reality and autonomy of unconscious complexes. To Jung we also owe an understanding of everyday terms like introverted and extraverted. Unlike Freud, who concentrated on retrieving repressed childhood memories in his patients, Jung was actually more interested in a prospective, future-oriented approach to analysis that emphasized the value of dream interpretation as the vehicle for understanding the messages of the unconscious as the guiding light of the soul.

Jung also recognized the therapeutic value of authentic, subjective religious experience, which is not necessarily to be found within the houses of worship of denominational religions but rather through the confrontation with the divine as wholly Other.

There is a widespread belief that Jung is not easy reading, and if *The Quotable Jung* can help to dispel that preconception, it will already have achieved its purpose. The breadth and depth of Jung's knowledge ranks among the highest of any civilization, spanning almost sixty years and thousands and thousands of pages. The wisdom to be found in even the necessarily abbreviated subject matter in this book should whet every reader's appetite for more. My faith is, then, that readers will find the Jung in these pages eminently readable and approachable, for he was a truly original thinker, a human being filled with kindness and compassion, and one of the greatest healers of all time.

NOTES

1. The Philemon Foundation prepares for publication previously unpublished works of C. G. Jung. Other titles from Princeton University Press in the Philemon Series (General Editor, Sonu Shamdasani) include *Analytical Psychology in Exile: The Correspondence of C. G. Jung and Erich Neumann*, edited by Martin Liebscher; *Children's Dreams: Notes of the Seminar Given in 1936–1940*, edited by Lorenz Jung, Maria Meyer-Grass; *Dream Interpretation Ancient and Modern: Notes from the Seminar Given in 1936–1941*, edited by John Peck, Lorenz Jung and Maria Meyer-Grass; *Introduction to Jungian Psychology: Notes of the Seminary on Analytical Psychology Given in 1925*, edited by William McGuire and Sonu Shamdasani; *Jung Contra Freud: The 1912 New York Lectures on the Theory of Psychoanalysis*; *The Question of Psychological Types: The Correspondence of C. G. Jung and Hans Schmid-Guisan, 1915–1916*, edited by John Beebe and Ernst Falzeder. Also in preparation is *On Psychological and Visionary Art: Notes from Jung's Lecture on Gérard de Nerval's "Aurélia"* edited by Craig Stephenson; and a comprehensive reconstruction of *Modern Psychology: Notes on the Lectures Given at the ETH Zurich, 1933–1940*, edited by Ernst Falzeder and Martin Liebscher (www.philemonfoundation.org).

2. Jolande Jacobi (1890–1973) was one of Jung's best-known students and a founding member of the C. G. Jung Institute in Zürich.

Readers of *The Quotable Jung* might be interested in knowing in more detail how I selected the quotations for this volume.

This work is actually a case study in how to make best use of the enormous potential of the modern-day computer as an incredible storage and filing system, far removed in the speed and the range of access to stored data from the little file cards so familiar to many of us hitherto accustomed to the typewriter.

About twenty-three years ago when I began my training at the C. G. Jung Institute in Küsnacht, Switzerland, I found myself drawn to the idea of assembling my own personal collection of quotations from Jung. At the same time I immediately set about figuring out how to store all the information in a simple yet useful way. Since that time I have continued to organize my "collection" of quotable material into many digital folders stored in the computer, each of which comprises even more files under various categories, such as The Unconscious, Dreams, Shadow, Active Imagination, and many others. It didn't seem to be long before I had amassed more than four hundred categories, the contents of which were often cross-referenced with each other. In effect I had already compiled a large concordance long before the idea for this book arose.

By the time I decided to take on this work, I had formulated a diagram that reveals a thread running from beginning to end, which comprises the theory and ideas of analytical psychology as conceived and developed by C. G. Jung. In other words, I have endeavored to provide the reader with a map, which he or she can use in several different ways, depending on the particular context at a given time and place.

I am sure that if a reader wants to know what Jung has to say about love, for example, he or she need only consult the index. A second stage might involve reading a particular chapter on a subject such as religion straight through from beginning to end. Other readers might choose to read the book from beginning to end following the map that I have laid out.

On the other hand, it could be tempting for the reader simply to open the book at random and read whatever appears on the page. This might be surprisingly beneficial, especially if one were grappling with some significant and vexing question.

Please note that the English translations are all copyright R.F.C. Hull, with the exception of *Memories, Dreams, Reflections* (Richard and Clara Winston), *Liber Novus: The Red Book* (Mark Kyburz, John Peck, and Sonu Shamdasani), *The Question of Psychological Types* (Ernst Falzeder with the collaboration of Tony Woolfson), and *Children's Dreams* (Ernst Falzeder with the collaboration of Tony Woolfson).

May the readers of this volume derive as much joy as I have in the study of the life and work of Carl Gustav Jung.

Acknowledgments

I am deeply appreciative of the guidance and inspiration I derived from Jolande Jacobi's anthology of Jung's writings, *Psychological Reflections*.

My profound thanks go to Sonu Shamdasani, who advised and encouraged me from beginning to end throughout the process.

In the initial stages, Dr. Anne Maguire (1921–2011) encouraged me with great enthusiasm to undertake this work.

I am also indebted to Ross Woodman (1922–2014), who was reading the first draft of the manuscript when he died. Our lengthy conversations on the spirit of Jung will always remain with me.

I thank Daryl Sharp for the warmth of his generosity; Andreas and Regine Schweizer, who understood the importance of this volume from the beginning; and Kevin Toohey, with whom I have shared Jung for many, many years.

Many thanks to Victoria Cowan for her expertise and dedication in compiling the index.

I am grateful to the members of the Board of The Foundation of the Works of C. G. Jung, in particular Ulrich Hoerni, Daniel Niehus, and Thomas Fischer, without whom this work would not be possible; the members of the Board of The Philemon Foundation, Michael Marsman, Craig Stephenson, Caterina Vezzoli, and Beverley Zabriskie, as well as our General Editor, Professor Sonu Shamdasani, in our joint endeavor in helping to bring Jung's unpublished works to light; and, in particular, to my editor at Princeton University Press, Fred Appel, for catalyzing the project and helping to keep it going thereafter.

To my husband, Tony Woolfson, who supported and aided me always with his unfailing spirit.

Zürich, April 2014.

C. G. Jung Chronology

1875   Carl Gustav Jung born on July 26 at Kesswil in Canton Thurgau, where his father, Johann Paul Achilles Jung, is parson. His mother is Emilie Jung, née Preiswerk.

1879   The family moves to Klein-Hüningen, near Basel.

1884   His sister, Gertrud, is born (dies in 1935).

1895   Jung begins medical studies at the University of Basel.

1896   His father, whose loss of religious faith the young Jung witnessed, dies.

1899   He decides to become a psychiatrist.

1900   Jung is appointed Assistant Staff Physician under Eugen Bleuler at the Burghölzli, the psychiatric hospital of the Canton of Zürich and psychiatric clinic of the University of Zürich.

1902   He attends Pierre Janet's lectures on theoretical psychopathology at the Collège de France in Paris. His first professional articles are published.

1903   Jung marries Emma Rauschenberg of Schaffhausen. They have one son and four daughters.

1903   He begins experimental researches on word associations and is appointed senior staff physician at the Burghölzli.

1906   He begins his correspondence with Sigmund Freud.

1907   At their first meeting in Vienna, Jung and Freud talk without a break for 13 hours.

1908   Jung organizes the First Congress for Freudian Psychology in Salzburg.

1909   The Jungs move to their newly built home in Küsnacht by the lake of Zürich. Their descendants still live there. Jung withdraws from the Burghölzli clinic to concentrate on his thriving private practice. In September he visits the United States for the first time, with Freud, and both receive honorary degrees at Clark University in Massachusetts.

1910   Jung is appointed first president of the International Psychoanalytic Association.

1913   Jung cannot accept Freud's dogma concerning infantile sexuality. They break off their relationship. Jung resigns from his professorship at the University of Zürich. He enters a long period of intense introversion, soul-searching, and confrontation with his unconscious, recorded first in the *Black Books* and then in the *Liber Novus*, the *Red Book*. This provides the foundation for all his subsequent work.

1916   The Psychological Club in Zürich is officially founded. Between 1913 and 1951 Jung gives fifty Lectures at the Club, presenting the first drafts of his new works.

1920   Jung travels to Algeria and Tunisia.

1921   *Psychological Types* is published and receives very favorable reviews.

1922–23   Jung purchases the land in Bollingen at the southern end of the Lake of Zürich, where construction of the first tower of his retreat at Bollingen is built. His mother dies.

1924   He visits the Pueblo Indians in Taos, New Mexico, and forms friendship with Chief Mountain Lake.

1925   Jung leads the first of many acclaimed Zürich Seminars in English, including *Analytical Psychology*, *Dream Analysis*, *The Visions Seminars*, *The Psychology of Kundalini Yoga*, *Nietzsche's Zarathustra*, and *Children's Dreams*.

1925–26   He undertakes an expedition to Kenya, Uganda, and the Nile. While with the Elgonyi tribe on Mt. Elgon, he is so inspired by the sight of gigantic herds of wild animals that he realizes that humans, through consciousness, are the second creators of the world.

1932   Jung begins 25-year collaboration with Wolfgang Pauli (1900–58), winner of the Nobel Prize for Physics in 1945. He is awarded Literature Prize of the City of Zürich.

1933   The first annual Eranos conference at Ascona in Southern Switzerland includes distinguished scholars from all over the world. Jung lectures nearly every year until 1951. Among the participants are Joseph Campbell, Henry Corbin, Gershom Scholem, Karl Kerényi, Erich Neumann, and Mircea Eliade.

1933–41	Jung lectures on "Modern Psychology" at the Swiss Federal Polytechnical Institute (ETH) in Zürich.
1935	He lectures at the Tavistock Clinic in London to about two hundred medical professionals from every "school" of psychotherapy. He is appointed Titular Professor at the ETH.
1936	Jung is awarded honorary doctorate from Harvard University.
1937	A large audience attends Jung's Terry Lectures at Yale, published as *Psychology and Religion*. He defines religion as "the attitude peculiar to a consciousness which has been altered by the experience of the numinosum."
1938	Jung receives an honorary doctorate from Oxford University and is appointed Honorary Fellow of the Royal Society of Medicine, London. He describes as a "decisive moment" his trip to India to receive honorary degrees from the Universities of Benares, Allahabad, and Calcutta.
1944	He breaks his foot, suffers a heart attack, and experiences mystic visions while near death in hospital.
1945	In honor of his 70th birthday, the University of Geneva awards Jung an honorary doctorate.
1951	The publication of *Answer to Job* is so controversial that it engenders a series of key late letters concerning the evolution of the Western God image and the dark side of God. The first of the twenty volumes of the English-language edition of Jung's *Collected Works* is published.
1955	In recognition of his 80th birthday, the ETH awards him an honorary doctorate. On November 27 his wife of 52 years, Emma Rauschenberg Jung, dies.
1957	Jung begins work on his memoirs, published posthumously in 1962. *Memories, Dreams, Reflections* is a best seller.
1959	John Freeman interviews Jung on the BBC television program "Face to Face." To the question, "Do you now believe in God?" Jung answers, "Now? [Pause.] Difficult to answer. I *know*. I don't need to believe, I know."

1959   Jung dreams he is addressing a multitude of people in a public space, and they understand him. He conceives and edits *Man and His Symbols*, thereby completing his *Introduction* 10 days before his death.

1960   Jung is declared an honorary citizen of Küsnacht, his home for more than 50 years and where, after a short illness, he dies on June 6, 1961.

2009   Many decades after he wrote it, Jung's original *Red Book* is meticulously photographed and a facsimile edition is published. It is an instant best seller, with more than 100,000 hardback copies in print worldwide.

Permissions

THE QUOTABLE JUNG

1
The Unconscious

Man started from an unconscious state and has ever striven for greater consciousness. The development of consciousness is the burden, the suffering, and the blessing of mankind.

"Men, Women, and God" (1955), *C. G. Jung Speaking*, p. 248.

[T]he attainment of consciousness was the most precious fruit of the tree of knowledge, the magical weapon which gave man victory over the earth, and which we hope will give him a still greater victory over himself.

"The Meaning of Psychology for Modern Man" (1933/1934), CW 10,
§ 289.

"All that is outside, also is inside," we could say with Goethe. But this "inside," which modern rationalism is so eager to derive from "outside," has an *a priori* structure of its own that antedates all conscious experience. It is quite impossible to conceive how "experience" in the widest sense, or, for that matter, anything psychic, could originate exclusively in the outside world. The psyche is part of the inmost mystery of life, and it has its own peculiar structure and form like every other organism. Whether this psychic structure and its elements, the archetypes, ever "originated" at all is a metaphysical question and therefore unanswerable. The structure is something given, the precondition that is found to be present in every case. And this is the *mother*, the matrix—the form into which all experience is poured.

"Psychological Aspects of the Mother Archetype" (1938/1954),
CW 9i, § 187.

The psyche is the starting point of all human experience, and all the knowledge we have gained eventually leads back to it. The psyche is the beginning and end of all cognition. It is not only the object of its science, but the subject also. This gives psychology a unique place among all the other sciences; on the one hand there is a constant doubt as to the possibility of its being a science at all, while on the other hand psychology acquires the right to state a theoretical problem the solution of which will be one of the most difficult tasks for a future philosophy.

"Psychological Factors Determining Human Behaviour" (1937),

CW 8, § 261.

What most people overlook or seem unable to understand is the fact that I regard the psyche as *real*.

Answer to Job (1952), CW 11, § 751.

Man knows only a small part of his psyche, just as he has only a very limited knowledge of the physiology of his body. The causal factors determining his psychic existence reside largely in unconscious processes outside consciousness, and in the same way there are final factors at work in him which likewise originate in the unconscious.

Aion (1951), CW 9ii, § 253.

The fact that individual consciousness means separation and opposition is something that man has experienced countless times in his long history.

"The Meaning of Psychology for Modern Man" (1933/1934), CW 10, § 290.

The world itself becomes a reflection of the psyche.

The Psychology of Kundalini Yoga: Notes of the Seminar Given in 1932 (26 October, 1932), p. 50.

I am of the opinion that the psyche is the most tremendous fact of human life. Indeed, it is the mother of all human facts; of civilization and of its destroyer, war.

"Concerning Rebirth" (1940/1950), CW 9i, § 206.

[T]he psyche consists essentially of images. It is a series of images in the truest sense, not an accidental juxtaposition or sequence, but a structure that is throughout full of meaning and purpose; it is a "picturing" of vital activities. And just as the material of the body that is ready for life has need of the psyche in order to be capable of life, so the psyche presupposes the living body in order that its images may live.

"Spirit and Life" (1926), CW 8, § 618.

[A]ll psychic processes whose energies are not under conscious control are instinctive.

Psychological Types (1921), CW 6, § 765.

It does not seem to have occurred to people that when we say "psyche" we are alluding to the densest darkness it is possible to imagine.

"Transformation Symbolism in the Mass" (1942/1954), CW 11,

§ 448.

Psychic energy is a very fastidious thing which insists on fulfilment of its own conditions. However much energy may be present, we cannot make it serviceable until we have succeeded in finding the right gradient.

On the Psychology of the Unconscious (1917/1926), CW 7, § 76.

"[A]t bottom" the psyche is simply "world."

"The Psychology of the Child Archetype" (1940), CW 9i, § 291.

We also speak of the "objective world," by which we do not mean that this objective world is the one we are conscious of. There is no object of which we are totally conscious. So, too, the collective unconscious becomes conscious in part and to that extent it is then a conscious object. But over and above that it is still present unconsciously, though it can be discovered. It behaves exactly like the world of things, which is partly known, partly unknown, the unknown being just as objectively real as that which is known to me. I chose the term "objective psyche" in contradistinction to "subjective psyche" because the subjective psyche coincides with consciousness, whereas the objective psyche does not always do so by any means.

Letter to Jolande Jacobi, 15 April 1948, Letters, Vol. I, p. 497.

No one who has undergone the process of assimilating the unconscious will deny that it gripped his very vitals and changed him.

The Relations between the Ego and the Unconscious (1916/1928),
CW 7, § 361.

There is no morality without freedom.

Psychological Types (1921), CW 6, § 357.

The psyche does not merely *react*, it gives its own specific answer to the influences at work upon it.

"Some Crucial Points in Psychoanalysis" (1914), CW 4, § 665.

I have been compelled, in my investigations into the structure of the unconscious, to make a conceptual distinction between *soul* and *psyche*. By psyche I understand the totality of all psychic processes, conscious and unconscious. By soul, on the other hand, I understand a clearly demarcated functional complex that can best be described as a "personality."

Psychological Types (1921), CW 6, § 797.

I have never asserted, nor do I think I know, what the unconscious is in itself. It is the unconscious region of the psyche. When I speak of psyche, I do not pretend to know what it is either, and how far this concept extends. For this concept is simply beyond all possibility of cognition. It is a mere convention of giving some kind of name to the unknown which appears to us psychic. This psychic factor, as experience shows, is something very different from our consciousness.

Letter to Pastor Jahn, 7 September 1935, Letters, Vol. I, p. 196.

[J]ust as the unconscious world of mythological images speaks indirectly, through the experience of external things, to the man who surrenders wholly to the outside world, so the real world and its demands find their way indirectly to the man who has surrendered wholly to the soul; for no man can escape both realities. If he is intent only on the outer reality, he must live his myth; if he is turned only towards the inner reality, he must dream his outer, so-called real life.

Psychological Types (1921) CW 6, § 280.

The primitive mentality does not *invent* myths, it *experiences* them.

"The Psychology of the Child Archetype" (1940), CW 9i, § 261.

The unconscious is on no account an empty sack into which the refuse of consciousness is collected, as it appears to be in Freud's view; it is the whole other half of the living psyche.

Letter to Dr. N.,[1] 5 February 1934, *Letters, Vol. I*, p. 143.

It is difficult for me to outline the special features of my teachings in a few words. For me the essential thing is the investigation of the unconscious. Whereas Freud holds that in order to cure the neuroses, all of which as you know he derives from sexual roots, it is sufficient to make the unconscious conscious, I maintain that it is necessary to coordinate with consciousness the activities streaming out of the matrix of the unconscious. I try to funnel the fantasies of the unconscious into the conscious mind, not in order to destroy them but to develop them.

"Three Versions of a Press Conference in Vienna" (1928), *C. G. Jung Speaking*, pp. 39–40.

[T]he unconscious is not just a receptacle for all unclean spirits and other odious legacies from the dead past—such as, for instance, that deposit of centuries of public opinion which constitutes Freud's "superego." It is in very truth the eternally living, creative, germinal layer in each of us, and though it may make use of age-old symbolical images it nevertheless intends them to be understood in

---

[1] Whenever Jung wrote a letter to Herr, Frau, Mr., or Mrs. N., it indicated a correspondent who wished to remain anonymous or who could not be identified.

a new way. Naturally a new meaning does not come ready-made out of the unconscious, like Pallas Athene springing fully-armed from the head of Zeus; a living effect is achieved only when the products of the unconscious are brought into serious relationship with the conscious mind.

"Introduction to Kranefeldt's *Secret Ways of the Mind*" (1930), CW 4,

§ 760.

In the Tower at Bollingen it is as if one lived many centuries simultaneously. The place will outlive me, and in its location and style it points backward to things of long ago. There is very little about it to suggest the present. If a man of the sixteenth century were to move into the house, only the kerosene lamp and the matches would be new to him; otherwise, he would know his way about without difficulty. There is nothing to disturb the dead, neither electric light nor telephone. Moreover, my ancestors' souls are sustained by the atmosphere of the house, since I answer for them the questions that their lives once left behind. I carve out rough answers as best I can. I have even drawn them on the walls. It is as if a silent, greater family, stretching down the centuries, were peopling the house.

Memories, Dreams, Reflections (1962), p. 237.

[T]he unconscious is that which we do not know, therefore we call it the unconscious.

Nietzsche's Zarathustra: *Notes of the Seminar Given in 1934–1939*,

Vol. II (19 October 1938), p. 1348.

[T]he unconscious is unfavourable or dangerous only because we are not at one with it and therefore in opposition to it. A negative attitude to the unconscious, or its splitting off, is detrimental in so far as the dynamics of the unconscious are identical with instinctual energy. Disalliance with the unconscious is synonymous with loss of instinct and rootlessness.

On the Psychology of the Unconscious (1917/1926/1943), CW 7, § 195.

[T]he unconscious can make a fool of you in no time.

Visions: Notes of the Seminar Given in 1930–1934, Vol. II (15 June 1932), p. 747.

The unconscious is useless without the human mind. It always seeks its collective purposes and never your individual destiny. Your destiny is the result of the collaboration between the conscious and the unconscious.

Letter to Mrs. N., 20 May 1940, *Letters, Vol. I*, p. 283.

I cannot see why it is a mystery how the unconscious can ever become known to consciousness. It is a fact of everyday experience that formerly unconscious contents more or less suddenly emerge into consciousness. As a matter of fact our consciousness couldn't function if the unconscious psychic process didn't support it by providing it with the necessary material. For instance, if you have forgotten a name and the unconscious obstinately retains it, then you depend almost entirely upon the good will of the unconscious that it allows you to recall it. It happens very often that your memory fails you in an almost diabolical way.

Letter to W. Y. Evans-Wentz, 9 February 1939, *Letters, Vol. I*, p. 262.

The world comes into being when man discovers it. But he only discovers it when he sacrifices his containment in the primal mother, the original state of unconsciousness.

Symbols of Transformation (1912/1952), CW 5, § 652.

[T]he unconscious itself initiates the process of renewal.

Mysterium Coniunctionis (1955–56), CW 14, § 548.

Where instinct predominates, *psychoid* processes set in which pertain to the sphere of the unconscious as elements incapable of consciousness. The psychoid process is not the unconscious as such, for this has a far greater extension.

"On the Nature of the Psyche" (1947/1954), CW 8, § 380.

The unconscious is not simply the unknown, it is rather the *unknown psychic*; and this we define on the one hand as all those things in us which, if they came to consciousness, would presumably differ in no respect from the known psychic contents, with the addition, on the other hand, of the psychoid system, of which nothing is known directly. So defined, the unconscious depicts an extremely fluid state of affairs: everything of which I know, but of which I am not at the moment thinking; everything of which I was once conscious but have now forgotten; everything perceived by my senses, but not noted by my conscious mind; everything which, involuntarily and without paying attention to it, I feel, think, remember, want, and do; all the future things that are taking shape in me and will sometime come to consciousness: all this is the content of the unconscious. These contents are all more or less capable, so to speak, of consciousness, or were once conscious and may become conscious again the next moment. Thus far the unconscious is "a fringe of consciousness," as William James put it. To this marginal phenomenon, which is born of alternating shades of light and darkness, there also belong the Freudian findings we have already noted. But, as I say, we must also include in the unconscious the psychoid functions that are not capable of consciousness and of whose existence we have only indirect knowledge.

"On the Nature of the Psyche" (1947/1954), CW 8, § 382.

It is as if you were ruler of a land which is only partially known to yourself, king of a country with an unknown number of inhabitants. You don't know who they are or what their condition may be; time and again you make the discovery that you have subjects in your country of whose existence you had no idea. Therefore, you cannot assume the responsibility; you can only say, "I find myself as the ruler of a country which has unknown borders and unknown inhabitants, possessing qualities of which I am not entirely aware." Then you are at once out of your subjectivity, and are confronted with a situation in which you are a sort of prisoner; you are confronted with unknown possibilities, because those many uncontrollable factors at any time may influence all your actions or decisions. So you are a funny kind of king in that country, a king who is not really a king, who is dependent upon so many known quantities and conditions that he often cannot carry through his own intentions. Therefore, it is better not to speak of being a king at all, and be only one of the inhabitants who has just a corner of that territory in which to rule. And the greater your experience, the more you see that your corner is infinitely small in comparison with the vast extent of the unknown against you.

Nietzsche's Zarathustra: Notes of the Seminar Given in 1934–1939,
Vol. I (20 February, 1935), p. 390.

There are a number of ways in which unconscious forces play their part. The collective unconscious is a real fact in human affairs. It would need volumes to explain its various ramifications. We all participate in it. In one sense it is the accumulated human wisdom which we unconsciously inherit; in other senses it implies the common human emotions which we all share.

"Jung Diagnoses the Dictators" (1939), *C. G. Jung Speaking*, p. 139.

The autonomy of the unconscious therefore begins where emotions are generated. Emotions are instinctive, involuntary reactions which upset the rational order of consciousness by their elemental outbursts. Affects are not "made" or wilfully produced; they simply happen. In a state of affect a trait of character sometimes appears which is strange even to the person concerned, or hidden contents may irrupt involuntarily. The more violent an affect the closer it comes to the pathological, to a condition in which the ego-consciousness is thrust aside by autonomous contents that were unconscious before. So long as the unconscious is in a dormant condition, it seems as if there were absolutely nothing in this hidden region. Hence we are continually surprised when something unknown suddenly appears "from nowhere."

"Conscious, Unconscious, and Individuation" (1939), CW 9i, § 497.

[T]ouching the personal unconscious already changes you and touching the collective unconscious changes you all the more: you are a different being, and no longer like the people who have not touched it.

Nietzsche's Zarathustra: Notes of the Seminar Given in 1934–1939,
Vol. I (15 May 1935), p. 483.

Indeed, the fate of the individual is largely dependent on unconscious factors.

"Conscious, Unconscious, and Individuation" (1939), CW 9i, § 504.

We know that the mask of the unconscious is not rigid—it reflects the face we turn towards it. Hostility lends it a threatening aspect, friendliness softens its features.

Psychology and Alchemy (1944), CW 12, § 29.

The role of the unconscious is to act compensatorily to the conscious contents of the moment. By this I do not mean that it sets up an opposition, for there are times when the tendency of the unconscious coincides with that of consciousness, namely, when the conscious attitude is approaching the optimum. The nearer it approaches the optimum, the more the autonomous activity of the unconscious is diminished, and the more its value sinks until, at the moment when the optimum is reached, it falls to zero. We can say, then, that so long as all goes well, so long as a person travels the road that is, for him, the individual as well as the social optimum, there is no talk of the unconscious. The very fact that we in our age come to speak of the unconscious at all is proof that everything is not in order.

"The Role of the Unconscious" (1918), CW 10, § 21.

The unconscious is not a demoniacal monster, but a natural entity which, as far as moral sense, aesthetic taste, and intellectual judgment go, is completely neutral. It only becomes dangerous when our conscious attitude is completely wrong. To the degree that we repress it, its danger increases. But the moment the patient begins to assimilate contents that were previously unconscious, its danger diminishes.

"The Practical Use of Dream-Analysis" (1934), CW 16, § 329.

The unconscious on one side is nothing but nature, and on the other hand it is the overcoming of nature; it is yea and nay in itself, two things in one. So we shall never understand what the unconscious is, as we shall never understand what the world is, because it is and it is not.

Visions: Notes of the Seminar Given in 1930–1934, Vol. I (19 November 1930), p. 89.

For not knowing about the unconscious means that one has deviated, one is not in harmony with it, and therefore it works against one.

Visions: Notes of the Seminar Given in 1930–1934, Vol. I (10 June 1931), p. 405.

[W]e have to distinguish in the unconscious a layer which we may call the *personal unconscious*. The materials contained in this layer are of a personal nature in so far as they have the character partly of acquisitions derived from the individual's life and partly of psychological factors which could just as well be conscious. It can readily be understood that incompatible psychological elements are liable to repression and therefore become unconscious. But on the other hand this implies the possibility of making and keeping the repressed contents conscious once they have been recognized. We recognize them as personal contents because their effects, or their partial manifestation, or their source can be discovered in our personal past.

The Relations between the Ego and the Unconscious (1916/1928), CW 7, § 218.

A more or less superficial layer of the unconscious is undoubtedly personal. I call it the *personal unconscious*. But this personal unconscious rests upon a deeper layer, which does not derive from personal experience and is not a personal acquisition but is inborn. This deeper layer I call the *collective unconscious*. I have chosen the term "collective" because this part of the unconscious is not individual but universal; in contrast to the personal psyche, it has contents and modes of behaviour that are more or less the same everywhere and in all individuals. It is, in other words, identical in all men and thus constitutes a common psychic substrate of a suprapersonal nature which is present in every one of us.

"Archetypes of the Collective Unconscious" (1934/1954),

CW 9i, § 3.

Whereas the contents of the personal unconscious are acquired during the individual's lifetime, the contents of the collective unconscious are invariably archetypes that were present from the beginning.

Aion (1951), CW 9ii, § 13.

This "personal unconscious" must always be dealt with first, that is, made conscious, otherwise the gateway to the collective unconscious cannot be opened.

Psychology and Alchemy (1944), CW 12, § 81.

I understand the unconscious rather as an *impersonal* psyche common to all men, even though it expresses itself through a personal unconscious. When anyone breathes, his breathing is not a phenomenon to be interpreted personally.

"The Psychological Aspects of the Kore" (1949), CW 9i, § 314.

The experience of the unconscious is a personal secret communicable only to very few, and that with difficulty.

Psychology and Alchemy (1944), CW 12, § 61.

Modern psychology knows that the personal unconscious is only the top layer, resting on a foundation of a wholly different nature which we call the collective unconscious. The reason for this designation is the circumstance that, unlike the personal unconscious and its purely personal contents, the images in the deeper unconscious have a distinctly mythological character. That is to say, in form and content they coincide with those widespread primordial ideas which underlie the myths. They are no longer of a personal but of a purely supra-personal nature and are therefore common to all men. For this reason they are to be found in the myths and legends of all peoples and all times, as well as in individuals who have not the slightest knowledge of mythology.

"The Psychology of Eastern Meditation" (1943), CW 11, § 944.

[I]n the unconscious it is not so terribly important whether a man is alive or dead, that seems to make very little impression upon the unconscious. But your attitude to it matters, how you will take it, whether you believe in immortality or not, how you react to such and such an event, that matters to the unconscious.

Visions: Notes of the Seminar Given in 1930–1934, Vol. II (1 February 1933), p. 903.

The unconscious is the only available source of religious experience. This is certainly not to say that what we call the unconscious is identical with God or is set up in his place. It is simply the medium from which religious experience seems to flow. As to what the further cause of such experience might be, the answer to this lies beyond the range of human knowledge. Knowledge of God is a transcendental problem.

The Undiscovered Self (1957), CW 10, § 565.

I was being compelled to go through this process of the unconscious. I had to let myself be carried along by the current, without a notion of where it would lead me.

Memories, Dreams, Reflections (1962), p. 196.

People who are unconscious always create unconsciousness, and in this way they influence others; they can get them into an unconscious condition so that they will behave exactly according to their intention. That is the real essence of witchcraft.

Visions: Notes of the Seminar Given in 1930–1934, Vol. II (31 January 1934), pp. 1272–73.

[T]he unconscious, as the totality of all archetypes, is the deposit of all human experience right back to its remotest beginnings. Not, indeed, a dead deposit, a sort of abandoned rubbish-heap, but a living system of reactions and aptitudes that determine the individual's life in invisible ways—all the more effective because invisible. It is not just a gigantic historical prejudice, so to speak, an *a priori* historical condition; it is also the source of the instincts, for the archetypes are simply the forms which the instincts assume. From the living fountain of instinct flows everything that is creative; hence the unconscious is not merely conditioned by history, but is the very source of the creative impulse. It is like Nature herself—prodigiously conservative, and yet transcending her own historical conditions in her acts of creation. No wonder, then, that it has always been a burning question for humanity how best to adapt to these invisible determinants. If consciousness had never split off from the unconscious—an eternally repeated event symbolized as the fall of the angels and the disobedience of the first parents—this problem would never have arisen, any more than would the question of environmental adaptation.

"The Structure of the Psyche" (1927/1931), CW 8, § 339.

[T]he archetype as an image of instinct is a spiritual goal toward which the whole nature of man strives; it is the sea to which all rivers wend their way, the prize which the hero wrests from the fight with the dragon.

"On the Nature of the Psyche" (1947/1954), CW 8, § 415.

A psychological reading of the dominant archetypal images reveals a continuous series of psychological transformations, depicting the autonomous life of archetypes behind the scenes of consciousness. This hypothesis has been worked out to clarify and make comprehensible our religious history.

"Jung and Religious Belief" (1958), CW 18, § 1686.

[W]hat we mean by "archetype" is in itself irrepresentable, but has effects which make visualizations of it possible, namely, the archetypal images and ideas.

"On the Nature of the Psyche" (1947/1954), CW 8, § 417.

Nobody has ever seen an archetype, and nobody has ever seen an atom either.

Letter to H. Haberlandt, 23 April 1952, *Letters, Vol. II*, p. 54.

[A]rchetypes are not whimsical inventions but autonomous elements of the unconscious psyche which were there before any invention was thought of. They represent the unalterable structure of a psychic world whose "reality" is attested by the determining effects it has upon the conscious mind.

"The Phenomenology of the Spirit in Fairytales" (1945/1948), CW 9i,
§ 451.

The archetype is essentially an unconscious content that is altered by becoming conscious and by being perceived, and it takes its colour from the individual consciousness in which it happens to appear.

"Archetypes of the Collective Unconscious" (1934/1954), CW 9i, § 6.

An archetype—so far as we can establish it empirically—is an *image*. An image, as the very term denotes, is a picture of something. An archetypal image is like the portrait of an unknown man in a gallery. His name, his biography, his existence in general are unknown, but we assume nevertheless that the picture portrays a once living subject, a man who was real. We find numberless images of God, but we cannot produce the original. There is no doubt in my mind that there is an original behind our images, but it is inaccessible.

"Jung and Religious Belief" (1958), CW 18, § 1589.

The archetype—let us never forget this—is a psychic organ present in all of us.

"The Psychology of the Child Archetype" (1963), CW 9i, § 271.

[I]t seems to me probable that the real nature of the archetype is not capable of being made conscious, that it is transcendent, on which account I call it psychoid.

"On the Nature of the Psyche" (1947/1954), CW 8, § 417.

Archetypes are like riverbeds which dry up when the water deserts them, but which it can find again at any time. An archetype is like an old watercourse along which the water of life has flowed for centuries, digging a deep channel for itself. The longer it has flowed in this channel the more likely it is that sooner or later the water will return to its old bed.

"Wotan" (1936), CW 10, § 395.

Archetypes are, by definition, factors and motifs that arrange the psychic elements into certain images, characterized as archetypal, but in such a way that they can be recognized only from the effects they produce. They exist preconsciously, and presumably they form the structural dominants of the psyche in general. They may be compared to the invisible presence of the crystal lattice in a saturated solution. As *a priori* conditioning factors they represent a special, psychological instance of the biological "pattern of behaviour," which gives all living organisms their specific qualities. Just as the manifestations of this biological ground plan may change in the course of development, so also can those of the archetype. Empirically considered, however, the archetype did not ever come into existence as a phenomenon of organic life, but entered into the picture with life itself.

"A Psychological Approach to the Dogma of the Trinity"
(1942/1948), CW 11, n. 2, § 222.

Do we ever understand what we think? We only understand that kind of thinking which is a mere equation, from which nothing comes out but what we have put in. That is the working of the intellect. But besides that there is a thinking in primordial images, in symbols which are older than the historical man, which are inborn in him from the earliest times, and, eternally living, outlasting all generations, still make up the groundwork of the human psyche. It is only possible to live the fullest life when we are in harmony with these symbols; wisdom is a return to them.

"The Stages of Life" (1930–31), CW 8, § 794.

[A]rchetypes probably represent typical situations in life.

"Psychological Factors Determining Human Behavior" (1937),
CW 8, § 254.

The archetypes are the numinous, structural elements of the psyche and possess a certain autonomy and specific energy which enables them to attract, out of the conscious mind, those contents which are best suited to themselves.

Symbols of Transformation, (1912/1952), CW 5, § 344.

[M]an must remain conscious of the world of the archetypes, because in it he is still a part of Nature and is connected with his own roots.

"Psychological Aspects of the Mother Archetype" (1938/1954),
CW 9i, § 174.

The archetypal is a powerful emotion brought into its original form. When someone is able to perform the art of touching on the archetypal, he can play on the souls of people like on the strings of a piano.

Children's Dreams: Notes of the Seminar Given in 1936–1940,

p. 150.

No archetype can be reduced to a simple formula. It is a vessel which we can never empty, and never fill. It has a potential existence only, and when it takes shape in matter it is no longer what it was. It persists throughout the ages and requires interpreting ever anew. The archetypes are imperishable elements of the unconscious, but they change their shape continually.

"The Psychology of the Child Archetype" (1940), CW 9i, § 301.

The archetype is, so to speak, an "eternal" presence, and it is only a question of whether it is perceived by the conscious mind or not.

Psychology and Alchemy (1944), CW 12, § 329.

Just as all archetypes have a positive, favourable, bright side that points upwards, so also they have one that points downwards, partly negative and unfavourable, partly chthonic, but for the rest merely neutral.

"The Phenomenology of the Spirit in Fairytales" (1945/1948), CW 9i,

§ 413.

The impact of an archetype, whether it takes the form of immediate experience or is expressed through the spoken word, stirs us because it summons up a voice that is stronger than our own. Whoever speaks in primordial images speaks with a thousand voices; he enthrals and overpowers, while at the same time he lifts the idea he is seeking to express out of the occasional and the transitory into the realm of the ever-enduring. He transmutes our personal destiny into the destiny of mankind, and evokes in us all those beneficent forces that ever and anon have enabled humanity to find a refuge from every peril and to outlive the longest night.

"On the Relation of Analytical Psychology to Poetry" (1922), CW 15,

§ 129.

Only that which acts upon me do I recognize as real and actual. But that which has no effect upon me might as well not exist.

Answer to Job (1952), CW 11, § 757.

The deposit of man's whole ancestral experience—so rich in emotional imagery—of father, mother, child, husband and wife, of the magic personality, of dangers to body and soul, has exalted this group of archetypes into the supreme regulating principles of religious and even of political life, in unconscious recognition of their tremendous psychic power.

"The Structure of the Psyche" (1927/1931), CW 8, § 337.

[T]he unconscious functions according to the archetypes. When it functions correctly, it could lead to the discovery of the world or to the reinvention of world history. It is not we who have those images, but they are within us, and we are shaped by them. These are preordained modes of functioning. The way it happens in us is how it happens in nature in general. An insect does by itself what it has to do after hatching. It is not welcomed by benevolent parents or midwives, and all the same it spins its threads correctly. It flies to the plant where it finds its food, and so on. It just does the right thing. Similarly, the mental functioning of human beings is not something that each individual has to learn anew for him- or herself. We do what our ancestors have always done. It is not the school that brings this about. On the contrary, we have to be careful that the school does not destroy the natural functioning of the psyche.

Children's Dreams: Notes from the Seminar Given in 1936–1940, p. 133.

When I was working on the stone tablets, I became aware of the fateful links between me and my ancestors. I feel very strongly that I am under the influence of things or questions which were left incomplete and unanswered by my parents and grandparents and more distant ancestors. It often seems as if there were an impersonal karma within a family, which is passed on from parents to children. It has always seemed to me that I had to answer questions which fate had posed to my forefathers, and which had not yet been answered, or as if I had to complete, or perhaps continue, things which previous ages had left unfinished. It is difficult to determine whether these questions are more of a personal or more of a general (collective) nature. It seems to me that the latter is the case. A collective problem, if not recognized as such, always appears as a personal problem, and in individual cases may give the impression that something is out of order in the realm of the personal psyche. The personal sphere is indeed disturbed, but such disturbances need not be primary; they may well be secondary, the consequence of an insupportable change in the social atmosphere. The cause of the disturbance is, therefore, not to be sought in the personal surroundings, but rather in the collective situation. Psychotherapy has hitherto taken this matter far too little into account.

Memories, Dreams, Reflections (1962), pp. 233–34.

[T]he indispensable condition is that you have an archetypal experience, and to have that means that you have surrendered to life. If your life has not three-dimensions, if you don't live in the body, if you live on the two-dimensional plane in the paper world that is flat and printed, as if you were only living your biography, then you are nowhere. You don't see the archetypal world, but live like a pressed flower in the pages of a book, a mere memory of yourself.

Nietzsche's Zarathustra: Notes of the Seminar Given in 1934–1939,
Vol. II (3 June 1936), p. 972.

[I]t is not surprising that when an archetypal situation occurs we suddenly feel an extraordinary sense of release, as though transported, or caught up by an overwhelming power. At such moments we are no longer individuals, but the race; the voice of all mankind resounds in us.

"On the Relation of Analytical Psychology to Poetry" (1922), CW 15,
§ 128.

Archetypes are forms of different aspects expressing the creative psychic background. They are and always have been numinous and therefore "divine." In a very generalizing way we can therefore define them as attributes of the creator.

Letter to Herbert Read, 22 October 1960, *Letters, Vol. II*, p. 606.

The great lure of the archetypal situation is that you yourself suddenly cease to be. You cease to think and are acted upon as though carried by a great river with no end. You are suddenly eternal.

Nietzsche's Zarathustra: Notes of the Seminar Given in 1934–1939,
Vol. I (14 November 1934), p. 240.

[A]nyone possessed by an archetype cannot help having all the symptoms of inflation. For the archetype is nothing human; no archetype is properly human. The archetype itself is an exaggeration and it reaches beyond the confines of humanity.

Nietzsche's Zarathustra: Notes of the Seminar Given in 1934–1939,
Vol. II (19 October 1938), p. 1343.

Man's capacity for consciousness alone makes him man.

"On the Nature of the Psyche" (1947/1954), CW 8, § 412.

And yet the attainment of consciousness was the most precious fruit of the tree of knowledge, the magical weapon which gave man victory over the earth, and which we hope will give him a still greater victory over himself.

"The Meaning of Psychology for Modern Man" (1933/1934), CW 10,
§ 289.

Without consciousness there would, practically speaking, be no world, for the world exists for us only in so far as it is consciously reflected by a psyche. *Consciousness is a precondition of being.* Thus the psyche is endowed with the dignity of a cosmic principle, which philosophically and in fact gives it a position co-equal with the principle of physical being. The carrier of this consciousness is the individual, who does not produce the psyche of his own volition but is, on the contrary, preformed by it and nourished by the gradual awakening of consciousness during childhood. If therefore the psyche is of overriding empirical importance, so also is the individual, who is the only immediate manifestation of the psyche.

The Undiscovered Self (1957), CW 10, § 528.

Consciousness, no matter how extensive it may be, must always remain the smaller circle within the greater circle of the unconscious, an island surrounded by the sea; and, like the sea itself, the unconscious yields an endless and self-replenishing abundance of living creatures, a wealth beyond our fathoming. We may long have known the meaning, effects, and characteristics of unconscious contents without ever having fathomed their depths and potentialities, for they are capable of infinite variation and can never be depotentiated. The only way to get at them in practice is to try to attain a conscious attitude which allows the unconscious to co-operate instead of being driven into opposition.

The Psychology of the Transference (1946), CW 16, § 366.

[W]e come to the paradoxical conclusion that there is no conscious content which is not in some other respect unconscious.

"On the Nature of the Psyche" (1947/1954), CW 8, § 385.

The greatest blessing in this world is the greatest curse in the unconscious.

The Psychology of Kundalini Yoga: Notes of the Seminar Given in 1932 (26 October, 1932), p. 51.

[N]o matter what your conscious attitude may be, the unconscious has an absolutely free hand and can do what it pleases.

Visions: Notes of the Seminar Given in 1930–1934, Vol. I (22 October 1930), p. 27.

The longing for light is the longing for consciousness.

Memories, Dreams, Reflections (1962), p. 269.

Conflict engenders fire, the fire of affects and emotions, and like every other fire it has two aspects, that of combustion and that of creating light. On the one hand, emotion is the alchemical fire whose warmth brings everything into existence and whose heat burns all superfluities to ashes. But on the other hand, emotion is the moment when steel meets flint and a spark is struck forth, for emotion is the chief source of consciousness. There is no change from darkness to light or from inertia to movement without emotion.

"Psychological Aspects of the Mother Archetype" (1938/1954),
CW 9i, § 179.

If there were no consciousness, there would be no world; the whole world, as far as it enters into our consideration, depends upon that little flame of consciousness, that is surely the decisive factor. In the unconscious one cannot judge because of the great darkness there, but in the conscious there is light, and so there are differences; there is a criterion in consciousness which gives one a measure by which to judge.

Visions: Notes of the Seminar Given in 1930–1934, Vol. II (1 February 1933), p. 898.

[C]onsciousness can take up no position which will not call up, somewhere in the dark corners of the psyche, a negation or a compensatory effect, approval or resentment. This process of coming to terms with the Other in us is well worth while, because in this way we get to know aspects of our nature which we would not allow anybody else to show us and which we ourselves would never have admitted.

Mysterium Coniunctionis (1955–56), CW 14, § 706.

The secret participation of the unconscious is everywhere present without our having to search for it, but as it remains unconscious we never really know what is going on or what to expect. What we are searching for is a way to make conscious those contents which are about to influence our actions, so that the secret interference of the unconscious and its unpleasant consequences can be avoided.

"The Transcendent Function" ([1916]/1958),[2] CW 8, § 158.

Anything conscious can be corrected. But anything that slips away into the unconscious is beyond the reach of correction and, its rank growth undisturbed, is subject to increasing degeneration. Happily, nature sees to it that the unconscious contents will irrupt into consciousness sooner or later and create the necessary confusion.

Mysterium Coniunctionis (1955–56), CW 14, § 672.

[M]an's greatest triumph was that God himself incarnated in man in order to illumine the world; that was a tremendous increase of consciousness. But every increase of consciousness means a further separation from the original animal-like condition, and I don't know where it will end: it is really a tragic problem. We have to discover more consciousness, to extend consciousness, and the more it is extended the more we get away from the original condition.

Nietzsche's Zarathustra: Notes of the Seminar Given in 1934–1939,
Vol. II (3 June 1936), p. 967.

[W]e cannot apply our notion of time to the unconscious. Our consciousness can conceive of things only in temporal succession, our time is, therefore, essentially linked to the chronological sequence. In the unconscious this is different, because there everything lies together, so to speak. To some extent, in the unconscious we all still live in the past; in a way we are still very little children, and often only very little is needed for the "child" to come to the surface. At the same time, we are standing in the shadow cast by a future, of which we still know nothing, but which is already somehow anticipated by the unconscious.

Children's Dreams: Notes from the Seminar Given in 1936–1940,
p. 360.

[2] A date in square brackets is the date when the work was composed; other dates refer to the year the work was published.

Projection is a terrific force. You are moved by it and you do not know why. The impact of the projection comes at you like a billiard ball. Through projection terrible things can be brought about. If you do not know of the hook in yourself or of the open door, then the devil creeps in (the projection) and has a tremendous effect. You cannot be indifferent to a projection.

Dream Analysis: Notes of a Seminar Given in 1928–1930 (13 March 1929), p. 165.

Practical analysis has shown that unconscious contents are invariably projected at first upon concrete persons and situations. Many projections can ultimately be integrated back into the individual once he has recognized their subjective origin; others resist integration, and although they may be detached from their original objects, they thereupon transfer themselves to the doctor.

The Psychology of the Transference (1946), CW 16, § 357.

Projection is one of the commonest psychic phenomena. It is the same as *participation mystique*, which Lévy-Bruhl, to his great credit, emphasized as being an especially characteristic feature of primitive man. We merely give it another name, and as a rule deny that we are guilty of it. Everything that is unconscious in ourselves we discover in our neighbour, and we treat him accordingly.

"Archaic Man" (1931), CW 10, § 131.

[T]here is always an attraction between conscious mind and projected content. Generally it takes the form of a fascination.

Psychology and Alchemy (1944), CW 12, § 436.

[S]o long as a content remains in the projected state it is inaccessible.

Psychology and Alchemy (1944), CW 12, § 555.

Projections change the world into the replica of one's unknown face.

Aion (1951), CW 9ii, § 17.

Everything that works from the unconscious appears projected on others. Not that these others are wholly without blame, for even the worst projection is at least hung on a hook, perhaps a very small one, but still a hook offered by the other person.

"On Psychic Energy" (1928), CW 8, § 99.

True, whoever looks into the mirror of the water will see first of all his own face. Whoever goes to himself risks a confrontation with himself. The mirror does not flatter, it faithfully shows whatever looks into it; namely, the face we never show to the world because we cover it with the *persona*, the mask of the actor. But the mirror lies behind the mask and shows the true face.

"Archetypes of the Collective Unconscious" (1934/1954), CW 9i, § 43.

The tendencies of the conscious and the unconscious are the two factors that together make up the transcendent function. It is called "transcendent" because it makes the transition from one attitude to another organically possible, without loss of the unconscious.

"The Transcendent Function" ([1916]/1958), CW 8, § 145.

The process of coming to terms with the unconscious is a true labour, a work which involves both action and suffering. It has been named the "transcendent function" because it represents a function based on real and "imaginary," or rational and irrational, data, thus bridging the yawning gulf between conscious and unconscious.

On the Psychology of the Unconscious (1917/1926), CW 7, § 121.

[Y]ou find no trace of the transcendent function in the psychology of a man with definite religious convictions. What the term "transcendent function" designates is really the transition from one condition to another. When a man is caught by a religious concept, he does not leave it; he stays with his religious conviction, and, furthermore, that is what he should do. If any conflict appears, it is immediately repressed or resolved by a definite religious idea. That is why the transcendent function can be observed only in people who no longer have their original religious conviction, or never had any, and who, in consequence, find themselves directly faced with their unconscious. This was the case with Christ. He was a religious innovator who opposed the traditional religion of his time and his people. Thus he was *extra ecclesiam* [outside the church][3] and in a state of *nulla salus* [no salvation]. That is why he experienced the transcendent function, whereas a Christian saint could never experience it, since for him no fundamental and total change of attitude would be involved.

Letter to M. Zarine, 3 May 1939, *Letters, Vol. I*, p. 268.

How the harmonizing of conscious and unconscious data is to be undertaken cannot be indicated in the form of a recipe. It is an irrational life-process which expresses itself in definite symbols. It may be the task of the analyst to stand by this process with all the help he can give. In this case, knowledge of the symbols is indispensable, for it is in them that the union of conscious and unconscious contents is consummated. Out of this union emerge new situations and new conscious attitudes. I have therefore called the union of opposites the "transcendent function." This rounding out of the personality into a whole may well be the goal of any psychotherapy that claims to be more than a mere cure of symptoms.

"Conscious, Unconscious, and Individuation" (1939), CW 9i, § 524.

If the mediatory product remains intact, it forms the raw material for a process not of dissolution but of construction, in which thesis and antithesis both play their part. In this way it becomes a new content that governs the whole attitude, putting an end to the division and forcing the energy of the opposites into a common channel. The standstill is overcome and life can flow on with renewed power towards new goals.

Psychological Types (1921), CW 6, § 827.

---

[3] Square brackets within quotations always enclose the editor's translation or insertion.

The psychology of an individual can never be exhaustively explained from himself alone: a clear recognition is needed of the way it is also conditioned by historical and environmental circumstances. His individual psychology is not merely a physiological, biological, or moral problem, it is also a contemporary problem. Again, no psychological fact can ever be exhaustively explained in terms of causality alone; as a living phenomenon, it is always indissolubly bound up with the continuity of the vital process, so that it is not only something evolved but also continually evolving and creative.

Anything psychic is Janus-faced—it looks both backwards and forwards. Because it is so evolving, it is also preparing the future. Were this not so, intentions, aims, plans, calculations, predictions, and premonitions would be psychological impossibilities.

> *Psychological Types* (1921), CW 6, § 717–18.

Meaningful coincidences—which are to be distinguished from meaningless chance groupings—therefore seem to rest on an archetypal foundation.

> "Synchronicity: An Acausal Connecting Principle" (1952), CW 8,
> § 846.

Where an archetype prevails, we can expect synchronistic phenomena, i.e., *acausal correspondences*, which consist in a parallel arrangement of facts in time. The arrangement is not the effect of a cause. It just happens, being a consequence of the fact that causality is a statistical truth.

> Letter to John Raymond Smythies, 29 February 1952, *Letters, Vol. II*,
> p. 46.

My researches into the psychology of unconscious processes long ago compelled me to look around for another principle of explanation, since the causality principle seemed to me insufficient to explain certain remarkable manifestations of the unconscious. I found that there are psychic parallelisms which simply cannot be related to each other causally, but must be connected by another kind of principle altogether. This connection seemed to lie essentially in the relative simultaneity of the events, hence the term "synchronistic."

"Richard Wilhelm: In Memoriam" (1930), CW 15, § 81.

Viewed from the psychological standpoint, extra-sensory perception appears as a manifestation of the *collective unconscious*. This particular psyche behaves as if it were *one* and not as if it were split up into many individuals. It is *non-personal*. (I call it the "objective psyche.") It is the same everywhere and at all times. (If it were not so, comparative psychology would be impossible.) As it is not limited to the person, it is also not limited to the body. It manifests itself therefore not only in human beings but also at the same time in animals and even in physical circumstances. (Cf. the oracle technique of the *I Ching* and character horoscopes.) I call these latter phenomena the synchronicity of archetypal events. For instance, I walk with a woman patient in a wood. She tells me about the first dream in her life that had made an everlasting impression upon her. She had seen a spectral fox coming down the stairs in her parental home. At this moment a real fox comes out of the trees not 40 yards away and walks quietly on the path ahead of us for several minutes. The animal behaves as if it were a partner in the human situation. (One fact is no fact, but when you have seen many, you begin to sit up.)

Answers to Rhine's Questions, November 1945, *Letters, Vol. I*, p. 395.

The concept of synchronicity says that a connection exists which is not of a causal nature. The connection consists firstly in the fact of coincidence and secondly in the fact of parallel meaning. It is a question of meaningful coincidences.

Letter to Karl Schmid, 11 June 1958, *Letters, Vol. II*, pp. 446–47.

[S]ynchronistic phenomena manifest themselves as pure chance. The essential thing about these phenomena is that an objective event coincides meaningfully with a psychic process; that is to say, a physical event and an endopsychic one have a common meaning. This presupposes not only an all-pervading, latent meaning which can be recognized by consciousness, but, during that preconscious time, a psychoid process with which a physical event meaningfully coincides. Here the meaning cannot be recognized because there is as yet no consciousness. It is through the archetype that we come closest to this early, "irrepresentable," psychoid stage of conscious development; indeed, the archetype itself gives us direct intimations of it. Unconscious synchronicities are, as we know from experience, altogether possible, since in many cases we are unconscious of their happening, or have to have our attention drawn to the coincidence by an outsider.

Letter to Erich Neumann, 10 March 1959, *Letters, Vol. II*, p. 495.

[J]ung said to me [Pierre Courthion, the interviewer], "Take the tendency to commit suicide—right from the beginning. What happens? You don't pay attention on the street. One day you fall down stairs. Then there is a little automobile accident. It doesn't look like anything. Yet these are the preliminaries. Chance? Primitive people never mention chance. That is why I say, 'Be careful when you are not at one with yourself, in your moments of dissociation.'"

"A Wartime Interview" (1942), *C. G. Jung Speaking*, p. 144.

Everyone knows nowadays that people "have complexes." What is not so well known, though far more important theoretically, is that complexes can *have us*. The existence of complexes throws serious doubt on the naïve assumption of the unity of consciousness, which is equated with "psyche," and on the supremacy of the will. Every constellation of a complex postulates a disturbed state of consciousness. The unity of consciousness is disrupted and the intentions of the will are impeded or made impossible. Even memory is often noticeably affected, as we have seen. The complex must therefore be a psychic factor which, in terms of energy, possesses a value that sometimes exceeds that of our conscious intentions, otherwise such disruptions of the conscious order would not be possible at all.

"A Review of the Complex Theory" (1934), CW 8, § 200.

Complexes are in truth the living units of the unconscious psyche, and it is only through them that we are able to deduce its existence and its constitution. The unconscious would in fact be—as it is in Wundt's psychology—nothing but a vestige of dim or "obscure" representations, or a "fringe of consciousness," as William James calls it, were it not for the existence of complexes. That is why Freud became the real discoverer of the unconscious in psychology, because he examined those dark places and did not simply dismiss them, with a disparaging euphemism, as "parapraxes." The *via regia* to the unconscious, however, is not the dream, as he thought, but the complex, which is the architect of dreams and of symptoms. Nor is this *via* so very "royal," either, since the way pointed out by the complex is more like a rough and uncommonly devious footpath that often loses itself in the undergrowth and generally leads not into the heart of the unconscious but past it.

"A Review of the Complex Theory" (1934), CW 8, § 210.

[C]omplexes are focal or nodal points of psychic life which we would not wish to do without; indeed, they should not be missing, for otherwise psychic activity would come to a fatal standstill.

Psychological Types (1921), CW 6, § 925.

What then, scientifically speaking, is a "feeling-toned complex?" It is the *image* of a certain psychic situation which is strongly accentuated emotionally and is, moreover, incompatible with the habitual attitude of consciousness. This image has a powerful inner coherence, it has its own wholeness and, in addition, a relatively high degree of autonomy, so that it is subject to the control of the conscious mind to only a limited extent, and therefore behaves like an animated foreign body in the sphere of consciousness. The complex can usually be suppressed with an effort of will, but not argued out of existence, and at the first suitable opportunity it reappears in all its original strength.

"A Review of the Complex Theory" (1934), CW 8, § 201.

A complex can be really overcome only if it is lived out to the full. In other words, if we are to develop further we have to draw to us and drink down to the very dregs what, because of our complexes, we have held at a distance.

"Psychological Aspects of the Mother Archetype" (1938/1954),

CW 9i, § 184.

Where the realm of the complexes begins the freedom of the ego comes to an end, for complexes are psychic agencies whose deepest nature is still unfathomed.

"A Review of the Complex Theory" (1934), CW 8, § 216.

Since the stars have fallen from heaven and our highest symbols have paled, a secret life holds sway in the unconscious. That is why we have a psychology today, and why we speak of the unconscious. All this would be quite superfluous in an age or culture that possessed symbols. Symbols are spirit from above, and under those conditions the spirit is above too. Therefore it would be a foolish and senseless undertaking for such people to wish to experience or investigate an unconscious that contains nothing but the silent, undisturbed sway of nature. Our unconscious, on the other hand, hides living water, spirit that has become nature, and that is why it is disturbed. Heaven has become for us the cosmic space of the physicists, and the divine empyrean a fair memory of things that once were. But "the heart glows," and a secret unrest gnaws at the roots of our being.

"Archetypes of the Collective Unconscious" (1934/1954), CW 9i,

§ 50.

2
The Structure of the Psyche

We understand the ego as the complex factor to which all conscious contents are related. It forms, as it were, the centre of the field of consciousness; and, in so far as this comprises the empirical personality, the ego is the subject of all personal acts of consciousness. The relation of a psychic content to the ego forms the criterion of its consciousness, for no content can be conscious until it is represented to a subject.

Aion (1951), CW 9ii, § 1.

The important fact about consciousness is that nothing can be conscious without an ego to which it refers. If something is not related to the ego then it is not conscious. Therefore you can define consciousness as a relation of psychic facts to the ego. What is that ego? The ego is a complex datum which is constituted first of all by a general awareness of your body, of your existence, and secondly by your memory data; you have a certain idea of having been, a long series of memories. Those two are the main constituents of what we call the ego. Therefore you can call the ego a complex of psychic facts. This complex has a great power of attraction, like a magnet; it attracts contents from the unconscious, from that dark realm of which we know nothing; it also attracts impressions from the outside, and when they enter into association with the ego they are conscious. If they do not, they are not conscious.

The Tavistock Lectures: On the Theory and Practice of Analytical Psychology (1935), CW 18, (1968), CW 18, § 18.

The ego, the subject of consciousness, comes into existence as a complex quantity which is constituted partly by the inherited disposition (character constituents) and partly by unconsciously acquired impressions and their attendant phenomena.

Analytical Psychology and Education (1926/1946), CW 17, § 169.

Since it is the point of reference for the field of consciousness, the ego is the subject of all successful attempts at adaptation so far as these are achieved by the will.

Aion (1951), CW 9ii, § 11.

As a conscious factor the ego could, theoretically at least, be described completely. But this would never amount to more than a picture of the *conscious personality*; all those features which are unknown or unconscious to the subject would be missing. A total picture would have to include these.

Aion (1951), CW 9ii, § 7.

Most people confuse "self-knowledge" with knowledge of their conscious ego-personalities. Anyone who has any ego-consciousness at all takes it for granted that he knows himself. But the ego knows only its own contents, not the unconscious and its contents.

The Undiscovered Self (1957), CW 10, § 491.

In mental disorder, for instance, you have to start by strengthening the ego. Sometimes it is necessary to say with vigor: "Come on, that's just a fantasy." First of all, the fantasy is devalued by this, the ego and the vision are torn apart, a distance is put between them. Sometimes you have to take very drastic measures to bring about the differentiation. So it can be necessary to shout at somebody to wake him up, when he is drifting into a kind of collective sleep, or to grab hold of people and shake them, so that they know who they are. A slap or a shove can work wonders, so that the person feels: "This is me." There are good circumstances when a good smack, morally or physically, is the most effective way to counter the great fascination of the images.

Children's Dreams: Notes from the Seminar Given in 1936–1940,
p. 184.

The personal unconscious is personified by the shadow.

Mysterium Coniunctionis (1955–1956), CW 14, § 128.

[W]e would call it the unconscious, and we distinguish between a personal unconscious which enables us to recognize the shadow and an impersonal unconscious which enables us to recognize the archetypal symbol of the self.

Aion (1951), CW 9ii, § 261.

The shadow is a living part of the personality and therefore wants to live with it in some form. It cannot be argued out of existence or rationalized into harmlessness.

"Archetypes of the Collective Unconscious" (1934/1954), CW 9i,
§ 44.

[W]hen one tries desperately to be good and wonderful and perfect, then all the more the shadow develops a definite will to be black and evil and destructive. People cannot see that; they are always striving to be marvellous, and then they discover that terrible destructive things happen which they cannot understand, and they either deny that such facts have anything to do with them, or if they admit them, they take them for natural afflictions, or they try to minimize them and to shift the responsibility elsewhere. The fact is that if one tries beyond one's capacity to be perfect, the shadow descends into hell and becomes the devil. For it is just as sinful from the standpoint of nature and of truth to be above oneself as to be below oneself. It is surely not the divine will in man that he should be something which he is not, for when one looks into nature, one sees that it is most definitely the divine will that everything should be what it is.

Visions: Notes of the Seminar Given in 1930–1934. Vol. I (10 February
1932), p. 569.

When you accept the fact of your inferiority, it lives with you; you are it too, but not exclusively. You are not only white, one part is black, but both make the whole man. It is not wiping out the white substance when you accept the black—on the contrary; it is only when you *can't* that things go wrong, when there is nothing but white and nothing but black. That is simply neurotic.

Visions: Notes of the Seminar Given in 1930–1934, Vol. I (3 June 1931), p. 391.

By not being aware of having a shadow, you declare a part of your personality to be non-existent. Then it enters the kingdom of the non-existent, which swells up and takes on enormous proportions. When you don't acknowledge that you have such qualities, you are simply feeding the devils. In medical language, each quality in the psyche represents a certain energic value, and if you declare an energic value to be non-existent, a devil appears instead. If you declare that the river which flows by your house is non-existent, it may swell up and fill your garden with pebbles and sand and undermine your house. If you give such a limitless possibility to nature to work by itself, nature can do what she pleases. If you see a herd of cattle or pigs and say they are non-existent, they are immediately all over the place, the cows will eat up the rose-garden and the pigs will climb into your bed and sleep there! In this way the non-existent grows fat. Meyrink's *Die Fledermäus* (otherwise very bad) describes very vividly a world in which are living some extremely poor specimens of people, pale, sad, unhealthy, and getting worse and worse; and then the discovery is made that as they decrease, certain corpses in the graveyard are growing proportionately fat. The thing you have buried grows fat while you grow thin. If you get rid of qualities you don't like by denying them, you become more and more unaware of what you are, you declare yourself more and more non-existent, and your devils will grow fatter and fatter.

Dream Analysis: Notes of the Seminar Given in 1928–1930 (28 November 1928), p. 53.

Assimilation of the shadow gives a man body, so to speak; the animal sphere of instinct, as well as the primitive or archaic psyche, emerge into the zone of consciousness and can no longer be repressed by fictions and illusions. In this way man becomes for himself the difficult problem he really is. He must always remain conscious of the fact that he is such a problem if he wants to develop at all.

The Psychology of the Transference (1946), CW 16, § 452.

The shadow is a tight passage, a narrow door, whose painful constriction no one is spared who goes down to the deep well. But one must learn to know oneself in order to know who one is. For what comes after the door is, surprisingly enough, a boundless expanse full of unprecedented uncertainty, with apparently no inside and no outside, no above and no below, no here and no there, no mine and no thine, no good and no bad. It is the world of water, where all life floats in suspension; where the realm of the sympathetic system, the soul of everything living, begins; where I am indivisibly this *and* that; where I experience the other in myself and the other-than-myself experiences me.

"Archetypes of the Collective Unconscious" (1934/1954), CW 9i, § 45.

[T]he more one turns to the light, the greater is the shadow behind one's back. Or, the more one turns one's eyes to the light of consciousness, the more one feels the shadow at one's back.

Dream Analysis: Notes of the Seminar Given in 1928–1930 (28 November 1928), p. 49.

[W]hen there is a light in the darkness which comprehends the darkness, darkness no longer prevails.

Mysterium Coniunctionis (1955–56), CW 14, § 345.

Light is followed by shadow, the other side of the Creator.

Memories, Dreams, Reflections (1962), p. 328.

Since human nature is not compounded wholly of light, but also abounds in shadows, the insight gained in practical analysis is often somewhat painful, the more so if, as is generally the case, one has previously neglected the other side. Hence there are people who take their newly won insight very much to heart, far too much in fact, quite forgetting that they are not unique in having a shadow-side. They allow themselves to get unduly depressed and are then inclined to doubt everything, finding nothing right anywhere. That is why so many excellent analysts with very good ideas can never bring themselves to publish them, because the psychic problem, as they see it, is so overwhelmingly vast that it seems to them almost impossible to tackle it scientifically.

The Relations between the Ego and the Unconscious (1916/1928),

CW 7, § 225.

[I]t is a therapeutic necessity, indeed, the first requisite of any thorough psychological method, for consciousness to confront its shadow. In the end this must lead to some kind of union, even though the union consists at first in an open conflict, and often remains so for a long time. It is a struggle that cannot be abolished by rational means. When it is wilfully repressed it continues in the unconscious and merely expresses itself indirectly and all the more dangerously, so no advantage is gained. The struggle goes on until the opponents run out of breath. What the outcome will be can never be seen in advance. The only certain thing is that both parties will be changed; but what the product of the union will be it is impossible to imagine. The empirical material shows that it usually takes the form of a subjective experience which, according to the unanimous testimony of history, is always of a religious order. If, therefore, the conflict is consciously endured and the analyst follows its course without prejudice, he will unfailingly observe compensations from the unconscious which aim at producing a unity.

Mysterium Coniunctionis (1955–56), CW 14, § 514.

[T]o be fully aware of the shadow would be an almost superhuman task, but we can reach a certain optimum of consciousness; we should be aware to a much higher degree than we are now.

Visions: Notes of the Seminar Given in 1930–1934, Vol. I (18 February 1931), p. 237.

Self-knowledge is an adventure that carries us unexpectedly far and deep. Even a moderately comprehensive knowledge of the shadow can cause a good deal of confusion and mental darkness, since it gives rise to personality problems which one had never remotely imagined before

Mysterium Coniunctionis (1955–56), CW 14, § 741.

The shadow is a moral problem that challenges the whole ego-personality, for no one can become conscious of the shadow without considerable moral effort. To become conscious of it involves recognizing the dark aspects of the personality as present and real. This act is the essential condition for any kind of self-knowledge, and it therefore, as a rule, meets with considerable resistance. Indeed, self-knowledge as a psychotherapeutic measure frequently requires much painstaking work extending over a long period.

Aion (1951), CW 9ii, § 14.

[W]hat is light without shadow? What is high without low? You deprive the deity of its omnipotence and its universality by depriving it of the dark quality of the world. To ascribe infinite evil to man and all the good to God would make man much too important: he would be as big as God, because light and the absence of light are equal, they belong together in order to make the whole.

Nietzsche's Zarathustra: Notes of the Seminar Given in 1934–1939,
Vol. II (20 May 1936), p. 929.

Our shadow is the last thing that has to be put on top of everything, and that is the thing we cannot swallow; we can swallow anything else, but not our own shadow because it makes us doubt our good qualities.

Nietzsche's Zarathustra: Notes of the Seminar Given in 1934–1939,
Vol. II (19 May 1937), p. 1090.

So whatever comes from behind comes from the shadow, from the darkness of the unconscious, and because you have no eyes there, and because you wear no neck amulet to ward off evil influences, that thing gets at you, possesses and obsesses you. It sits on top of you.

Nietzsche's Zarathustra: Notes of the Seminar Given in 1934–1939, Vol. II (25 May 1938), p.1265.

One realizes, first of all, that one cannot project one's shadow on to others, and next that there is no advantage in insisting on their guilt, as it is so much more important to know and possess one's own, because it is part of one's own self and a necessary factor without which nothing in this sublunary world can be realized.

Mysterium Coniunctionis (1955–56), CW 14, § 203.

This process of coming to terms with the Other in us is well worth while, because in this way we get to know aspects of our nature which we would not allow anybody else to show us and which we ourselves would never have admitted.

Mysterium Coniunctionis (1955–56), CW 14, § 706.

Confrontation with the shadow produces at first a dead balance, a standstill that hampers moral decisions and makes convictions ineffective or even impossible. Everything becomes doubtful.

Mysterium Coniunctionis (1955–56), CW 14, § 708.

We are inflated because we don't know or because we have forgotten what we are. We substitute our ignorance with gas; modern people are all gas bags inasmuch as they are ignorant of what they really are. We have simply forgotten what a human being really is, so we have men like Nietzsche and Freud and Adler, who tell us what we are, quite mercilessly. We have to discover our shadow. Otherwise we are driven into a world war in order to see what beasts we are.

Visions: Notes of the Seminar Given in 1930–1934, Vol. I (18 February 1931), p. 235.

I have defined the anima as a personification of the unconscious in general, and have taken it as a bridge to the unconscious, in other words, as a function of relationship to the unconscious.

"Commentary on *The Secret of the Golden Flower*" (1929), CW 13, § 62.

Every man carries within him the eternal image of woman, not the image of this or that particular woman, but a definite feminine image. This image is fundamentally unconscious, a hereditary factor of primordial origin engraved in the living organic system of the man, an imprint or "archetype" of all the ancestral experiences of the female, a deposit, as it were, of all the impressions ever made by a woman—in short, an inherited system of psychic adaptation. Even if no woman existed, it would still be possible, at any given time, to deduce from this unconscious image exactly how a woman would have to be constituted psychically. The same is true of the woman: she too has her inborn image of man. Actually, we know from experience that it would be more accurate to describe it as an image of *men*, whereas in the case of the man it is rather the image of *woman*. Since this image is unconscious, it is always unconsciously projected upon the person of the beloved, and is one of the chief reasons for passionate attraction or aversion. I have called this image the "anima."

"Marriage as a Psychological Relationship" (1925), CW 17, § 338.

You are not responsible for your constitution but you are stuck with it, and so it is with the anima, which is likewise a constitutional factor one is stuck with. For what we are stuck with we have a certain responsibility, namely for the way we act towards it, but not for the fact that it exists. At any rate we can never treat the anima with moral reprimands; instead of this we have, or there is, wisdom, which in our days seems to have passed into oblivion.

Letter to Ewald Jung, 31 July 1935, *Letters, Vol. I*, p. 193.

In the Middle Ages, long before the physiologists demonstrated that by reason of our glandular structure there are both male and female elements in all of us, it was said that "every man carries a woman within himself." It is this female element in every male that I have called the "anima." This "feminine" aspect is essentially a certain inferior kind of relatedness to the surroundings, and particularly to women, which is kept carefully concealed from others as well as from oneself. In other words, though an individual's visible personality may seem quite normal, he may well be concealing from others—or even from himself—the deplorable condition of "the woman within."

"Approaching the Unconscious" (1964), *Man and His Symbols*, p. 31.

Woman is compensated by a masculine element and therefore her unconscious has, so to speak, a masculine imprint. This results in a considerable psychological difference between men and women, and accordingly I have called the projection-making factor in women the animus, which means mind or spirit. The animus corresponds to the paternal Logos just as the anima corresponds to the maternal Eros.

Aion (1951), CW 9ii, § 29.

Though the effects of anima and animus can be made conscious, they themselves are factors transcending consciousness and beyond the reach of perception and volition. Hence they remain autonomous despite the integration of their contents, and for this reason they should be borne constantly in mind.

Aion (1951), CW 9ii, § 40.

In its primary "unconscious" form the animus is a compound of spontaneous, unpremeditated opinions which exercise a powerful influence on the woman's emotional life, while the anima is similarly compounded of feelings which thereafter influence or distort the man's understanding ("she has turned his head"). Consequently the animus likes to project himself upon "intellectuals" and all kinds of "heroes," including tenors, artists, sporting celebrities, etc. The anima has a predilection for everything that is unconscious, dark, equivocal, and unrelated in woman, and also for her vanity, frigidity, helplessness, and so forth.

The Psychology of the Transference (1946), CW 16, § 521.

One must separate the shadow from the animus or anima. Therefore one of the most important parts of analysis consists in the understanding of the negative aspects of oneself, all the negative qualities one possesses.

Visions: Notes of the Seminar Given in 1930–1934, Vol. II (25 January 1933), p. 890.

The animus does not belong to the function of conscious relationship; his function is rather to facilitate relations with the unconscious. Instead of the woman merely associating opinions with external situations—the animus, as an associative function, should be directed inwards, where it could associate the contents of the unconscious. The technique of coming to terms with the animus is the same in principle as in the case of the anima; only here the woman must learn to criticize and hold her opinions at a distance; not in order to repress them, but, by investigating their origins, to penetrate more deeply into the background, where she will then discover the primordial images, just as the man does in his dealings with the anima. The animus is the deposit, as it were, of all woman's ancestral experiences of man—and not only that, he is also a creative and procreative being, not in the sense of masculine creativity, but in the sense that he brings forth something we might call the spermatic word. Just as a man brings forth his work as a complete creation out of his inner feminine nature, so the inner masculine side of a woman brings forth creative seeds which have the power to fertilize the feminine side of the man.

The Relations between the Ego and the Unconscious (1916/1928), CW 7, § 336.

[T]he animus is not created by the conscious, it is a creation of the unconscious, and therefore it is a personification of the unconscious.

Visions: Notes of the Seminar Given in 1930–1934, Vol. I (11 February 1931), p. 208.

For a woman, the typical danger emanating from the unconscious comes *from above*, from the "spiritual" sphere personified by the animus, whereas for a man it comes from the chthonic realm of the "world and woman," i.e., the anima projected on to the world.

"A Study in the Process of Individuation" (1934/1950), CW 9i, § 559.

[T]he "soul" which accrues to ego-consciousness during the *opus* has a feminine character in the man and a masculine character in the woman. His anima wants to reconcile and unite; her animus tries to discern and discriminate.

The Psychology of the Transference (1946), CW 16, § 522.

A woman possessed by the animus is always in danger of losing her femininity, her adapted feminine persona, just as a man in like circumstances runs the risk of effeminacy. These psychic changes of sex are due entirely to the fact that a function which belongs inside has been turned outside. The reason for this perversion is clearly the failure to give adequate recognition to an inner world which stands autonomously opposed to the outer world, and makes just as serious demands on our capacity for adaptation.

The Relations between the Ego and the Unconscious (1916/1928), CW 7, § 337.

Man understands his relation to his anima as being a highly emotional affair, while woman's relation to her animus is more in the Logos field. When a man is possessed by his anima, he is under peculiar feelings, he cannot control his emotions, but is controlled by them. A woman dominated by her animus is one who is possessed by opinions. Nor is she too discriminating about these opinions.

> *Introduction to Jungian Psychology: Notes of a Seminar on Analytical Psychology Given in 1925*, p. 122.

[T]he integration of the shadow, or the realization of the personal unconscious, marks the first stage in the analytic process, and without it a recognition of anima and animus is impossible. The shadow can be realized only through a relation to a partner, and anima and animus only through a relation to a partner of the opposite sex, because only in such a relation do their projections become operative. The recognition of the anima gives rise, in a man, to a triad, one third of which is transcendent: the masculine subject, the opposing feminine subject, and the transcendent anima. With a woman the situation is reversed.

> *Aion* (1951), CW 9ii, § 42.

No matter how friendly and obliging a woman's Eros may be, no logic on earth can shake her if she is ridden by the animus.

> *Aion* (1951), CW 9ii, § 29.

Like the anima, the animus too has a positive aspect. Through the figure of the father he expresses not only conventional opinion but—equally—what we call "spirit," philosophical or religious ideas in particular, or rather the attitude resulting from them. Thus the animus is a psychopomp, a mediator between the conscious and the unconscious and a personification of the latter. Just as the anima becomes, through integration, the Eros of consciousness, so the animus becomes a Logos; and in the same way that the anima gives relationship and relatedness to a man's consciousness, the animus gives to woman's consciousness a capacity for reflection, deliberation, and self-knowledge.

> *Aion* (1951), CW 9ii, § 33.

The animus is a sort of film between reality and a woman's mind, she always talks about things as they should be, so when she says a thing is really so, it is really not so at all. She never realizes how difficult it is to establish the truth about things, she thinks truth is established by saying something.

Visions: Notes of the Seminar Given in 1930–1934, Vol. I (2 March
1932), p. 615.

[T]he animus is meant to be cosmic. It is a function which should widen out the spiritual or mental possibilities into infinite space, as it were, into the infinity of the collective mind. Inasmuch as the animus is expanding into the great unconscious cosmos, he is really in his own element—there he belongs, that is his home.

Visions: Notes of the Seminar Given in 1930–1934, Vol. II (13
December 1933), p. 1228.

[T]he animus when on his way, on his quest, is really a *psychopompos*, leading the soul back to the stars whence it came. On the way back out of the existence in the flesh, the *psychopompos* develops such a cosmic aspect, he wanders among the constellations, he leads the soul over the rainbow bridge into the blossoming fields of the stars.

Visions: Notes of the Seminar Given in 1930–1934, Vol. II (13
December 1933), p. 1229.

This function of mediation between the opposites I have termed the *transcendent function*, by which I mean nothing mysterious, but merely a combined function of conscious and unconscious elements, or, as in mathematics, a common function of real and imaginary qualities.

Psychological Types (1921), CW 6, § 184.

[T]he animus and the mind of a woman are those functions in which the data of the unconscious and of the conscious can be united. Therefore the Logos element would carry the transcendent function in a woman, as the Eros would function in a man; his Eros, his personal relatedness, together with the anima, carry the symbol which unites the data of the unconscious and the conscious, and thus makes the transcendent function possible.

Visions: Notes of the Seminar Given in 1930–1934, Vol. II (29 November 1933), p. 1209.

Eros is a *kosmogonos*, a creater and father-mother of all higher consciousness.

Memories, Dreams, Reflections (1962), p. 353.

Though the shadow is a motif as well known to mythology as anima and animus, it represents first and foremost the personal unconscious, and its content can therefore be made conscious without too much difficulty. In this it differs from anima and animus, for whereas the shadow can be seen through and recognized fairly easily, the anima and animus are much further away from consciousness and in normal circumstances are seldom if ever realized. With a little self-criticism one can see through the shadow— so far as its nature is personal. But when it appears as an archetype, one encounters the same difficulties as with anima and animus. In other words, it is quite within the bounds of possibility for a man to recognize the relative evil of his nature, but it is a rare and shattering experience for him to gaze into the face of absolute evil.

Aion (1951), CW 9ii, §19.

[I]t is easier to gain insight into the shadow than into the anima or animus. With the shadow, we have the advantage of being prepared in some sort by our education, which has always endeavoured to convince people that they are not one-hundred-per-cent pure gold. So everyone immediately understands what is meant by "shadow," "inferior personality," etc. And if he has forgotten, his memory can easily be refreshed by a Sunday sermon, his wife, or the tax collector. With the anima and animus, however, things are by no means so simple. Firstly, there is no moral education in this respect, and secondly, most people are content to be self-righteous and prefer mutual vilification (if nothing worse!) to the recognition of their projections. Indeed, it seems a very natural state of affairs for men to have irrational moods and women irrational opinions.

Aion (1951), CW 9ii, § 35.

The anima and animus have tremendous influence because we leave the shadow to them.

Dream Analysis: Notes of the Seminar Given in 1928–1930 (28 November 1928), p. 53.

[W]hen animus and anima meet, the animus draws his sword of power and the anima ejects her poison of illusion and seduction. The outcome need not always be negative, since the two are equally likely to fall in love (a special instance of love at first sight).

Aion (1951), CW 9ii, § 30.

The animus and anima are unconscious factors which can never completely disappear from discussion; wherever you are, in whatever condition you are, they remain a problem. I could even go as far as to say that without the anima and animus there would be no object, no other human being, because you perceive differences only through that which is a likeness to the differences in yourself.

Visions: Notes of the Seminar Given in 1930–1934, Vol. II (14 March 1934), p. 1357.

[A] content can only be integrated when its double aspect has become conscious and when it is grasped not merely intellectually but understood according to its feeling-value. Intellect and feeling, however, are difficult to put into one harness—they conflict with one another by definition. Whoever identifies with an intellectual standpoint will occasionally find his feeling confronting him like an enemy in the guise of the anima; conversely, an intellectual animus will make violent attacks on the feeling standpoint. Therefore, anyone who wants to achieve the difficult feat of achieving something not only intellectually, but also according to its feeling-value, must for better or for worse come to grips with the anima/animus problem in order to open the way for a higher union, a *coniunctio oppositorum* [a union of the opposites]. This is an indispensable prerequisite for wholeness.

Aion (1951), CW 9ii, § 58.

I may define "self" as the totality of the conscious and unconscious psyche, but this totality transcends our vision; it is a veritable *lapis invisibilitatis* [stone of invisibility]. In so far as the unconscious exists it is not definable; its existence is a mere postulate and nothing whatever can be predicated as to its possible contents.

Psychology and Alchemy (1944), CW 12, § 247.

I have suggested calling the total personality which, though present, cannot be fully known, the *self*. The ego is, by definition, subordinate to the self and is related to it like a part to the whole.

Aion (1951), CW 9ii, § 9.

[O]ne man alone cannot reach the self.

Nietzsche's Zarathustra: Notes of the Seminar Given in 1934–1939,
Vol. II (29 January 1936), p. 787.

The self is merely a term that designates the whole personality. The whole personality of man is indescribable. His consciousness *can* be described, his unconscious *cannot* be described because the unconscious—and here I must repeat myself—is always unconscious. It is really unconscious, we really don't know it, so we don't know our unconscious personality. We have hints, we have certain ideas, but we don't know it really. Nobody can say where man ends. That is the beauty of it, you know; it's very interesting. The unconscious of man can reach God knows where. There we are going to make discoveries.

"The Houston Films" (1957), *C. G. Jung Speaking*, p. 301.

The self is by definition the totality of all psychic facts and contents. It consists on one side of our ego consciousness that is included in the unconscious like a smaller circle in a greater one. So the self is not only an unconscious fact, but also a conscious fact: the ego is the visibility of the self. Of course, in the ego the self only becomes dimly visible, but you get under favourable conditions a fair idea of it through the ego—not a very true picture, yet it is an attempt. You see, it is as if the self were trying to manifest in space and time, but since it consists of so many elements that have neither space nor time qualities, it cannot bring them altogether into space and time. And those efforts of the self to manifest in the empirical world result in man: he is the result of the attempt. So much of the self remains outside, it doesn't enter this three-dimensional empirical world. The self consists, then, of the most recent acquisitions of the ego consciousness and on the other side, of the archaic material. The self is a fact of nature and always appears as such in immediate experiences, in dreams and visions, and so on; it is the spirit in the stone, the great secret which has to be worked out, to be extracted from nature, because it is buried in nature herself. It is also most dangerous, just as dangerous as an archetypal invasion because it contains *all* the archetypes: one could say an archetypal experience was the experience of the self. It is like a personification of nature and of anything that can be experienced in nature, including what we call God.

Nietzsche's Zarathustra: Notes of the Seminar Given in 1934–1939,
Vol. II (3 June 1936), p. 977.

[T]he symbol for the Self[4] is an idea of a totality that is not identical with the ego. It is a consciousness which is not exactly our consciousness, a light which is not exactly our light.

Visions: Notes of the Seminar Given in 1930–1934, Vol. I (11
November 1931), p. 445.

Through the self we are plunged into the torrent of cosmic events. Everything essential happens in the self and the ego functions as a receiver, spectator, and transmitter.

Letter to Aniela Jaffé, 22 December 1942, *Letters, Vol. I*, p. 326.

[4] In the original (English) version of the *Visions Seminars*, *Self* is always capitalized.

[E]very light, every fire, comes to an end, and there would be utter darkness, but there is still left the light of the self, which is the supreme light.

Nietzsche's Zarathustra: Notes of the Seminar Given in 1934–1939,
Vol. II (29 January 1936), p. 792.

The self, as a symbol of wholeness, is a *coincidentia oppositorum* [coming together of the opposites], and therefore contains light and dark simultaneously.

Symbols of Transformation (1912/1952), CW 5, § 576.

During those years, between 1918 and 1920, I began to understand that the goal of psychic development is the self. There is no linear evolution; there is only a circumambulation of the self. Uniform development exists, at most, only at the beginning; later, everything points toward the center. This insight gave me stability, and gradually my inner peace returned. I knew that in finding the mandala as an expression of the self I had attained what was for me the ultimate. Perhaps someone else knows more, but not I.

Memories, Dreams, Reflections (1962), pp. 196–97.

The ego stands to the self as the moved to the mover, or as object to subject, because the determining factors which radiate out from the self surround the ego on all sides and are therefore supraordinate to it. The self, like the unconscious, is an *a priori* existent out of which the ego evolves. It is, so to speak, an unconscious prefiguration of the ego. It is not I who create myself, rather I happen to myself.

"Transformation Symbolism in the Mass" (1942/1954), CW 11,
§ 391.

Whatever man's wholeness, or the self, may mean *per se*, empirically it is an image of the goal of life spontaneously produced by the unconscious, irrespective of the wishes and fears of the conscious mind. It stands for the goal of the total man, for the realization of his wholeness and individuality with or without the consent of his will. The dynamic of this process is instinct, which ensures that everything which belongs to an individual's life shall enter into it, whether he consents or not, or is conscious of what is happening to him or not. Obviously, it makes a great deal of difference subjectively whether he knows what he is living out, whether he understands what he is doing, and whether he accepts responsibility for what he proposes to do or has done.

Answer to Job (1952), CW 11, § 745.

That tiny thing, that unique individual, the Self, is small as the point of a needle, yet because it is so small it is also greater than great.

Visions: Notes of the Seminar Given in 1930–1934, Vol. I (21 May 1931), p. 358.

The self, in its efforts at self-realization, reaches out beyond the ego-personality on all sides; because of its all-encompassing nature it is brighter and darker than the ego, and accordingly confronts it with problems which it would like to avoid. Either one's moral courage fails, or one's insight, or both, until in the end fate decides. The ego never lacks moral and rational counterarguments, which one cannot and should not set aside so long as it is possible to hold on to them. For you only feel yourself on the right road when the conflicts of duty seem to have resolved themselves, and you have become the victim of a decision made over your head or in defiance of the heart. From this we can see the numinous power of the self, which can hardly be experienced in any other way. For this reason *the experience of the self is always a defeat for the ego*.

Mysterium Coniunctionis (1955–56), CW 14, § 778.

So the Self is part of the collective unconscious, but it is not the collective unconscious; it is that unit which apparently comes from the union of the ego and the shadow. We designate that totality as the Self, where everything conscious is united with everything unconscious, with the exception of those things that reach beyond our limitation in time and space. The Self is in its structure like the collective unconscious, and it is also a non-ego because it is beyond our grasp; it reaches over our heads. We can never say, "I *know* this Self of mine." We don't know it, we can never know it because it is the bigger circle that includes the smaller circle of our consciousness. Just as the Self is a unit in the collective unconscious, so we are units in the Self. And how can we know the whole of which we are only a part?

Visions: Notes of the Seminar Given in 1930–1934, Vol. II (15 June 1932), p. 754.

The forest philosophers didn't go out into the forests in the beginning to try to find the self. They first live a full human life in the world and then comes the wood life. They are rooted in the world. They never shunned the individual social life, but gathered all the experience from their worldly existence, and then carried it into the wood. And that was the case in Buddha's own existence; he was a prince, a man of the world, and he had a wife, he had concubines, he had a child—then he went over to the saintly life. I could say just as well that you could never attain the self without isolation; it is both being alone and in relationship.

Nietzsche's Zarathustra: Notes of the Seminar Given in 1934–1939, Vol. II (29 January 1936), p. 797.

[T]he term *self* is often mixed up with the idea of God. I would not do that. I would say that the term *self* should be reserved for that sphere which is within the reach of human experience, and we should be very careful not to use the word *God* too often. As we use it, it borders on impertinence; it is unlawful to use such a concept too often. The experience of the self is so marvelous and so complete that one is of course tempted to use the conception of God to express it. I think it is better not to, because the self has the peculiar quality of being specific yet universal. It is a restricted universality or a universal restrictedness, a paradox; so it is a relatively universal being and therefore doesn't deserve to be called "God." You could think of it as an intermediary, or a hierarchy of ever-widening-out figures of the self *till* one arrives at the conception of a deity. So we should reserve that term *God* for a remote deity that is supposed to be the absolute unity of all singularities. The self would be the preceding stage, a being that is more than man and that definitely manifests; that is the thinker of our thoughts, the doer of our deeds, the maker of our lives, yet it is still within the reach of human experience.

Nietzsche's Zarathustra: Notes of the Seminar Given in 1934–1939,
Vol. II (3 June 1936), pp. 977–78.

Intellectually the self is no more than a psychological concept, a construct that serves to express an unknowable essence which we cannot grasp as such, since by definition it transcends our powers of comprehension. It might equally well be called the "God within us." The beginnings of our whole psychic life seem to be inextricably rooted in this point, and all our highest and ultimate purposes seem to be striving towards it. This paradox is unavoidable, as always, when we try to define something that lies beyond the bourn of our understanding.

The Relations between the Ego and the Unconscious (1916/1928),
CW 7, § 399.

I am unable to envisage anything beyond the self, since it is—by definition—a borderline concept designating the unknown totality of man: there are no known limits to the unconscious. There is no reason whatsoever why you should or should not call the beyond-self Christ or Buddha or Purusha or Tao or Khidr or Tifereth. All these terms are recognizable formulations of what I call the "self."

"Jung and Religious Belief" (1958), CW 18, § 1672.

[P]eople often say that they can in a measure do what they like, but that the main thing is done by the will of God. God is doing it through them; that is, of course, the religious form of confessing the quality of the self. Therefore, my definition of the self is a non-personal center, the center of the psychical non-ego—of all that in the psyche which is not ego—and presumably is to be found everywhere in all people. You can call it the center of the collective unconscious. It is as if our unconscious psychology or psyche were centered, just as our conscious psyche is centered in the ego consciousness. The very word *consciousness* is a term expressing association of the contents of a center to the ego, and the same would be the case with the unconscious, yet there it is obviously not *my* ego, because the unconscious condition *is* unconscious: it is not related to me. I am very much related to the unconscious because the unconscious can influence me all the time, yet I cannot influence the unconscious. It is just as if I were the *object* of a consciousness, as if somebody knew of me though I didn't know of him. That center, that other order of consciousness which to me is unconscious, would be the self, and that doesn't confine itself to myself, to my ego: it can include I don't know how many other people.

Nietzsche's Zarathustra: Notes of the Seminar Given in 1934–1939,
Vol. II (22 January, 1936), p. 783.

[T]he self is timeless, and that assembly of facts which characterizes the self has been chosen before time. Therefore, one cannot help having the feeling of being chosen, and that this whole thing is chosen, premeditated. There is no getting away from it: one is embedded in a course of events that is meaningful. Now, if that is not realized consciously, it simply spreads out unconsciously, and instead of the chosen self, realized by consciousness as the choice that has taken place before time, the whole people is chosen; and then you have that funny fact of a people imagining that it has a mission or something like that—that they are God's own people, chosen by God himself.

Nietzsche's Zarathustra: Notes of the Seminar Given in 1934–1939,
Vol. II (12 February 1936), pp. 827–28.

If we go further and consider the fact that man is also what neither he himself nor other people know of him—an unknown something which can yet be proved to exist—the problem of identity becomes more difficult still. Indeed, it is quite impossible to define the extent and the ultimate character of psychic existence. When we now speak of man we mean the indefinable whole of him, an ineffable totality, which can only be formulated symbolically. I have chosen the term "self" to designate the totality of man, the sum total of his conscious and unconscious contents. I have chosen this term in accordance with Eastern philosophy, which for centuries has occupied itself with the problems that arise when even the gods cease to incarnate.

Psychology and Religion (1938/1940), CW 11, § 140.

3
The Symbolic Life

[E]very psychological expression is a symbol if we assume that it states or signifies something more and other than itself which eludes our present knowledge.

Psychological Types (1921), CW 6, § 817.

The functional importance of the symbol is clearly shown in the history of civilization. For thousands of years the religious symbol proved a most efficacious device in the moral education of mankind. Only a prejudiced mind could deny such an obvious fact. Concrete values cannot take the place of the symbol; only new and more effective symbols can be substituted for those that are antiquated and outworn and have lost their efficacy through the progress of intellectual analysis and understanding. The further development of the individual can be brought about only by means of symbols which represent something far in advance of himself and whose intellectual meanings cannot yet be grasped entirely. The individual unconscious produces such symbols, and they are of the greatest possible value in the moral development of the personality.

"Preface to *Collected Papers on Analytical Psychology*" (1916), CW 4, § 680.

[S]ymbols may be found among the relics of prehistoric man as well as among the most primitive human types living today. Symbol-formation, therefore, must obviously be an extremely important biological function.

Psychological Types (1921), CW 6, § 402.

There are not too many truths, there are only a few. Their meaning is too deep to grasp other than in symbols.

The Red Book (1915/2009), p. 291.

The symbol has a very complex meaning because it defies reason; it always presupposes a lot of meanings that can't be comprehended in a single logical concept. The symbol has a future. The past does not suffice to interpret it, because germs of the future are included in every actual situation.

"A Wartime Interview" (1942), *C. G. Jung Speaking*, p. 143.

Our civilization has long since forgotten how to think symbolically.

Symbols of Transformation (1912/1952), CW 5, § 683.

You see, man is in need of a symbolic life—badly in need. We only live banal, ordinary, rational, or irrational things—which are naturally also within the scope of rationalism, otherwise you could not call them irrational. But we have no symbolic life. Where do we live symbolically? Nowhere, except where we participate in the ritual of life. But who, among the many, are really participating in the ritual of life? Very few.

"The Symbolic Life" (1939), CW 18, § 625.

What to the causal view is *fact* to the final view is *symbol*, and vice versa.

"On Psychic Energy" (1928), CW 8, § 45.

If the word is a sign, it means nothing. But if the word is a symbol, it means everything.

The Red Book (1915/2009), p. 310.

The symbol is the middle way along which the opposites flow together in a new movement, like a watercourse bringing fertility after a long drought.

Psychological Types (1921), CW 6, § 443.

The symbol is not a sign that disguises something generally known. Its meaning resides in the fact that it is an attempt to elucidate, by a more or less apt analogy, something that is still entirely unknown or still in the process of formation. If we reduce this by analysis to something that is generally known, we destroy the true value of the symbol; but to attribute hermeneutic significance to it is consistent with its value and meaning.

"The Structure of the Unconscious" (1916), CW 7, § 492.

One might say that every symbol seeks to be concretized.

Introduction to Jungian Psychology: Notes of the Seminar on Analytical Psychology Given in 1925, p. 13.

[O]ne creates inner freedom only through the symbol.

The Red Book (1915/2009), p. 311.

Concepts are coined and negotiable values; images are life.

Mysterium Coniunctionis (1955–56), CW 14, § 226.

I am of the opinion that the union of rational and irrational truth is to be found not so much in art as in the symbol *per se*; for it is the essence of the symbol to contain both the rational and the irrational. It always expresses the one through the other; it comprises both without being either.

"The Role of the Unconscious" (1918), CW 10, § 24.

How the harmonizing of conscious and unconscious data is to be undertaken cannot be indicated in the form of a recipe. It is an irrational life-process which expresses itself in definite symbols. It may be the task of the analyst to stand by this process with all the help he can give. In this case, the knowledge of the symbols is indispensable, for it is in them that the union of conscious and unconscious contents is consummated. Out of this union emerge new situations and new conscious attitudes.

"Conscious, Unconscious, and Individuation" (1939), CW 9i, § 524.

The symbol is the word that goes out of the mouth, that one that does not simply speak, but that rises out of the depths of the self as a word of power and great need and places itself unexpectedly on the tongue. It is an astonishing and perhaps seemingly irrational word, but one recognizes it as a symbol since it is alien to the conscious mind. If one accepts the symbol, it is as if a door opens leading into a new room whose existence one previously did not know. But if one does not accept the symbol, it is as if one carelessly went past this door; and since this was the only door leading to the inner chambers, one must pass outside into the streets again, exposed to everything external. But the soul suffers great need, since outer freedom is of no use to it. Salvation is a long road that leads through many gates. These gates are symbols. Each new gate is at first invisible; indeed it seems at first that it must be created, for it exists only if one has dug up the spring's root, the symbol.

The Red Book (1915/2009), p. 311.

[A] symbol is the sensuously perceptible *expression of an inner experience*. A religious experience strives for expression and can be expressed only "symbolically" because it transcends understanding. It *must* be expressed one way or another, for therein is revealed its immanent vital force. It wants to step over, as it were, into visible life, to take concrete shape.

Letter to Kurt Plachte, 10 January 1929, *Letters, Vol. I*, p. 59.

The soul gives birth to images that from the rational standpoint of consciousness are assumed to be worthless. And so they are, in the sense that they cannot immediately be turned to account in the objective world.

Psychological Types (1921), CW 6, § 426.

Psychic development cannot be accomplished by intention and will alone; it needs the attraction of the symbol, whose value quantum exceeds that of the cause. But the formation of a symbol cannot take place until the mind has dwelt long enough on the elementary facts, that is to say until the inner or outer necessities of the life-process have brought about a transformation of energy.

"On Psychic Energy" (1928), CW 8, § 47.

[G]ood and bad must always be united first if the symbol is to be created. The symbol can neither be thought up nor found; it becomes. Its becoming is like the becoming of human life in the womb. Pregnancy comes about through voluntary copulation. It goes on through willing attention. But if the depths have conceived, then the symbol grows out of itself and is born from the mind, as befits a God.

The Red Book (1915/2009), p. 311.

[A] symbol is a psychic image expressing something unknown. In a certain sense the symbol has a life of its own which guides the subject and eases his task; but it cannot be invented or fabricated because the experience of it does not depend on our will.

Letter to A. Zarine, 3 May, 1939, *Letters, Vol. I*, p. 269.

Analysis and reduction lead to causal truth; this by itself does not help us to live but only induces resignation and hopelessness. On the other hand, the recognition of the intrinsic value of a symbol leads to constructive truth and helps us to live; it inspires hopefulness and furthers the possibility of future development.

"Preface to *Collected Papers on Analytical Psychology*" (1916), CW 4,
§ 679.

[H]er life makes sense, and makes sense in all continuity, and for the whole of humanity. That gives peace, when people feel that they are living the symbolic life, that they are actors in the divine drama. That gives the only meaning to human life; everything else is banal and you can dismiss it. A career, producing of children, are all *maya* compared with that one thing, that your life is meaningful.

"The Symbolic Life" (1954), CW 18, § 630.

How are we to explain religious processes, for instance, whose nature is essentially symbolical? In abstract form, symbols are religious ideas; in the form of action, they are rites or ceremonies. They are the manifestation and expression of excess libido. At the same time they are stepping-stones to new activities, which must be called cultural in order to distinguish them from the instinctual functions that run their regular course according to natural law.

"On Psychic Energy" (1928), CW 8, § 91.

The symbol, you see, is a special term. The symbolic expression in a dream is a manifestation of the situation of the unconscious, looked at from the unconscious.

"The Houston Films (1957)," *C. G. Jung Speaking*, p. 319.

Luckily for us, symbols mean very much more than can be known at first glance. Their meaning resides in the fact that they compensate an unadapted attitude of consciousness, an attitude that does not fulfil its purpose, and that they would enable it to do this if they were understood. But it becomes impossible to interpret their meaning if they are reduced to something else. That is why some of the later alchemists, particularly in the sixteenth century, abhorred all vulgar substances and replaced them by "symbolic" ones which allowed the nature of the archetype to glimmer through. This does not mean that the adept ceased to work in the laboratory, only that he kept an eye on the symbolic aspect of his transmutations. This corresponds exactly to the situation in the modern psychology of the unconscious: while personal problems are not overlooked (the patient himself takes very good care of that!), the analyst keeps an eye on their symbolic aspects, for healing comes only from what leads the patient beyond himself and beyond his entanglement with the ego.

"The Philosophical Tree" (1945/1954), CW 13, § 397.

Since, as a rule, the unconscious can create only symbolic expressions, the constructive method seeks to elucidate the symbolically expressed meaning in such a way as to indicate how the conscious orientation may be corrected, and how the subject may act in harmony with the unconscious.

Psychological Types (1921), CW 6, § 702.

[A]ll knowledge of the psyche is itself psychic; in spite of all this the soul is the only experient of life and existence. It is, in fact, the only immediate experience we can have and the *sine qua non* of the subjective reality of the world. The symbols it creates are always grounded in the unconscious archetype, but their manifest forms are moulded by the ideas acquired by the conscious mind. The archetypes are the numinous, structural elements of the psyche and possess a certain autonomy and specific energy which enables them to attract, out of the conscious mind, those contents which are best suited to themselves. The symbols act as *transformers*, their function being to convert libido from a "lower" into a "higher" form. This function is so important that feeling accords it the highest values. The symbol works by suggestion; that is to say, it carries conviction and at the same time expresses the content of that conviction. It is able to do this because of the numen, the specific energy stored up in the archetype. Experience of the archetype is not only impressive, it seizes and possesses the whole personality, and is naturally productive of faith.

Symbols of Transformation (1912/1952), CW 5, § 344.

The symbol becomes my lord and unfailing commander. It will fortify its reign and change itself into a fixed and riddling image, whose meaning turns completely inward, and whose pleasure radiates outward like blazing fire, a Buddha in the flames. Because I sink into my symbol to such an extent, the symbol changes me from my one into my other.

The Red Book (1915/2009), p. 250.

[T]he more the libido is invested—or, to be more accurate, invests itself—in the unconscious, the greater becomes its influence or potency: all the rejected, disused, outlived functional possibilities that have been lost for generations come to life again and begin to exert an ever-increasing influence on the conscious mind, despite its desperate struggles to gain insight into what is happening. The saving factor is the symbol, which embraces both conscious and unconscious and unites them. For while the consciously disposable libido gets gradually used in the differentiated function and is replenished more and more slowly and with increasing difficulty, the symptoms of inner disunity multiply and there is a growing danger of inundation and destruction by the unconscious contents, but all the time the symbol is developing that is destined to resolve the conflict. The symbol, however, is so intimately bound up with the dangerous and menacing aspect of the unconscious that it is easily mistaken for it, or its appearance may actually call forth evil and destructive tendencies. At all events the appearance of the redeeming symbol is closely connected with destruction and devastation.

If the old were not ripe for death, nothing new would appear; and if the old were not injuriously blocking the way for the new; it could not and need not be rooted out.

Psychological Types (1921), CW 6, § 446.

[C]hildlikeness or lack of prior assumptions is of the very essence of the symbol and its function.

Psychological Types (1921), CW 6, § 442.

A symbol loses its magical or, if you prefer, its redeeming power as soon as its liability to dissolve is recognized. To be effective, a symbol must be by its very nature unassailable. It must be the best possible expression of the prevailing world-view, an unsurpassed container of meaning; it must also be sufficiently remote from comprehension to resist all attempts of the critical intellect to break it down; and finally, its aesthetic form must appeal so convincingly to our feelings that no argument can be raised against it on that score.

Psychological Types (1921), CW 6, § 401.

[T]he symbol presupposes a function that creates symbols, and in addition a function that understands them. This latter function takes no part in the creation of the symbol, it is a function in its own right, which one could call symbolic thinking or symbolic understanding. The essence of the symbol consists in the fact that it represents in itself something that is not wholly understandable, and that it hints only intuitively at its possible meaning. The creation of a symbol is not a rational process, for a rational process could never produce an image that represents a content which is at bottom incomprehensible. To understand a symbol we need a certain amount of intuition which apprehends, if only approximately, the meaning of the symbol that has been created, and then incorporates it into consciousness. Schiller calls the symbol-creating function a third instinct, the *play* instinct; it bears no resemblance to the two opposing functions, but stands between them and does justice to both their natures.

Psychological Types (1921), CW 6, § 171.

Symbols are not allegories and not signs; they are images of contents which for the most part transcend consciousness.

Symbols of Transformation (1912/1952), CW 5, § 114.

The symbol always says: in some such form as this a new manifestation of life will become possible, a release from bondage and world-weariness. The libido that is freed from the unconscious by means of the symbol appears as a rejuvenated god, or actually as a new god; in Christianity, for instance, Jehovah is transformed into a loving Father with a higher and more spiritual morality. The motif of the god's renewal is universal and may be assumed to be familiar to most readers.

Psychological Types (1921), CW 6, § 435.

The redeeming symbol is a highway, a way upon which life can move forward without torment and compulsion.

Psychological Types (1921), CW 6, § 445.

[T]he mediating position between the opposites can be reached only by the symbol. The reality presupposed by one instinct is different from the reality of the other. To the other it would be quite unreal or bogus, and vice versa. This dual character of real and unreal is inherent in the symbol. If it were only real, it would not be a symbol, for it would then be a real phenomenon and hence unsymbolic. Only that can be symbolic which embraces both. And if it were altogether unreal, it would be mere empty imagining, which, being related to nothing real, would not be a symbol either.

Psychological Types (1921), CW 6, § 178.

The core of the individual is a mystery of life, which dies when it is "grasped." That is also why *symbols want to keep their secrets*; they are mysterious not only because we are unable to clearly see what is at their bottom. For the symbol wants to prevent Freudian interpretations, which are indeed so pseudo-correct that they never fail to have an effect. For ill people, "analytical" understandings is as healingly destructive as cauterization or thermocautery, but healthy tissue is banefully destroyed by it. After all, it is a technique we learned from the devil, always destructive, but useful where destruction is necessary. We can commit no greater error, however, than to apply the principles of this technique to an analyzed psychology.

But there's still more to this! All understanding, as such, being an integration into general viewpoints, contains the devil's element, and kills. It tears another life out from its own peculiar course, and forces it into something foreign in which it cannot live. That is why, in the later stages of analysis, we must help the other to come to those hidden and unopenable symbols, in which the second half of life lies securely hidden like the tender seed in the hard shell.

The Question of Psychological Types: The Correspondence of C. G. Jung and Hans Schmidt-Guisan, 1915–1916, pp. 140–41 (6 November 1915).

[T]he vision of the symbol is a pointer to the onward course of life, beckoning with the libido towards a still distant goal—but a goal that henceforth will burn unquenchably within him, so that his life, kindled as by a flame, moves steadily towards the far-off beacon. This is the specific life-promoting significance of the symbol, and such, too, is the meaning and value of religious symbols. I am speaking, of course, not of symbols that are dead and stiffened by dogma, but of living symbols that rise up from the creative unconscious of the living man.

Psychological Types (1921), CW 6, § 202.

A sign is always less than the thing it points to, and a symbol is always more than we can understand at first sight. Therefore we never stop at the sign but go on to the goal it indicates; but we remain with the symbol because it promises more than it reveals.

"Symbols and the Interpretation of Dreams" (1961), CW 18, § 482.

[T]hat is the symbol. In it all paradoxes are abolished.

Letter to Kurt Plachte, 10 January 1929, *Letters, Vol, I*, p. 61.

If symbols mean anything at all, they are tendencies which pursue a definite but not yet recognizable goal and consequently can express themselves only in analogies. In this uncertain situation one must be content to leave things as they are, and give up trying to know anything beyond the symbol.

Mysterium Coniunctionis (1955–56), CW 14, § 667.

It is a fact that symbols, by their very nature, can so unite the opposites that these no longer diverge or clash, but mutually supplement one another and give meaningful shape to life.

Memories, Dreams, Reflections (1962), p. 338.

The ancients lived their symbols, since the world had not yet become real for them. Thus they went into the solitude of the desert to teach us that the place of the soul is a lonely desert. There they found the abundance of visions, the fruits of the desert, the wondrous flowers of the soul. Think diligently about the images that the ancients have left behind. They show the way of what is to come. Look back at the collapse of empires, of growth and death, of the desert and monasteries, they are the images of what is to come. Everything has been foretold. But who knows how to interpret it?

The Red Book (1915/2009), p. 236.

[D]ream symbols are the essential message carriers from the instinctive to the rational parts of the human mind, and their interpretation enriches the poverty of consciousness so that it learns to understand again the forgotten language of the instincts.

"Approaching the Unconscious" (1964), *Man and His Symbols*, p. 52.

The sign is always less than the concept it represents, while a symbol always stands for something more than its obvious and immediate meaning. Symbols, moreover, are natural and spontaneous products. No genius has ever sat down with a pen or a brush in his hand and said: "Now I am going to invent a symbol." No one can take a more or less rational thought, reached as a logical conclusion or by deliberate intent, and then give it "symbolic" form. No matter what fantastic trappings one may put upon an idea of this kind, it will still remain a sign, linked to the conscious thought behind it, not a symbol that hints at something not yet known. In dreams, symbols occur spontaneously, for dreams happen and are not invented; they are, therefore, the main source of all our knowledge about symbolism.

"Approaching the Unconscious" (1964), *Man and His Symbols*, p. 55.

4
Dreams

The dream is a little hidden door in the innermost and most secret recesses of the soul, opening into that cosmic night which was psyche long before there was any ego-consciousness, and which will remain psyche no matter how far our ego-consciousness extends. For all ego-consciousness is isolated; because it separates and discriminates, it knows only particulars, and it sees only those that can be related to the ego. Its essence is limitation, even though it can reach to the farthest nebulae among the stars. All consciousness separates; but in dreams we put on the likeness of that more universal, truer, more eternal man dwelling in the darkness of primordial night. There he is still the whole, and the whole is in him, indistinguishable from nature and bare of all egohood. It is from these all-uniting depths that the dream arises, be it never so childish, grotesque, and immoral.

"The Meaning of Psychology for Modern Man" (1933/1934), CW 10, §§ 304–5.

[T]he dream is a living thing, by no means a dead thing that rustles like dry paper. It is a living situation, it is like an animal with feelers, or with many umbilical cords. We don't realize that while we are talking of it, it is producing.

Dream Analysis: Notes of the Seminar Given in 1928–1930 (28 November 1928), p. 44.

The dream, we would say, originates in an unknown part of the psyche and prepares the dreamer for the events of the following day.

Symbols of Transformation (1912/1952), CW 5, § 5.

It is only in modern times that the dream, this fleeting and insignificant-looking product of the psyche, has met with such profound contempt. Formerly it was esteemed as a harbinger of fate, a portent and comforter, a messenger of the gods. Now we see it as the emissary of the unconscious, whose task it is to reveal the secrets that are hidden from the conscious mind, and this it does with astounding completeness.

On the Psychology of the Unconscious (1917/1926), CW 7, § 21.

[The dream] shows the inner truth and reality of the patient as it really is: not as I conjecture it to be, and not as he would like it to be, but *as it is*.

"The Practical Use of Dream-Analysis" (1934), CW 16, § 304.

The dream is in large part a warning of something to come.

"Americans Must Say 'No'" (1931), *C. G. Jung Speaking*, p. 49.

As against Freud's view that the dream is essentially a wish-fulfilment, I hold with my friend and collaborator Alphonse Maeder that the dream is a *spontaneous self-portrayal, in symbolic form, of the actual situation in the unconscious.*

"General Aspects of Dream Psychology" (1916/1928/1948), CW 8, § 505.

Apart from the efforts that have been made for centuries to extract a prophetic meaning from dreams, Freud's discoveries are the first successful attempt in practice to find their real significance. His work merits the term "scientific" because he has evolved a technique which not only he but many other investigators assert achieves its object, namely the understanding of the meaning of the dream.

"General Aspects of Dream Psychology" (1916/1928/1948), CW 8,
§ 447.

I was never able to agree with Freud that the dream is a "façade" behind which its meaning lies hidden—a meaning already known but maliciously, so to speak, withheld from consciousness. To me dreams are a part of nature, which harbors no intention to deceive, but expresses something as best it can, just as a plant grows or an animal seeks its food as best it can. These forms of life, too, have no wish to deceive our eyes, but we may deceive ourselves because our eyes are shortsighted. Or we hear amiss because our ears are rather deaf—but it is not our ears that wish to deceive us. Long before I met Freud I regarded the unconscious, and dreams, which are its direct exponents, as natural processes to which no arbitrariness can be attributed, and above all no legerdemain. I knew no reasons for the assumption that the tricks of consciousness can be extended to the natural processes of the unconscious. On the contrary, daily experience taught me what intense resistance the unconscious opposes to the tendencies of the conscious mind.

Memories, Dreams, Reflections (1962), pp. 161–62.

We must take the dream for what it is. We must not assume that one thing is merely a symbol for something else, as if we controlled the sources of the dream. We must be grateful if we discover the sources of the dream, but we have absolutely no control over them.

Visions: Notes of the Seminar Given in 1930–1934, Vol. I (22 October 1930), p. 23.

[W]e apply a structure to the dream that corresponds to the pattern of a drama. We distinguish four elements: the *introduction* often specifies place and time, as well as the actors (dramatis personae) of the dream action. There follows the *exposition*, which unfolds the problem of the dream. It contains, so to speak, the theme, or maybe the question posed by the unconscious. From this arises the *peripeteia*: the dream action leads to increasing complexity, until it reaches a climax and changes—sometimes in the form of a catastrophe. Finally, the *lysis* gives a solution or the result of the dream.

> *Children's Dreams: Notes of the Seminar Given in 1936–1940*,
> p. 236.

The art of interpreting dreams cannot be learned from books. Methods and rules are good only when we can get along without them. Only the man who can do it anyway has real skill, only the man of understanding really understands.

> "The Meaning of Psychology for Modern Man" (1933/1934), CW 10,
> § 325.

My respect for dreams goes very far, and I am impressed again and again by the extraordinary independence of the unconscious, the most extraordinary mental independence that I know. The independence of the conscious is ridiculous in comparison.

> *Visions: Notes of the Seminar Given in 1930–1934, Vol. I* (22 October
> 1930), p. 26.

[D]reams are as simple or as complicated as the dreamer is himself, only they are always a little bit ahead of the dreamer's consciousness. I do not understand my own dreams any better than any of you, for they are always somewhat beyond my grasp and I have the same trouble with them as anyone who knows nothing about dream interpretation. Knowledge is no advantage when it is a matter of one's own dreams.

> *The Tavistock Lectures: On the Theory and Practice of Analytical*
> *Psychology* (1935), CW 18, § 244.

You always have to imagine a dream as like a conversation you overhear on the radio or the phone. Somebody says something, you hear a sentence of conversation, then the conversation breaks off again, and now you should reconstruct what had been said. That's how you should think of dreams. It is always a "listening in." You just overhear something for a moment. Something becomes clear subliminally. You wake up with a sentence on your lips, but perhaps you've even forgotten the dream, too.

Children's Dreams: Notes of the Seminar Given in 1936–1940,
p. 359.

As Freud says, dream-analysis is the *via regia* to the unconscious. It leads straight to the deepest personal secrets, and is, therefore, an invaluable instrument in the hand of the physician and educator of the soul.

On the Psychology of the Unconscious (1917/1926), CW 7, § 25.

[I]f one approaches the unconscious, it loses its dangerous aspect, and what has been entirely negative becomes positive. One sees that from dreams. One often has dreams which seem destructive and evil, the thing one cannot accept, but it is merely due to the fact that one's conscious attitude is wrong. If one says, "It seems quite black but perhaps I must accept it," instantly the thing changes color, it becomes compatible with consciousness.

Visions: Notes of the Seminar Given in 1930–1934, Vol. I (10 June 1931), pp. 405–6.

It is Freud's great achievement to have put dream-interpretation on the right track. Above all, he recognized that no interpretation can be undertaken without the dreamer. The words composing a dream-narrative have not just *one* meaning, but many meanings. If, for instance, someone dreams of a table, we are still far from knowing what the "table" of the dreamer signifies, although the word "table" sounds unambiguous enough. For the thing we do not know is that this "table" is the very one at which his father sat when he refused the dreamer all further financial help and threw him out of the house as a good-for-nothing. The polished surface of this table stares at him as a symbol of his lamentable worthlessness in his daytime consciousness as well as in his dreams at night. This is what our dreamer understands by "table." Therefore we need the dreamer's help in order to limit the multiple meanings of words to those that are essential and convincing. That the "table" stands as a mortifying landmark in the dreamer's life may be doubted by anyone who was not present. But the dreamer does not doubt it, nor do I. Clearly, dream-interpretation is in the first place an experience which has immediate validity for only two persons.

"On the Nature of Dreams" (1945/1948), CW 8, § 539.

There are, as you know, numerous works on the phenomenology of dreams, but very few that deal with their psychology. This for the obvious reason that a psychological interpretation of dreams is an exceedingly ticklish and risky business. Freud has made a courageous attempt to elucidate the intricacies of dream psychology with the help of views which he gathered in the field of psychopathology. Much as I admire the boldness of his attempt, I cannot agree either with his method or with its results. He explains the dream as a mere façade behind which something has been carefully hidden. There is no doubt that neurotics hide disagreeable things, probably just as much as normal people do. But it is a serious question whether this category can be applied to such a normal and world-wide phenomenon as the dream. I doubt whether we can assume that a dream is something other than it appears to be. I am rather inclined to quote another Jewish authority, the Talmud, which says: "The dream is its own interpretation." In other words *I take the dream for what it is.* The dream is such a difficult and complicated thing that I do not dare to make any assumptions about its possible cunning or its tendency to deceive. The dream is a natural occurrence, and there is no earthly reason why we should assume that it is a crafty device to lead us astray. It occurs when consciousness and will are to a large extent extinguished. It seems to be a natural product which is also found in people who are not neurotic. Moreover, we know so little about the psychology of the dream process that we must be more than careful when we introduce into its explanation elements that are foreign to the dream itself.

Psychology and Religion (1938/1940), CW 11, § 41.

Never apply any theory, but always ask the patient how *he* feels about his dream-images. For dreams are always about a particular problem of the individual about which he has a wrong conscious judgment. The dreams are the reaction to our conscious attitude in the same way that the body reacts when we overeat or do not eat enough or when we ill-treat it in some other way. *Dreams are the natural reaction of the self-regulating psychic system.* This formulation is the nearest I can get to a theory about the structure and function of dreams, I hold that dreams are just as manifold and unpredictable and incalculable as a person you observe during the day. If you watch an individual at one moment and then at another you will see and hear the most varied reactions, and it is exactly the same with dreams. In our dreams we are just as many-sided as in our daily life, and just as you cannot form a theory about those many aspects of the conscious personality you cannot make a general theory of dreams. Otherwise we would have an almost divine knowledge of the human mind, which we certainly do not possess. We know precious little about it, therefore we call the things we do not know unconscious.

The Tavistock Lectures: On the Theory and Practice of Analytical Psychology (1935), CW 18, § 248.

So when I counsel my patient to pay attention to his dreams, I mean: "Turn back to the most subjective part of yourself, to the source of your being, to that point where you are making world history without being aware of it. Your apparently insoluble difficulty must, it is obvious, remain insoluble, for otherwise you would wear yourself out seeking for remedies of whose ineptitude you are convinced from the start. Your dreams are an expression of your inner life, and they can show you through what false attitude you have landed yourself in this blind alley."

"The Meaning of Psychology for Modern Man" (1933/1934), CW 10,
§ 316.

This is the secret of dreams—that we do not dream, but rather we *are dreamt*. We are the object of the dream, not its maker. The French say: "Faire un rêve." [To make a dream.] This is wrong. The dream is dreamed to us. We are the objects. We simply find ourselves put into a situation. If a fatal destiny is awaiting us, we are already seized by what will lead us to this destiny in the dream, in the same way it will overcome us in reality.

Children's Dreams: Notes of the Seminar Given in 1936–1940,
p. 159.

The dream is often occupied with apparently very silly details, thus producing an impression of absurdity, or else it is on the surface so unintelligible as to leave us thoroughly bewildered. Hence we always have to overcome a certain resistance before we can seriously set about disentangling the intricate web through patient work. But when at last we penetrate to its real meaning, we find ourselves deep in the dreamer's secrets and discover with astonishment that an apparently quite senseless dream is in the highest degree significant, and that in reality it speaks only of important and serious matters. This discovery compels rather more respect of the so-called superstition that dreams have a meaning, to which the rationalistic temper of our age has hitherto given short shrift.

On the Psychology of the Unconscious (1917/1926), CW 7, § 24.

So difficult is it to understand a dream that for a long time I have made it a rule, when someone tells me a dream and asks for my opinion, to say first of all to myself: "I have no idea what this dream means." After that I can begin to examine the dream.

"On the Nature of Dreams" (1945/1948), CW 8, § 533.

My intuition consisted in a sudden and most unexpected insight into the fact that my dream meant myself, *my* life and *my* world, my whole reality as against a theoretical structure erected by another, alien mind for reasons and purposes of its own.

"Symbols and The Interpretation of Dreams" (1961), CW 18, § 490.

[A] dream can be an experience of the greatest importance for somebody. If he grasps its meaning, it will become an experience for him that he will value more than all the kingdoms on earth. These are experiences we cannot rationalize. Neither can we argue about them, just as we cannot argue about Paul and the great vision he had on the road to Damascus. The transformation occurs when that inner growth, with all its original values and implicit meanings, enters into the empirical world. The experience of this wholeness can be so all-embracing that it has actually been called the *medicina catholica*, the panacea, the *alexipharmakon*, the antitoxin against all toxins. The highest attributes have always been ascribed to this idea, not out of rational consideration but because it expresses the deepest inner experiences of man.

Children's Dreams: Notes from the Seminar Given in 1936–1940,
p. 299.

The dream rectifies the situation. It contributes the material that was lacking and thereby improves the patient's attitude. That is the reason we need dream-analysis in our therapy.

"General Aspects of Dream Psychology" (1916/1928/1948), CW 8,
§ 482.

The general function of dreams is to try to restore our psychological balance by producing dream material that re-establishes, in a subtle way, the total psychic equilibrium. This is what I call the complementary (or compensatory) role of dreams in our psychic make-up. It explains why people who have unrealistic ideas or too high an opinion of themselves, or who make grandiose plans out of proportion to their real capacities, have dreams of flying or falling.

The dream compensates for the deficiencies of their personalities, and at the same time it warns them of the dangers in their present course. If the warnings of the dream are disregarded, real accidents may take place. The victim may fall downstairs or may have a motor accident.

"Approaching the Unconscious" (1964), *Man and His Symbols*, p. 50.

We now must make it clear what is required to produce the transcendent function. First and foremost, we need the unconscious material. The most readily accessible expression of unconscious processes is undoubtedly dreams. The dream is, so to speak, a pure product of the unconscious.

"The Transcendent Function" ([1916]/1958), CW 8, § 152.

The unconscious is the unknown at any given moment, so it is not surprising that dreams add to the conscious psychological situation of the moment all those aspects which are essential for a totally different point of view. It is evident that this function of dreams amounts to a psychological adjustment, a compensation absolutely necessary for properly balanced action. In a conscious process of reflection it is essential that, so far as possible, we should realize all the aspects and consequences of a problem in order to find the right solution. This process is continued automatically in the more or less unconscious state of sleep, where, as experience seems to show, all those aspects occur to the dreamer (at least by way of allusion) that during the day were insufficiently appreciated or even totally ignored—in other words, were comparatively unconscious.

"General Aspects of Dream Psychology" (1916/1928/1948), CW 8, § 469.

If we want to interpret a dream correctly, we need a thorough knowledge of the conscious situation at that moment, because the dream contains its unconscious complement, that is, the material which the conscious situation has constellated in the unconscious.

Without this knowledge it is impossible to interpret a dream correctly, except by a lucky fluke.

"General Aspects of Dream Psychology" (1916/1928/1948), CW 8,

§ 477.

Nature commits no errors.

*The Tavistock Lectures: On the Theory and Practice of Analytical
Psychology* (1935), CW 18, § 95.

[D]reams may sometimes announce certain situations long before
they actually happen. This is not necessarily a miracle or a form of
precognition. Many crises in our lives have a long unconscious history. We move toward them step by step, unaware of the dangers
that are accumulating. But what we consciously fail to see is frequently perceived by our unconscious, which can pass the information on through dreams.

"Approaching the Unconscious" (1964), *Man and His Symbols*, p. 51.

The "manifest" dream-picture is the dream itself and contains the
whole meaning of the dream. When I find sugar in the urine, it is
sugar and not just a façade for albumen. What Freud calls the
"dream-façade" is the dream's obscurity, and this is really only a
projection of our own lack of understanding. We say that the dream
has a false front only because we fail to see into it. We would do
better to say that we are dealing with something like a text that is
unintelligible not because it has a façade—a text has no façade—
but simply because we cannot read it. We do not have to get behind
such a text, but must first learn to read it.

"The Practical Use of Dream-Analysis" (1934), CW 16, § 319.

I leave theory aside as much as possible when analysing dreams—
not entirely, of course, for we always need some theory to make
things intelligible. It is on the basis of theory, for instance, that I
expect dreams to have a meaning. I cannot prove in every case that
this is so, for there are dreams which the doctor and the patient

simply do not understand. But I have to make such an hypothesis in order to find courage to deal with dreams at all.

"The Practical Use of Dream-Analysis" (1934), CW 16, § 318.

A dream that is not understood remains a mere occurrence; understood, it becomes a living experience.

"Fundamental Questions of Psychotherapy" (1951), CW 16, § 252.

Together the patient and I address ourselves to the 2,000,000-year-old man that is in all of us. In the last analysis, most of our difficulties come from losing contact with our instincts, with the age-old unforgotten wisdom stored up in us. And where do we make contact with this old man in us? In our dreams.

"The 2,000,000-Year-Old Man" (1936), *C. G. Jung Speaking*, p. 89.

One of the most important sources of the primitive belief in spirits is dreams. People very often appear as the actors in dreams, and the primitive readily believes them to be spirits or ghosts. The dream has for him an incomparably higher value than it has for civilized man. Not only does he talk a great deal about his dreams, he also attributes an extraordinary importance to them, so that it often seems as though he were unable to distinguish between them and reality. To the civilized man dreams as a rule appear valueless, though there are some people who attach great significance to certain dreams on account of their weird and impressive character. This peculiarity lends plausibility to the view that dreams are inspirations.

"The Psychological Foundations of Belief in Spirits" (1920/1948), CW 8, § 574.

In each of us there is another whom we do not know. He speaks to us in dreams and tell us how differently he sees us from the way we see ourselves. When, therefore, we find ourselves in a difficult situation to which there is no solution, he can sometimes kindle a light that radically alters our attitude—the very attitude that led us into the difficult situation.

"The Meaning of Psychology for Modern Man" (1933/1934), CW 10,
§ 325.

The unconscious is the unknown at any given moment, so it is not surprising that dreams add to the conscious psychological situation of the moment all those aspects which are essential for a totally different point of view. It is evident that this function of dreams amounts to a psychological adjustment, a compensation absolutely necessary for properly balanced action. In a conscious process of reflection it is essential that, so far as possible, we should realize all the aspects and consequences of a problem in order to find the right solution. This process is continued automatically in the more or less unconscious state of sleep, where, as experience seems to show, all those aspects occur to the dreamer (at least by way of allusion) that during the day were insufficiently appreciated or even totally ignored—in other words, were comparatively unconscious.

"General Aspects of Dream Psychology" (1916/1928/1948), CW 8,
§ 469.

One would do well to treat every dream as though it were a totally unknown object. Look at it from all sides, take it in your hand, carry it about with you, let your imagination play round it, and talk about it with other people. Primitives tell each other impressive dreams, in a public palaver if possible, and this custom is also attested in late antiquity, for all the ancient peoples attributed great significance to dreams. Treated in this way, the dream suggests all manner of ideas and associations which lead us closer to its meaning. The ascertainment of the meaning is, I need hardly point out, an entirely arbitrary affair, and this is where the hazards begin. Narrower or wider limits will be set to the meaning, according to one's experience, temperament, and taste. Some people will be satisfied with little, for others much is still not enough. Also the meaning of the dream, or our interpretation of it, is largely dependent on the intentions of the interpreter, on what he expects the meaning to be or requires it to do. In eliciting the meaning he will involuntarily be guided by certain presuppositions, and it depends very much on the scrupulousness and honesty of the investigator whether he gains something by his interpretation or perhaps only becomes still more deeply entangled in his mistakes.

"The Meaning of Psychology for Modern Man" (1933/1934), CW 10, § 320.

I call every interpretation which equates the dream images with real objects an *interpretation on the objective level*. In contrast to this is the interpretation which refers every part of the dream and all the actors in it back to the dreamer himself. This I call *interpretation on the subjective level*.

On the Psychology of the Unconscious (1917/1926), CW 7, § 130.

There is no reason to believe that the unconscious does not say what it means; in sharpest contradiction to Freud I say that the unconscious says what it means. Nature is never diplomatic. If nature produces a tree, it is a tree and not a mistake for a dog. And so the unconscious does not make disguises, that is what we do.

Dream Analysis: Notes of the Seminar Given in 1928–1930 (21 November 1928), p. 30.

Just as dreams do not conceal something already known, or express it under a disguise, but try rather to formulate an as yet unconscious fact as clearly as possible, so myths and alchemical symbols are not euhemeristic allegories that hide artificial secrets. On the contrary, they seek to translate natural secrets into the language of consciousness and to declare the truth that is the common property of mankind. By becoming conscious, the individual is threatened more and more with isolation, which is nevertheless the *sine qua non* of conscious differentiation. The greater this threat, the more it is compensated by the production of collective and archetypal symbols which are common to all men.

"The Philosophical Tree" (1945/1954), CW 13, § 395.

It is idle to speculate on how great a share consciousness has in dreams. A dream presents itself to us: we do not consciously create it. Conscious reproduction, or even the perception of it, certainly alters the dream in many ways, without, however, doing away with the basic fact of the unconscious source of creative activity.

Psychological Types (1921), CW 6, § 842.

The collective unconscious is more dangerous than dynamite, but there are ways of handling it without too many risks. Then, when a psychological crisis launches itself, you are in a better position than any other to solve it. You have dreams and waking dreams: take the trouble to observe them. One could almost say that every dream, in its own manner, carries a message. It not only tells you that something is amiss in the depths of your being, it also brings you a solution for getting out of the crisis. For the collective unconscious which sends you these dreams already possesses the solution: nothing has been lost from the whole immemorial experience of humanity, every imaginable situation and every solution seem to have been foreseen by the collective unconscious. You have only to observe carefully the message sent by the unconscious and then decode it. Analysis helps you to read these messages correctly.

"Eliade's Interview for *Combat*" (1952), *C. G. Jung Speaking*, p. 231.

I remember a very revealing case of three girls who had a *most* devoted mother. When they were approaching puberty they confessed shamefacedly to each other that for years they had suffered from horrible dreams about her. They dreamt of her as a witch or a dangerous animal, and they could not understand it at all, since their mother was so lovely and so utterly devoted to them. Years later the mother became insane, and in her insanity would exhibit a sort of lycanthropy in which she crawled about on all fours and imitated the grunting of pigs, the barking of dogs, and the growling of bears.

"Child Development and Education" (1928), CW 17, § 107.

[O]ur dreams are like windows that allow us to look in, or to listen in, to that psychological process which is continually going on in our unconscious. It is a process of continuous transformation with no end if we don't interfere. It needs our conscious interference to bring it to a goal—by our interference we make a goal. Otherwise it is like the eternal change of the seasons in nature, a building up and a pulling down, integration and disintegration without end. No crops are brought home by nature; only the consciousness of man knows about crops. He gathers the apples under the trees, for they simply disintegrate if left to themselves. And that is true of our unconscious mental process: it revolves within itself. It builds up and it pulls down; it integrates and disintegrates—and then integrates again. It is like the seasons, or the eternal sunrise and sunset, from which nothing comes unless a human consciousness interferes and realizes the result. Perhaps one suddenly sees something and says, "This is a flower." Now we have reached something. But left to itself the process would come to nothing.

Nietzsche's Zarathustra: *Notes of the Seminar Given in 1934–1939*, *Vol. I* (14 November 1934), pp. 236–37.

[I] concluded that only the material that is clearly and visibly part of a dream should be used in interpreting it. The dream has its own limitation. Its specific form itself tells us what belongs to it and what leads away from it. While "free" association lures one away from that material in a kind of zigzag line, the method I evolved is more like a circumambulation whose center is the dream picture. I work all around the dream picture and disregard every attempt that the dreamer makes to break away from it. Time and time again, in my professional work, I have had to repeat the words: "Let's get back to your dream. What does the *dream* say?"

"Approaching the Unconscious" (1941), *Man and His Symbols*, p. 29.

[D]reams have influenced all the important changes in my life and theories.

Introduction to Jungian Psychology: Notes of the Seminar on Analytical Psychology Given in 1925, p. 25.

[T]he simpler the dream is, the more we are confronted with general and fundamental problems. For it is only a deceptive simplicity, due to the fact that the dream, despite the importance of its content, has not found enough substance to express itself. We could compare it to a framework of archetypes, for which there is already a disposition at the beginning of life, and which is gradually filled with substance in the course of development. If a primordial image forces itself onto consciousness, we have to fill it with as much substance as possible to grasp the whole scope of its meaning.

Children's Dreams: Notes from the Seminar Given in 1936–1940, p. 368.

A symbol in a dream is meant to be what it is.

Dream Analysis: Notes of the Seminar Given in 1928–1930 (30 January 1929), pp. 93–94.

On paper the interpretation of a dream may look arbitrary, muddled, and spurious; but the same thing in reality can be a little drama of unsurpassed realism. *To experience* a dream and its interpretation is very different from having a tepid rehash set before you on paper. Everything about this psychology is, in the deepest sense, experience; the entire theory, even where it puts on the most abstract airs, is the direct outcome of something experienced.

On the Psychology of the Unconscious (1917/1926), CW 7, § 199.

5
The Analytic Process

My method, like Freud's, is built up on the practice of confession. Like him, I pay close attention to dreams, but when it comes to the unconscious our views part company. For Freud it is essentially an appendage of consciousness, in which all the individual's incompatibilities are heaped up. For me the unconscious is a collective psychic disposition, creative in character. This fundamental difference of viewpoint naturally produces an entirely different evaluation of the symbolism and the method of interpreting it. Freud's procedure is, in the main, analytical and reductive. To this I add a synthesis which emphasizes the purposiveness of unconscious tendencies with respect to personality development.

"Yoga and the West" (1936), CW 11, § 875.

[I] say to the young psychotherapist: Learn the best, know the best— and then forget everything when you face the patient. No one has yet become a good surgeon by learning the text-books off by heart. Yet the danger that faces us today is that the whole of reality will be replaced by words. This accounts for that terrible lack of instinct in modern man, particularly the city-dweller. He lacks all contact with the life and breath of nature. He knows a rabbit or a cow only from the illustrated paper, the dictionary, or the movies, and thinks he knows what it is really like-and is then amazed that cowsheds "smell," because the dictionary didn't say so. It is the same with the danger of making a diagnosis. One knows that this disease is treated by So-and-so in chapter seventeen, and one thinks that this is the important thing. But the poor patient goes on suffering.

"Good and Evil in Analytical Psychology" (1960), CW 10, § 882.

In all cases after the preliminaries, such as the history of the family, the whole medical anamnesis, etc., we come to that question, What is it in your unconscious that makes you wrong, that hinders you from thinking normally? Then we reach a point where we can begin with the observation of the unconscious, and day by day we proceed by the data the unconscious produces. We discuss the dream and that gives a new surface to the whole problem. Then he will have another dream, and the next dream again gives an answer, because the unconscious is in a compensatory relation to consciousness, and after a while we get the full picture. And if he has the full picture and has the necessary moral stamina, well then he can be cured. But in the end it is a moral question whether a man applies what he has learned or not.

"The Houston Films" (1957), *C. G. Jung Speaking*, p. 319.

[A]nyone who wants to know the human psyche will learn next to nothing from experimental psychology. He would be better advised to abandon exact science, put away his scholar's gown, bid farewell to his study, and wander with human heart through the world. There, in the horrors of prisons, lunatic asylums and hospitals, in drab suburban pubs, in brothels and gambling-hells, in the salons of the elegant, the Stock Exchanges, Socialist meetings, churches, revivalist gatherings and ecstatic sects, through love and hate, through the experience of passion in every form in his own body, he would reap richer stores of knowledge than text-books a foot thick could give him, and he will know to doctor the sick with real knowledge of the human soul.

"New Paths in Psychology" (1912), CW 7, § 409.

There is a widespread prejudice that analysis is something like a "cure," to which one submits for a time and is then discharged healed. That is a layman's error left over from the early days of psychoanalysis. Analytical treatment could be described as a readjustment of psychological attitude achieved with the help of the doctor. Naturally this newly won attitude, which is better suited to the inner and outer conditions, can last a considerable time, but there are very few cases where a single "cure" is permanently successful.

It is true that medical optimism has never stinted itself of publicity and has always been able to report definitive cures. We must, however, not let ourselves be deceived by the all-too-human attitude of the practitioner, but should always remember that the life of the unconscious goes on and continually produces problematical situations. There is no need for pessimism; we have seen too many excellent results achieved with good luck and honest work for that. But this need not prevent us from recognizing that analysis is no once-and-for-all "cure"; it is no more, at first, than a more or less thorough readjustment. There is no change that is unconditionally valid over a long period of time. Life has always to be tackled anew. There are, of course, extremely durable collective attitudes which permit the solution of typical conflicts. A collective attitude enables the individual to fit into society without friction, since it acts upon him like any other condition of life. But the patient's difficulty consists precisely in the fact that his individual problem cannot be fitted without friction into a collective norm; it requires the solution of an individual conflict if the whole of his personality is to remain viable. No rational solution can do justice to this task, and there is absolutely no collective norm that could replace an individual solution without loss.

The new attitude gained in the course of analysis tends sooner or later to become inadequate in one way or another, and necessarily so, because the constant flow of life again and again demands fresh adaptation. Adaptation is never achieved once and for all. One might certainly demand of analysis that it should enable the patient to gain new orientations in later life, too, without undue difficulty. And experience shows that this is true up to a point. We often find that patients who have gone through a thorough analysis have considerably less difficulty with new adjustments later on. Nevertheless, these difficulties prove to be fairly frequent and may at times be really troublesome. That is why even patients who have had a thorough analysis often turn to their old analyst for help at some later period. In the light of medical practice in general there is nothing very unusual about this, but it does contradict a certain misplaced enthusiasm on the part of the therapist as well as the view that analysis constitutes a unique "cure." In the last resort it is highly improbable that there could ever be a therapy that got rid of all difficulties. Man needs difficulties; they are necessary for health. What concerns us here is only an excessive amount of them.

"The Transcendent Function" ([1916]/1958), CW 8, §§ 142–43.

[T]he patient must learn to go his own way.

"Principles of Practical Psychotherapy" (1935), CW 16, § 26.

Practice often turns out to be rather different from theory. You want, of course, to put a whole man on his feet and not just a part of him. You soon discover that there is nothing for him to stand on and nothing for him to hold on to. Return to the parents has become impossible, so he hangs on to the analyst. He can go neither backwards nor forwards, for he sees nothing before him that could give him a hold. All so-called reasonable possibilities have been tried out and have proved useless. Not a few patients then remember the faith in which they were brought up, and some find their way back to it, but not all. They know, perhaps, what their faith ought to mean to them, but they have found to their cost how little can be achieved with will and good intentions if the unconscious does not lend a hand.

Mysterium Coniunctionis (1955–56), CW 14, § 751.

Although I was the first to demand that the analyst should himself be analysed, we are largely indebted to Freud for the invaluable discovery that analysts too have their complexes and consequently one or two blind spots which act as so many prejudices. The psychotherapist gained this insight in cases where it was no longer possible for him to interpret or to guide the patient from on high or *ex cathedra*, regardless of his own personality, but was forced to admit that his personal idiosyncrasies or special attitude hindered the patient's recovery. When one possesses no very clear idea about something, because one is unwilling to admit it to oneself, one tries to hide it from the patient as well, obviously to his very great disadvantage. The demand that the analyst must be analysed culminates in the idea of a dialectical procedure, where the therapist enters into relationship with another psychic system both as questioner and answerer. No longer is he the superior wise man, judge, and counsellor; he is a fellow participant who finds himself involved in the dialectical process just as deeply as the socalled patient.

"Principles of Practical Psychotherapy" (1935), CW 16, §8.

One of the commonest consequences of preoccupation with unconscious contents is the development of what Freud called "the transference." Strictly speaking, transference is the projection of unconscious contents upon the person analysing the unconscious. The term "transference," however, is used in a much wider sense and embraces all the exceedingly complex processes which bind the patient to the analyst.

"The Significance of the Unconscious in Individual Education"
(1928), CW 17, § 260.

In contradistinction to all previous methods, psychoanalysis endeavours to overcome the disorders of the neurotic psyche through the unconscious, and not from the conscious side. In this work we naturally have need of the patient's conscious contents, for only in this way can we reach the unconscious. The conscious content from which our work starts is the material supplied by the anamnesis. In many cases the anamnesis provides useful clues which make the psychic origin of his symptoms clear to the patient.

"General Aspects of Psychoanalysis" (1913), CW 4, § 528.

Analysis, thus understood, is by no means a therapeutic method of which the medical profession holds a monopoly. It is an art, a technique, a science of psychological life, which the patient, when cured, should continue to practise for his own good and for the good of those amongst whom he lives. If he understands it in this

way, he will not set himself up as a prophet, nor as a world reformer; but, with a sound sense of the general good, he will profit
by the knowledge he has acquired during treatment, and his influence will make itself felt more by the example of his own life than
by any high discourse or missionary propaganda.

"The Structure of the Unconscious" (1916), CW 7, § 502.

Experience has shown, however, that even professional analysts,
who might be expected to have mastered the art of dream interpretation, often capitulate before their own dreams and have to call in
the help of a colleague. If even one who purports to be an expert in
the method proves unable to interpret his own dreams satisfacto-
rily, how much less can this be expected of the patient. Freud's hope
that the unconscious could be "exhausted" has not been fulfilled.
Dreamlife and intrusions from the unconscious continue—*mutatis
mutandis* [given also that things do change]—unimpeded.

"The Transcendent Function" ([1916]/1958), CW 8, § 141.

The doctor knows that always, wherever he turns, man is dogged
by his fate. Even the simplest illness may develop surprising complications; or, equally unexpectedly, a condition that seemed very
serious may take a turn for the better. Sometimes the doctor's art
helps, sometimes it is useless. In the domain of psychology especially, where we still know so little, we often stumble upon the un-
foreseen, the inexplicable—something of which we can make neither head nor tail.

The Psychology of the Transference (1946), CW 16, § 463.

The patient, by bringing an activated unconscious content to bear
upon the doctor, constellates the corresponding unconscious material in him, owing to the inductive effect which always emanates
from projections in greater or lesser degree. Doctor and patient
thus find themselves in a relationship founded on mutual unconsciousness.

The Psychology of the Transference (1946), CW 16, § 364.

The doctor knows—or at least he should know—that he did not choose this career by chance; and the psychotherapist in particular should clearly understand that psychic infections, however superfluous they seem to him, are in fact the predestined concomitants of his work, and thus fully in accord with the instinctive disposition of his own life. This realization also gives him the right attitude to his patient. The patient then means something to him personally, and this provides the most favourable basis for treatment.

The Psychology of the Transference (1946), CW 16, § 365.

This bond is often of such intensity that we could almost speak of a "combination." When two chemical substances combine, both are altered. This is precisely what happens in the transference. Freud rightly recognized that this bond is of greatest therapeutic importance in that it gives rise to a *mixtum compositum* [composite mixture] of the doctor's own mental health and the patient's maladjustment.

The Psychology of the Transference (1946), CW 16, § 358.

The transference is far from being a simple phenomenon with only one meaning, and we can never make out beforehand what it is all about.

The Psychology of the Transference (1946), CW 16, § 362.

The transference, however, alters the psychological stature of the doctor, though this is at first imperceptible to him. He too becomes affected, and has as much difficulty in distinguishing between the patient and what has taken possession of him as has the patient himself. This leads both of them to a direct confrontation with the daemonic forces lurking in the darkness.

The Psychology of the Transference (1946), CW 16, § 375.

We have come to understand that psychic suffering is not a definitely localized, sharply delimited phenomenon, but rather the symptom of a wrong attitude assumed by the total personality. We can therefore never hope for a thorough cure from a treatment restricted to the illness itself, but only from a treatment of the personality as a whole.

"Basic Postulates of Analytical Psychology" (1931), CW 8, § 684.

I am often asked about my psychotherapeutic or analytic method. I cannot reply unequivocally to the question. Therapy is different in every case. When a doctor tells me that he adheres strictly to this or that method, I have my doubts about his therapeutic effect. So much is said in the literature about the resistance of the patient that it would almost seem as if the doctor were trying to put something over on him, whereas the cure ought to grow naturally out of the patient himself. Psychotherapy and analysis are as varied as are human individuals. I treat every patient as individually as possible, because the solution of the problem is always an individual one. Universal rules can only be postulated with a grain of salt. A psychological truth is valid only if it can be reversed. A solution which would be out of the question for me may be just the right one for someone else.

Memories, Dreams, Reflections (1962), p. 131.

I once had a patient, a highly intelligent woman, who for various reasons aroused my doubts. At first the analysis went very well, but after a while I began to feel that I was no longer getting at the correct interpretation of her dreams, and I thought I also noticed an increasing shallowness in our dialogue. I therefore decided to talk with my patient about this, since it had of course not escaped her that something was going wrong. The night before I was to speak with her, I had the following dream.

I was walking down a highway through a valley in late-afternoon sunlight. To my right was a steep hill. At its top stood a castle, and on the highest tower there was a woman sitting on a kind of balustrade. In order to see her properly, I had to bend my head far back. I awoke with a crick in the back of my neck. Even in the dream I had recognized the woman as my patient.

The interpretation was immediately apparent to me. If in the dream I had to look up at the patient in this fashion, in reality I had probably been looking down on her. Dreams are, after all, compensations for the conscious attitude. I told her of the dream and my interpretation. This produced an immediate change in the situation, and the treatment once more began to move forward.

Memories, Dreams, Reflections (1962), p. 133.

I never try to convert a patient to anything, and never exercise any compulsion. What matters most to me is that the patient should reach his own view of things. Under my treatment a pagan becomes a pagan, a Christian a Christian, a Jew a Jew, according to what his destiny prescribes for him.

Memories, Dreams, Reflections (1962), p. 138.

Years ago I once drew up statistics on the results of my treatments. I no longer recall the figures exactly; but, on a conservative estimate, a third of my cases were really cured, a third considerably improved, and a third not essentially influenced. But it is precisely the unimproved cases which are hardest to judge, because many things are not realized and understood by the patients until years afterward, and only then can they take effect. How often former patients have written to me: "I did not realize what it was really all about until ten years after I had been with you."

Memories, Dreams, Reflections (1962), p. 143.

My patients brought me so close to the reality of human life that I could not help learning essential things from them. Encounters with people of so many different kinds and on so many different psychological levels have been for me incomparably more important than fragmentary conversations with celebrities. The finest and most significant conversations of my life were anonymous.

Memories, Dreams, Reflections (1962), p. 145.

No analysis is capable of banishing all unconsciousness for ever. The analyst must go on learning endlessly, and never forget that each new case brings new problems to light and thus gives rise to unconscious assumptions that have never before been constellated. We could say, without too much exaggeration, that a good half of every treatment that probes at all deeply consists in the doctor's examining himself, for only what he can put right in himself can he hope to put right in the patient. It is no loss, either, if he feels that the patient is hitting him, or even scoring off him: it is his own hurt that gives the measure of his power to heal. This, and nothing else, is the meaning of the Greek myth of the wounded physician.

"Fundamental Questions of Psychotherapy" (1951), CW 16, § 239.

Zarathustra's chief teaching was that the physician had to heal himself, that he should see himself with his own eyes and make himself whole.

Nietzsche's Zarathustra: Notes of the Seminar Given in 1934–1939,

Vol. I (19 February 1936), p. 850.

[T]he therapist must be guided by the patient's own irrationalities. Here we must follow nature as a guide, and what the doctor then does is less a question of treatment than of developing the creative possibilities latent in the patient himself.

"The Aims of Psychotherapy" (1931), CW 16, § 82.

As a doctor it is my task to help the patient to cope with life. I cannot presume to pass judgment on his final decisions, because I know from experience that all coercion—be it suggestion, insinuation, or any other method of persuasion—ultimately proves to be nothing but an obstacle to the highest and most decisive experience of all, which is to be alone with his own self, or whatever else one chooses to call the objectivity of the psyche. The patient must be alone if he is to find out what it is that supports him when he can no longer support himself. Only this experience can give him an indestructible foundation.

Psychology and Alchemy (1944), CW 12, § 32.

Today, instead of the sea or leviathan, we say analysis, which is equally dangerous. One goes under the water, makes the acquaintance of the leviathan there, and that is either the source of regeneration or destruction.

> *The Psychology of Kundalini Yoga*: *Notes of the Seminar Given in 1932*
> (12 October, 1932), p. 17.

People have a transference to their analyst because they suppose that he is in possession of the treasure. It is like rubbing up against the shrine containing the bones of the saint; they get the grace, as if he were the savings bank of divine treasures. It is inevitable at a certain stage. When the idea of the crystal becomes formed in the unconscious it is projected, and then they suspect somebody of possessing that particular treasure which is really in themselves.

> *Visions*: *Notes of the Seminar Given in 1930–1934, Vol. I* (25 March
> 1931), p. 319.

My aim was to protect and preserve my patient's dignity and freedom, so that he could live his life according to his own wishes.

> "Approaching the Unconscious" (1964), *Man and His Symbols*, p. 58.

It wants the *human* connection. That is the core of the transference phenomenon, and it is impossible to argue it away, because relationship to the self is at once relationship to our fellow man, and no one can be related to the latter until he is related to himself.

> *The Psychology of the Transference* (1946), CW 16, § 445.

Now and then it happened in my practice that a patient grew beyond himself because of unknown potentialities, and this became an experience of prime importance to me. In the meantime, I had learned that all the greatest and most important problems of life are fundamentally insoluble. They must be so, for they express the necessary polarity inherent in every self-regulating system. They can never be solved, but only outgrown.

> "Commentary on *The Secret of the Golden Flower*" (1929), CW 13,
> § 18.

All rational therapy leaves them stuck where they were, although on the face of it their illness is quite curable.

"Principles of Practical Psychotherapy" (1935), CW 16, § 22.

A therapist with a neurosis is a contradiction in terms. One cannot help any patient to advance further than one has advanced oneself.

"Psychotherapy and a Philosophy of Life" (1943), CW 16, § 179.

[A]ll psychotherapeutic methods are, by and large, useless. I merely want to stress the fact that there are not a few cases where the doctor has to make up his mind to deal fundamentally with the unconscious, to come to a real settlement with it. This is of course something very different from interpretation. In the latter case it is taken for granted that the doctor *knows* beforehand, so as to be able to interpret. But in the case of a real settlement it is not a question of interpretation: it is a question of releasing unconscious processes and letting them come into the conscious mind in the form of fantasies. We can try our hand at interpreting these fantasies if we like. In many cases it may be quite important for the patient to have some idea of the meaning of the fantasies produced. But it is of vital importance that he should experience them to the full and, in so far as intellectual understanding belongs to the totality of experience, also understand them. Yet I would not give priority to understanding. Naturally the doctor must be able to assist the patient in his understanding, but, since he will not and indeed cannot understand everything, the doctor should assiduously guard against clever feats of interpretation. For the important thing is not to interpret and understand the fantasies, but primarily to experience them.

The Relations between the Ego and the Unconscious (1916/1928),
CW 7, § 342.

An ancient adept has said: "If the wrong man uses the right means, the right means work in the wrong way." This Chinese saying, unfortunately only too true, stands in sharp contrast to our belief in the "right" method irrespective of the man who applies it. In reality, everything depends on the man and little or nothing on the method.

"Commentary on *The Secret of the Golden Flower*" (1929), CW 13, § 4.

The greatest mistake an analyst can make is to assume that his patient has a psychology similar to his own.

"General Aspects of Dream Psychology" (1916/1948), CW 8, § 498.

An analyst who cannot risk his authority will be sure to lose it.

"Foreword to Michael Fordham: *New Developments in Analytical Psychology*" (1957), CW 18, § 1172.

If the doctor wants to guide another, or even accompany him a step of the way, he must *feel* with that person's psyche. He never feels it when he passes judgment. Whether he puts his judgments into words, or keeps them to himself, makes not the slightest difference.

"Psychotherapists or the Clergy" (1932), CW 11, § 519.

Psychotherapy is at bottom a dialectical relationship between doctor and patient. It is an encounter, a discussion between two psychic wholes, in which knowledge is used only as a tool. The goal is transformation—not one that is predetermined, but rather an indeterminable change, the only criterion of which is the disappearance of egohood. No efforts on the part of the doctor can compel this experience. The most he can do is to smooth the path for the patient and help him to attain an attitude which offers the least resistance to the decisive experience.

"Foreword to Suzuki's *Introduction to Zen Buddhism*" (1939), CW 11, § 904.

I cannot "tell" my patient, I have to seek him and must learn his language and think his thoughts, until he knows that I understand him correctly. Then only is he ready to understand me and at the same time the strange language of the unconscious, that tells him of eternal truths, and incidentally he will discover that he has heard similar things before. That's the practical way. But to get there you have to avoid "suggestions."

Letter to Victor White, 5 October 1945, *The Jung-White Letters*, p. 10.

The great healing factor in psychotherapy is the doctor's personality.

"Medicine and Psychotherapy" (1945), CW 16, § 198.

Analysis is not only a "diagnosis" but rather an understanding and a moral support in the honest experimental attempt one calls "life." For the *individual* you never can know better or ahead. You only can help people to understand themselves and to gather up courage enough to try and risk. The invisible part of the work goes much further than whatever you can publish in a scientific journal. You have got to leave room for the irrational factor, although you hate it.

Letter to J. Allen Gilbert, 19 June 1929, *Letters, Vol. I*, p. 47.

Nobody can meddle with fire or poison without being affected in some vulnerable spot; for the true physician does not stand outside his work but is always in the thick of it.

Psychology and Alchemy, (1944), CW 12, § 5.

So long as you feel the human contact, the atmosphere of mutual confidence, there is no danger; and even if you have to face the terrors of insanity, or the shadowy menace of suicide, there is still that area of human faith, that certainty of understanding and of being understood, no matter how black the night.

Analytical Psychology and Education (1926/1946), CW 17, § 181.

We cannot demand of our patients a faith which they reject because they do not understand it, or which does not suit them even though we may hold it ourselves. We have to rely on the curative powers inherent in the patient's own nature, regardless of whether the ideas that emerge agree with any known creed or philosophy.

"Religion and Psychology: A Reply to Martin Buber" (1952), CW 18, § 1512.

In psychology it is very important that the doctor should not strive to heal at all costs. One has to be exceedingly careful not to impose one's own will and conviction on the patient. You have to give him a certain amount of freedom. You can't wrest people away from their fate, just as in medicine you cannot cure a patient if nature means him to die. Sometimes it is really a question whether you are allowed to rescue a man from the fate he must undergo for the sake of his further development.

The Tavistock Lectures: On the Theory and Practice of Analytical Psychology (1935), CW 18, § 291.

What are religions? Religions are psychotherapeutic systems. What are we doing, we psychotherapists? We are trying to heal the suffering of the human mind, of the human psyche or the human soul, and the religions deal with the same problem. Therefore our Lord himself is a healer; he is a doctor; he heals the sick and he deals with the troubles of the soul; and that is exactly what we call psychotherapy.

The Tavistock Lectures: On the Theory and Practice of Analytical Psychology (1935), CW 18, § 370.

[N]early all of my patients are people for whom the traditional symbols do not work.

Introduction to Jungian Psychology: Notes of a Seminar on Analytical Psychology Given in 1925, p. 87.

The labours of the doctor as well as the quest of the patient are directed towards that hidden and as yet unmanifest "whole" man, who is at once the greater and the future man. But the right way to wholeness is made up, unfortunately, of fateful detours and wrong turnings. It is a *longissima via* [longest way], not straight but snakelike, a path that unites the opposites in the manner of the guiding caduceus, a path whose labyrinthine twists and turns are not lacking in terrors. It is on the *longissima via* that we meet with those experiences which are said to be "inaccessible." Their inaccessibility really consists in the fact that they cost us an enormous amount of effort: they demand the very thing we most fear, namely the "wholeness" which we talk about so glibly and which lends itself to endless theorizing, though in actual life we give it the widest possible berth. It is infinitely more popular to go in for "compartment psychology," where the left-hand pigeon-hole does not know what is in the right.

Psychology and Alchemy (1944), CW 12, § 6.

The doctor has to cope with actual suffering for better or worse, and ultimately has nothing to rely on except the mystery of divine Providence.

"On the Discourses of the Buddha" (1956), CW 18, § 1578.

No one should deny the danger of the descent, but it *can* be risked. No one *need* risk it, but it is certain that some will. And let those who go down the sunset way do so with open eyes, for it is a sacrifice which daunts even the gods. Yet every descent is followed by an ascent; the vanishing shapes are shaped anew, and a truth is valid in the end only if it suffers change, and bears new witnesses in new images, in new tongues, like a new wine that is put into old bottles.

Symbols of Transformation (1912/1952), CW 5, § 553.

6
The Development of the Personality

The mother-child relationship is certainly the deepest and most poignant one we know; in fact, for some time the child is, so to speak, a part of the mother's body. Later it is part of the psychic atmosphere of the mother for several years, and in this way everything original in the child is indissolubly blended with the mother-image. This is true not only for the individual, but still more in a historical sense.

"Analytical Psychology and *Weltanschauung*" (1928/1931), CW 8,
§ 723.

The carrier of the archetype is in the first place the personal mother, because the child lives at first in complete participation with her, in a state of unconscious identity. She is the psychic as well as the physical precondition of the child. With the awakening of ego-consciousness the participation gradually weakens, and consciousness begins to enter into opposition to the unconscious, its own precondition. This leads to differentiation of the ego from the mother, whose personal peculiarities gradually become more distinct. All the fabulous and mysterious qualities attaching to her image begin to fall away and are transferred to the person closest to her, for instance the grandmother. As the mother of the mother, she is "greater" than the latter; she is in truth the "grand" or "Great Mother." Not infrequently she assumes the attributes of wisdom as well as those of a witch. For the further the archetype recedes from consciousness and the clearer the latter becomes, the more distinctly does the archetype assume mythological features. The transition from mother to grandmother means that the archetype is elevated to a higher rank.

"Psychological Aspects of the Mother Archetype" (1938/1954),
CW 9i, § 188.

The negative relationship to the mother is always an affront to nature, unnatural. Hence distance from the earth, identification with the father, heaven, light, wind, spirit, Logos. Rejection of the earth, of what is below, dark, feminine. Negative relationship to material things, also to children. Flight from personal feelings.

Letter to Count Hermann Keyserling, 25 August 1928, *Letters, Vol. I*,
p. 52.

For the parental imago is possessed of a quite extraordinary power; it influences the psychic life of the child so enormously that we must ask ourselves whether we may attribute such magical power to an ordinary human being at all. Obviously he possesses it, but we are bound to ask whether it is really his property. Man "possesses" many things which he has never acquired but has inherited from his ancestors. He is not born as a *tabula rasa* [blank slate], he is merely born unconscious. But he brings with him systems that are organized and ready to function in a specifically human way, and these he owes to millions of years of human development. Just as the migratory and nest-building instincts of birds were never learnt or acquired individually, man brings with him at birth the ground-plan of his nature, and not only of his individual nature but of his collective nature. These inherited systems correspond to the human situations that have existed since primeval times: youth and old age, birth and death, sons and daughters, fathers and mothers, mating, and so on. Only the individual consciousness experiences these things for the first time, but not the bodily system and the unconscious. For them they are only the habitual functioning of instincts that were preformed long ago.

"The Significance of the Father in the Destiny of the Individual"
(1909/1949), CW 4, § 728.

No man can begin with the present; he must slowly grow into it, for there would be no present but for the past. A young person has not yet acquired a past, therefore he has no present either. He does not create culture, he merely exists. It is the privilege and the task of maturer people, who have passed the meridian of life, to create culture.

"Woman in Europe" (1927), CW 10, § 272.

But no matter how much the parents and grandparents may have sinned against the child, the man who is really adult will accept these sins as his own condition which has to be reckoned with.

Only a fool is interested in other people's guilt, since he cannot alter it. The wise man learns only from his own guilt. He will ask himself: Who am I that all this should happen to me? To find the answer to this fateful question he will look into his own heart.

Psychology and Alchemy (1944), CW 12, § 152.

Psychologically, the central point of a human personality is the place where the ancestors are reincarnated.

Dream Analysis: Notes of the Seminar Given in 1928–1930 (9 October 1929), p. 304.

[F]or as the son of his father, he must, as if often the case with children, re-enact under unconscious compulsion the unlived lives of his parents.

Psychological Types (1921), CW 6, § 307.

A childish consciousness is always tied to father and mother, and is never by itself. Return to childhood is always the return to father and mother, to the whole burden of the psychic non-ego as represented by the parents, with its long and momentous history. Regression spells disintegration into historical and hereditary determinants, and it is only with the greatest effort that we can free ourselves from their embrace. Our psychic prehistory is in truth the spirit of gravity, which needs steps and ladders because, unlike the disembodied airy intellect, it cannot fly at will. Disintegration into the jumble of historical determinants is like losing one's way, where even what is right seems an alarming mistake.

Psychology and Alchemy (1944), CW 12, § 79.

That complete surrender to the present necessities means of course a fulfilment, a redemption of the past generations, and of the unfulfilled lives that are waiting to be fulfilled. If we live completely, we surrender to their lives and redeem them. Also, we prepare for a future generation, because we have lived out our own lives; we have

fulfilled them, and we leave no curse for the following generations—the curse of economized life.

Nietzsche's Zarathustra: *Notes of the Seminar Given in 1934–1939,*
Vol. I (6 June 1934), p. 89.

So long as the child is in that state of unconscious identity with the
mother, he is still one with the animal psyche and is just as unconscious as it. The development of consciousness inevitably leads not
only to separation from the mother, but to separation from the parents and the whole family circle and thus to a relative degree of
detachment from the unconscious and the world of instinct. Yet
the longing for this lost world continues and, when difficult adap-
tations are demanded, is forever tempting one to make evasions
and retreats, to regress to the infantile, which then starts throwing
up the incestuous symbolism.

Symbols of Transformation (1912/1952), CW 5, § 351.

One of the essential features of the child motif is its futurity. The
child is potential future. Hence the occurrence of the child motif in
the psychology of the individual signifies as a rule an anticipation
of future developments, even though at first sight it may seem like
a retrospective configuration. Life is a flux, a flowing into the future, and not a stoppage or a backwash. It is therefore not surprising that so many of the mythological saviours are child gods. This
agrees exactly with our experience of the psychology of the individual, which shows that the "child" paves the way for a future
change of personality. In the individuation process, it anticipates
the figure that comes from the synthesis of conscious and unconscious elements in the personality. It is therefore a symbol which
unites the opposites; a mediator, bringer of healing, that is, one
who makes whole. Because it has this meaning, the child motif is
capable of the numerous transformations mentioned above: it can
be expressed by roundness, the circle or sphere, or else by the quaternity as another form of wholeness. I have called this wholeness

that transcends consciousness the "self." The goal of the individuation process is the synthesis of the self.

"The Psychology of the Child Archetype" (1940), CW 9i, § 278.

"Child" means something evolving towards independence. This it cannot do without detaching itself from its origins: abandonment is therefore a necessary condition, not just a concomitant symptom.

"The Psychology of the Child Archetype" (1940), CW 9i, § 287.

The "child" is born out of the womb of the unconscious, begotten out of the depths of human nature, or rather out of living Nature herself. It is a personification of vital forces quite outside the limited range of our conscious mind; of ways and possibilities of which our one-sided conscious mind knows nothing; a wholeness which embraces the very depths of Nature. It represents the strongest, the most ineluctable urge in every being, namely the urge to realize itself. It is, as it were, an incarnation of *the inability to do otherwise*, equipped with all the powers of nature and instinct, whereas the conscious mind is always getting caught up in its supposed ability to do otherwise. The urge and compulsion to self-realization is a law of nature and thus of invincible power, even though its effect, at the start, is insignificant and improbable.

"The Psychology of the Child Archetype" (1940), CW 9i, § 289.

The "child" is therefore *renatus in novam infantiam* [reborn into a new infancy]. It is thus both beginning and end, an initial and a terminal creature. The initial creature existed before man was not, and the terminal creature will be when man is not. Psychologically speaking, this means that the "child" symbolizes the pre-conscious and the post-conscious essence of man. His pre-conscious essence is the unconscious state of earliest childhood; his post-conscious essence is an anticipation by analogy of life after death. In this idea the all-embracing nature of psychic wholeness is expressed. Wholeness is never comprised within the compass of the conscious mind—it includes the indefinite and indefinable extent of the unconscious as well. Wholeness, empirically speaking, is therefore of immeasurable extent, older and younger than consciousness and enfolding it in time and space. This is no speculation, but an immediate psychic experience. Not only is the conscious process continually accompanied, it is often guided, helped, or interrupted, by unconscious happenings. The child had a psychic life before it had consciousness.

"The Psychology of the Child Archetype" (1940), CW 9i, § 299.

The "child" is all that is abandoned and exposed and at the same time divinely powerful; the insignificant, dubious beginning, and the triumphal end. The "eternal" child in man is an indescribable experience, an incongruity, a handicap, and a divine prerogative; an imponderable that determines the ultimate worth or worthlessness of a personality.

"The Psychology of the Child Archetype" (1940), CW 9i, § 300.

Abandonment, exposure, danger, etc. are all elaborations of the "child's" insignificant beginnings and of its mysterious and miraculous birth. This statement describes a certain psychic experience of a creative nature, whose object is the emergence of a new and as yet unknown content.

"The Psychology of the Child Archetype" (1940), CW 9i, § 285.

No man can change himself into anything from sheer reason; he can only change into what he potentially is. When such a change becomes necessary, the previous mode of adaptation, already in a state of decay, is unconsciously compensated by the archetype of another mode. If the conscious mind now succeeds in interpreting the constellated archetype in a meaningful and appropriate manner, then a viable transformation can take place. Thus the most important relationship of childhood, the relation to the mother, will be compensated by the mother archetype as soon as detachment from the childhood state is indicated. One such successful interpretation has been, for instance, Mother Church, but once this form begins to show signs of age and decay a new interpretation becomes inevitable.

Symbols of Transformation (1912/1952), CW 5, § 351.

[A] child always means a beginning, a new attempt at life.

Visions: Notes of the Seminar Given in 1930–1934, Vol. I (6 May 1931), p. 342.

Young children have a consciousness which is remarkable. I find the psychology of little children exceedingly difficult; their dreams, for instance, are amazingly difficult. One would assume that they would be quite simple but they are far from that. Of course some are obvious, but they have an unusual number of great dreams, and great visions too, and to deal with them requires an hypothesis which makes one quite dizzy. One has to assume that they have a consciousness of the collective unconscious, an amazing thing. It makes little children seem quite old, like people who have lived a full life and who have a very profound idea of what consciousness really is. Hence the saying: fools and children speak the truth. It is because they know it. Children have the vision still hanging over them of things which they have never seen, and could not possibly have seen, and which are in accordance with the theory of reincarnation. It is just as if reminiscences of a former life were carried over into this life, or from the ancestral life perhaps, we don't know. I could tell you children's dreams which are simply uncanny, and if you want to interpret them at all, you have to use uncanny means. They cannot be explained even by the psychology of the parents. They must come from the psychology of the collective unconscious; one could say they were remnants of things they had seen before they were born, and that is really vision. I know a case where a vision affected a whole life. Individuals can be stunted all through their lives by a vision in childhood. Such children are not quite born—their birth takes place much later, when they can detach. But many people are never quite born; they live in the flesh but a part of them is still in what Lamaistic philosophy would call the *Bardo*, in the life between death and birth, and that prenatal state is filled with extraordinary visions.

Visions: Notes of the Seminar Given in 1930–1934, Vol. I (24 June
1931), p. 424.

Childhood dreams still remembered by adults are not just any dreams, but have been preserved by memory because they completely contain human life in either longer or shorter periods. When we have a cursory glance at such a dream, at first we do not understand why it has been remembered. If we are able to trace it back, however, we can in most cases find clues as to why it has gained such importance. If things have made a deep impression on us in childhood, we may assume that something highly important lies within what impressed us as such, or that a very important event happened in the neighbourhood of what we kept in our memory, something which is meaningful for the whole later course of life.

Children's Dreams: Notes from the Seminar Given in 1936–1940,
p. 136.

Our life is like the course of the sun. In the morning it gains continually in strength until it reaches the zenith-heat of high noon. Then comes the enantiodromia [running counter to]: the steady forward movement no longer denotes an increase, but a decrease, in strength. Thus our task in handling a young person is different from the task of handling an older person. In the former case, it is enough to clear away all the obstacles that hinder expansion and ascent; in the latter, we must nurture everything that assists the descent.

On the Psychology of the Unconscious (1917/1926), CW 7, § 114.

One looks back with appreciation to the brilliant teachers, but with gratitude to those who touched our human feelings. The curriculum is so much necessary raw material, but warmth is the vital element for the growing plant and for the soul of the child.

"The Gifted Child" (1943), CW 17, § 249.

Childhood is important not only because various warpings of instinct have their origin there, but because this is the time when, terrifying or encouraging, those far-seeing dreams and images appear before the soul of the child, shaping his whole destiny, as well as those retrospective intuitions which reach back far beyond the range of childhood experience into the life of our ancestors. Thus in the child-psyche the natural condition is already opposed by a "spiritual" one.

"On Psychic Energy" (1928), CW 8, § 98.

It is of course impossible to free oneself from one's childhood without devoting a great deal of work to it, as Freud's researches have long since shown. Nor can it be achieved through intellectual knowledge only; what is alone effective is a remembering that is also a re-experiencing. The swift passage of the years and the overwhelming inrush of the newly discovered world leave a mass of material behind that is never dealt with. We do not shake this off; we merely remove ourselves from it. So that when, in later years, we return to the memories of childhood we find bits of our personality still alive, which cling round us and suffuse us with the feeling of earlier times. Being still in their childhood state, these fragments are very powerful in their effect. They can lose their infantile aspect and be corrected only when they are reunited with adult consciousness.

Psychology and Alchemy (1944), CW 12, § 81.

Nothing exerts a stronger psychic effect upon the human environment, and especially upon children, than the life which the parents have not lived.

"Paracelsus" (1929), CW 15, § 4.

An individual is infantile because he has freed himself insufficiently, or not at all, from his childish environment and his adaptation to his parents, with the result that he has a false reaction to the world: on the one hand he reacts as a child towards his parents, always demanding love and immediate emotional rewards, while on the other hand he is so identified with his parents through his close ties with them that he behaves like his father or his mother. He is incapable of living his own life and finding the character that belongs to him.

Symbols of Transformation (1912/1952), CW 5, § 431.

All the life which the parents could have lived, but of which they thwarted themselves for artificial motives, is passed on to the children in substitute form. That is to say, the children are driven unconsciously in a direction that is intended to compensate for everything that was left unfulfilled in the lives of their parents. Hence it is that excessively moral-minded parents have what are called "unmoral" children, or an irresponsible wastrel of a father has a son with a positively morbid amount of ambition, and so on.

"Marriage as a Psychological Relationship" (1925), CW 17, § 328.

To remain a child too long is childish, but it is just as childish to move away and then assume that childhood no longer exists because we do not see it. But if we return to the "children's land" we succumb to the fear of becoming childish, because we do not understand that everything of psychic origin has a double face. One face looks forward, the other back. It is ambivalent and therefore symbolic, like all living reality.

Psychology and Alchemy (1944), CW 12, § 74.

The nearer we approach to the middle of life, and the better we have succeeded in entrenching ourselves in our personal attitudes and social positions, the more it appears as if we had discovered the right course and the right ideals and principles of behaviour. For this reason we suppose them to be eternally valid, and make a virtue of unchangeably clinging to them. We overlook the essential fact that the social goal is attained only at the cost of a diminution of personality. Many—far too many—aspects of life which should also have been experienced lie in the lumber-room among dusty memories; but sometimes, too, they are glowing coals under grey ashes.

"The Stages of Life" (1930–31), CW 8, § 772.

The middle period of life is a time of enormous psychological importance. The child begins its psychological life within very narrow limits, inside the magic circle of the mother and the family. With progressive maturation it widens its horizon and its own sphere of influence; its hopes and intentions are directed to extending the scope of personal power and possessions; desire reaches out to the world in ever-widening range; the will of the individual becomes more and more identical with the natural goals pursued by unconscious motivations. Thus man breathes his own life into things, until finally they begin to live of themselves and to multiply; and imperceptibly he is overgrown by them. Mothers are overtaken by their children, men by their own creations, and what was originally brought into being only with labour and the greatest effort can no longer be held in check. First it was passion, then it became duty, and finally an intolerable burden, a vampire that battens on the life of its creator.

"Marriage as a Psychological Relationship" (1925), CW 17, § 331a.

The wine of youth does not always clear with advancing years; sometimes it grows turbid.

"The Stages of Life" (1930–31), CW 8, § 774.

Wholly unprepared, we embark upon the second half of life. Or are there perhaps colleges for forty-year-olds which prepare them for their coming life and its demands as the ordinary colleges introduce our young people to a knowledge of the world? No, thoroughly unprepared we take the step into the afternoon of life; worse still, we take this step with the false assumption that our truths and ideals will serve us as hitherto. But we cannot live the afternoon of life according to the program of life's morning; for what was great in the morning will be little at evening, and what in the morning was true will at evening have become a lie.

"The Stages of Life" (1930–31), CW 8, § 784.

Our personality develops in the course of life from germs that are hard or impossible to discern, and it is only our deeds that reveal who we are. We are like the sun, which nourishes the life of the earth and brings forth every kind of strange, wonderful, and evil thing; we are like the mothers who bear in their wombs untold happiness and suffering. At first we do not know what deeds or misdeeds, what destiny, what good and evil we have in us, and only the autumn can show what the spring has engendered, only in the evening will it be seen what the morning began.

"The Development of Personality" (1934), CW 17, § 290.

There are experiences which one must go through and for which reason is no substitute. Such experiences are often of inestimable value to the patient.

The Theory of Psychoanalysis (1913), CW 4, § 446.

To become a personality is not the absolute prerogative of the genius, for a man may be a genius without being a personality. In so far as every individual has the law of his life inborn in him, it is theoretically possible for any man to follow this law and so become a personality, that is, to achieve wholeness. But since life only exists in the form of living units, i.e., individuals, the law of life always tends towards a life individually lived.

"The Development of Personality" (1934), CW 17, § 307.

Behind a man's actions there stands neither public opinion nor the moral code, but the personality of which he is still unconscious. Just as a man still is what he always was, so he already is what he will become. The conscious mind does not embrace the totality of a man, for this totality consists only partly of his conscious contents, and for the other and far greater part, of his unconscious, which is of indefinite extent with no assignable limits. In this totality the conscious mind is contained like a smaller circle within a larger one.

"Transformation Symbolism in the Mass" (1942/1954), CW 11,
§ 390.

The ego-conscious personality is only a part of the whole man, and its life does not yet represent his total life. The more he is merely "I," the more he splits himself off from the collective man, of whom he is also a part, and may even find himself in opposition to him. But since everything living strives for wholeness, the inevitable one-sidedness of our conscious life is continually being corrected and compensated by the universal human being in us, whose goal is the ultimate integration of conscious and unconscious, or better, the assimilation of the ego to a wider personality.

"On the Nature of Dreams" (1945/1948), CW 8, § 557.

We know that the first impressions of childhood accompany us inalienably throughout life, and that, just as indestructibly, certain educational influences can keep people all their lives within those limits. In these circumstances it is not surprising that conflicts break out between the personality moulded by educational and other influences of the infantile milieu and one's own individual style of life. It is a conflict which all those must face who are called upon to live a life that is independent and creative.

The Theory of Psychoanalysis (1913), CW 4, § 310.

[T]he development of personality from the germ-state to full consciousness is at once a charisma and a curse, because its first fruit is the conscious and unavoidable segregation of the single individual from the undifferentiated and unconscious herd. This means isolation, and there is no more comforting word for it. Neither family nor society nor position can save him from this fate, nor yet the most successful adaptation to his environment, however smoothly he fits in. The development of personality is a favour that must be paid for dearly.

"The Development of Personality" (1934), CW 17, § 294.

The personality is seldom, in the beginning, what it will be later on. For this reason the possibility of enlarging it exists, at least during the first half of life. The enlargement may be effected through an accretion from without, by new vital contents finding their way into the personality from outside and being assimilated. In this way a considerable increase of personality may be experienced. We therefore tend to assume that this increase comes *only* from without, thus justifying the prejudice that one becomes a personality by stuffing into oneself as much as possible from outside. But the more assiduously we follow this recipe, and the more stubbornly we believe that all increase has to come from without, the greater becomes our inner poverty. Therefore, if some great idea takes hold of us from outside, we must understand that it takes hold of us only because something in us responds to it and goes out to meet it. Richness of mind consists in mental receptivity, not in the accumulation of possessions. What comes to us from outside, and, for that matter, everything that rises up from within, can only be made our own if we are capable of an inner amplitude equal to that of the incoming content. Real increase of personality means consciousness of an enlargement that flows from inner sources. Without psychic depth we can never be adequately related to the magnitude of our object. It has therefore been said quite truly that a man grows with the greatness of his task. But he must have within himself the capacity to grow; otherwise, even the most difficult task is of no benefit to him. More likely he will be shattered by it.

"Concerning Rebirth" (1940/1950), CW 9i, § 215.

All beginnings are small. Therefore we must not mind doing tedious but conscientious work on obscure individuals, even though the goal towards which we strive seems unattainably far off. But one goal we can attain, and that is to develop and bring to maturity individual personalities. And inasmuch as we are convinced that the individual is the carrier of life, we have served life's purpose if one tree at least succeeds in bearing fruit, though a thousand others remain barren. Anyone who proposed to bring all growing things to the highest pitch of luxuriance would soon find the weeds—those hardiest of perennials—waving above his head. I therefore consider it the prime task of psychotherapy today to pursue with singleness of purpose the goal of individual development. So doing, our efforts will follow nature's own striving to bring life to the fullest possible fruition in each individual, for only in the individual can life fulfil its meaning—not in the bird that sits in a gilded cage.

"Fundamental Questions of Psychotherapy" (1951), CW 16, § 229.

Personality is a seed that can only develop by slow stages throughout life. There is no personality without definiteness, wholeness, and ripeness. These three qualities cannot and should not be expected of the child, as they would rob it of childhood.

Analytical Psychology and Education (1926/1946), CW 17, § 288.

In every adult there lurks a child—an eternal child, something that is always becoming, is never completed, and calls for unceasing care, attention, and education. That is the part of the human personality which wants to develop and become whole. But the man of today is far indeed from this wholeness.

"The Development of Personality" (1934), CW 17, § 286.

[C]hildren also contain a future personality within themselves, the being that they *will* be in the following years. The experiences of the coming years are, so to speak, there already, but only unconsciously, as they have not yet been made. The children already live in a tomorrow, only they are not aware of it. This figure exists *in potential*, naturally in a projected form.

Children's Dreams: Notes from the Seminar Given in 1936–1940,
p. 50.

Only the man who can consciously assent to the power of the inner voice becomes a personality; but if he succumbs to it he will be swept away by the blind flux of psychic events and destroyed. That is the great and liberating thing about any genuine personality: he voluntarily sacrifices himself to his vocation, and consciously translates into his own individual reality what would only lead to ruin if it were lived unconsciously by the group.

"The Development of Personality" (1934), CW 17, § 308.

Everything good is costly, and the development of personality is one of the most costly of all things. It is a matter of saying yea to oneself, of taking oneself as the most serious of tasks, of being conscious of everything one does, and keeping it constantly before one's eyes in all its dubious aspects—truly a task that taxes us to the utmost.

"Commentary on *The Secret of the Golden Flower*" (1929), CW 13,
§ 24.

Personality is the supreme realization of the innate idiosyncrasy of a living being. It is an act of high courage flung in the face of life, the absolute affirmation of all that constitutes the individual, the most successful adaptation to the universal conditions of existence coupled with the greatest possible freedom for self-determination.

"The Development of Personality" (1934), CW 17, § 289.

Personality consists of two things: first, consciousness and whatever this covers, and second, an indefinitely large hinterland of unconscious psyche. So far as the former is concerned, it can be more or less clearly defined and delimited; but as for the sum total of personality, one has to admit the impossibility of a complete description or definition. In other words, there is bound to be an illimitable and indefinable addition to every personality, because the latter consists of a conscious and observable part which does not contain certain factors whose existence, however, we are forced to assume in order to explain certain observable facts. The unknown factors form what we call the unconscious part of the personality.

Psychology and Religion (1938/1940), CW 11, § 66.

The wider the gap between conscious and unconscious, the nearer creeps the fatal splitting of the personality, which in neurotically disposed individuals leads to neurosis, and, in those with a psychotic constitution, to schizophrenia and fragmentation of personality.

Symbols of Transformation (1912/1952), CW 5, § 683.

If we follow the history of a neurosis with attention, we regularly find a critical moment when some problem emerged that was evaded. This evasion is just as natural and just as common a reaction as the laziness, slackness, cowardice, anxiety, ignorance, and unconsciousness which are at the back of it. Whenever things are unpleasant, difficult, and dangerous, we mostly hesitate and if possible give them a wide berth.

On the Psychology of the Unconscious (1917/1926), CW 7, § 23.

We should not try to "get rid" of a neurosis, but rather to experience what it means, what it has to teach, what its purpose is. We should even learn to be thankful for it, otherwise we pass it by and miss the opportunity of getting to know ourselves as we really are. A neurosis is truly removed only when it has removed the false attitude of the ego. We do not cure it—it cures us. A man is ill, but the illness is nature's attempt to heal him. From the illness itself we can learn so much for our recovery, and what the neurotic flings away as absolutely worthless contains the true gold we should never have found elsewhere.

"The State of Psychotherapy Today" (1934), CW 10, § 361.

Neurosis is always a substitute for legitimate suffering.

Psychology and Religion (1938/1940), CW 11, § 129.

Once we have made up our minds to treat the soul, we can no longer close our eyes to the fact that neurosis is not a thing apart but the whole thing of the pathologically disturbed psyche. It was Freud's momentous discovery that the neurosis is not a mere agglomeration of symptoms, but a wrong functioning which affects the whole psyche. The important thing is not the neurosis, but the man who has the neurosis. We have to set to work on the human being, and we must be able to do him justice as a human being.

"Psychotherapy and a Philosophy of Life" (1943), CW 16, § 190.

There are no magical cures for neurosis. The moment we begin to map out the lines of advance that are symbolically indicated, the patient himself must proceed along them. If he shirks this by his own deceit, he automatically precludes any cure. He must in very truth take the way of the individual lifeline he has recognized as his own, and continue along it until such time as an unmistakable reaction from the unconscious tells him that he is on the wrong track.

"The Structure of the Unconscious" (1916), CW 7, § 497.

Neurosis—let there be no doubt about this—may be any number of things, but never a "nothing but." It is the agony of a human soul in all its vast complexity—so vast, indeed, that any and every theory of neurosis is little better than a worthless sketch, unless it be a gigantic picture of the psyche which not even a hundred Fausts could conceive.

"The State of Psychotherapy Today" (1934), CW 10, § 357.

A neurosis is by no means merely a negative thing, it is also something positive. Only a soulless rationalism reinforced by a narrow materialistic outlook could possibly have overlooked this fact. In reality the neurosis contains the patient's psyche, or at least an essential part of it; and if, as the rationalist pretends, the neurosis could be plucked from him like a bad tooth, he would have gained nothing but would have lost something very essential to him. That is to say, he would have lost as much as the thinker deprived of his doubt, or the moralist deprived of his temptation, or the brave man deprived of his fear. To lose a neurosis is to find oneself without an object; life loses its point and hence its meaning. This would not be a cure, it would be a regular amputation.

"The State of Psychotherapy Today" (1934), CW 10, § 355.

He who does not possess this moral function, this loyalty to himself, will never get rid of his neurosis. But he who has this capacity will certainly find the way to cure himself.

"The Structure of the Unconscious" (1916), CW 7, § 498.

[I]f we understand anything of the unconscious, we know that it cannot be swallowed. We also know that it is dangerous to suppress it, because the unconscious is life and this life turns against us if suppressed, as happens in neurosis.

"Conscious, Unconscious, and Individuation" (1939), CW 9i, § 521.

In the neurosis is hidden one's worst enemy and best friend. One cannot rate him too highly, unless of course fate has made one hostile to life. There are always deserters, but they have nothing to say to us, nor we to them.

"The State of Psychotherapy Today" (1934), CW 10, § 359.

Among the so-called neurotics of our day there are a good many who in other ages would not have been neurotic—that is, divided against themselves. If they had lived in a period and in a milieu in which man was still linked by myth with the world of the ancestors, and thus with nature truly experienced and not merely seen from outside, they would have been spared this division within themselves.

Memories, Dreams, Reflections (1962), pp. 143–44.

[I] quite generally take the view that a neurosis is not of traumatic origin, that is, that it can't be traced back to a singular frightening experience; I try to understand it in the context of the present meaning. For what lives and takes effect today is also recreated today, again and again. I also relate frequently *recurring dreams* to what is currently going on, therefore, and to what is *recreated* over and over again, and not to something that lies many years back.

Children's Dreams: Notes from the Seminar Given in 1936–1940,
p. 276.

You know how long it takes to change the whole viewpoint of the patient, yet in nearly all neuroses it is almost indispensable that the whole outlook on life undergoes a complete change.

Letter to Elined Kotschnig, 18 February 1941, *Letters, Vol. I,*
p. 295.

[H]idden in the neurosis is a bit of still undeveloped personality, a precious fragment of the psyche lacking which a man is condemned to resignation, bitterness, and everything else that is hostile to life. A psychology of neurosis that sees only the negative elements empties out the baby with the bath-water, since it neglects the positive meaning and value of these "infantile"—i.e., creative—fantasies.

The State of Psychotherapy Today (1934), CW 10, § 355.

It may be that in schizophrenia a normal consciousness is confronted with an unusually strong unconscious: it may also be that the patient's consciousness is just weak and therefore unable to keep back the inrush of unconscious material. In practice I must allow for the existence of two groups of schizophrenia: one with a weak consciousness and the other with a strong unconscious. We have here a certain analogy with the neuroses, where we also find plenty of patients with a markedly weak consciousness and little willpower, and others who possess remarkable energy but are subjected to an almost overwhelmingly strong unconscious determination. This is particularly the case when creative impulses (artistic or otherwise) are coupled with unconscious incompatibilities.

"On the Psychogenesis of Schizophrenia" (1939), CW 3, § 531.

What, then, is a latent psychosis exactly? It is obviously nothing but the possibility that an individual may become mentally deranged at some period of his life. The existence of strange unconscious material proves nothing. You find the same material in neurotics, modern artists, and poets, and also in fairly normal people who have submitted to a careful investigation of their dreams. Moreover, you find most suggestive parallels in the mythology and symbolism of all races and times. The possibility of a future psychosis has nothing to do with the peculiar contents of the unconscious. But it has everything to do with whether the individual can stand a certain panic, or the chronic strain of a psyche at war with itself. Very often it is simply a matter of a little bit too much, of the drop that falls into a vessel already full, or of the spark that accidentally lands on a heap of gunpowder.

"On the Psychogenesis of Schizophrenia" (1939), CW 3, § 520.

The chief danger is that of succumbing to the fascinating influence of the archetypes, and this is most likely to happen when the archetypal images are not made conscious. If there is already a predisposition to psychosis, it may even happen that the archetypal figures, which are endowed with a certain autonomy on account of their natural numinosity, will escape from conscious control altogether and become completely independent, thus producing the phenomena of possession.

"Archetypes of the Collective Unconscious" (1934/1954), CW 9i, § 82.

People may even be destroyed by an archetype, their own existence wiped out forever. In *dementia praecox*, for instance, it often happens that people are just blasted by an archetype, exploded. They cannot resist it. If they have an experience which the ordinary religious man would call an experience of God, instead of realizing it as such and thanking heaven for the grace, they think they *are* God or three times more than God. The archetype has sucked them in and swallowed them. The individual ego is far less resistant; it is futile in comparison. Therefore the appearance of an archetype in our psychology is always a moment of the greatest danger as well as the greatest hope.

Visions: Notes of the Seminar Given in 1930–1934, Vol. I (5 November 1930), p. 67.

l once had a case of schizophrenia, a girl who was so caught by that redemption mystery which was going on in her that she could no longer speak to people. She was locked up in a lunatic asylum for about sixteen months, and I had a chance somehow to get behind her screen and discover where she went. She went to the moon and became the savior of the moon people. She became the redeemer of the world, she built temples and did all sorts of wonderful things, it was a most amazing story. And the thing which was difficult for her to bear was that, in telling me that story, she cut the thread to the moon and could not go back; she had to be sane, she was caught to the earth because she had betrayed the mystery. She wanted to kill me because I had cured her, because her life in the moon was so much more beautiful. She had no idea that the moon was a symbol, so that one called people like herself lunatics; she went into the un-conscious—into the moon—and there she did the only thing that was worth living for, redemption; she succeeded in saving the moon people. But she got stuck in the moon, she became the prisoner of the moon spirit. Then when I came in and she could tell me that story, she was caught in this world and could not go back. She hated me for a long time and said to me: "Oh, it was so much more beauti-ful. I hate to live on this earth." Since then I am not so compassionate about insane people; it may not be so bad, it only looks so.

Visions: Notes of the Seminar Given in 1930–1934, Vol. I (8 December 1930), p. 146.

Through my work with the patients, I realized that paranoid ideas and hallucinations contain a germ of meaning, personality. A life history, a pattern of hopes and desires lie behind the psychosis. The fault is ours if we do not understand them. It dawned upon me then for the first time that a general psychology of the personality lies concealed within psychosis, and that even here we come upon the old human conflicts. Although patients may appear dull and apathetic, or totally imbecilic, there is more going on in their minds, and more that is meaningful, than there seems to be. At bottom we discover nothing new and unknown in the mentally ill; rather, we encounter the substratum of our own natures.

Memories, Dreams, Reflections (1962), p. 127.

[I]t *is* madness to fall out of one's conscious world into an unconscious condition. Insanity means just that, being overcome by an invasion of the unconscious. Consciousness is swept over by unconscious contents in which all orientation is lost. The ego then becomes a sort of fish swimming in a sea among other fishes, and of course fishes don't know who they are, don't even know the name of their own species.

Nietzsche's Zarathustra: Notes of the Seminar Given in 1934–1939,
Vol. II (19 May 1937), pp. 1088–89.

I have given a detailed description of a purely psychological typology in my book *Psychological Types*. My investigation was based on twenty years of work as a doctor, which brought me into contact with people of all classes from all the great nations. When one begins as a young doctor, one's head is still full of clinical pictures and diagnoses. In the course of the years, impressions of quite another kind accumulate. One is struck by the enormous diversity of human individuals, by the chaotic profusion of individual cases, the special circumstances of whose lives and whose special characters produce clinical pictures that, even supposing one still felt any desire to do so, can be squeezed into the straitjacket of a diagnosis only by force. The fact that the disturbance can be given such and such a name appears completely irrelevant beside the overwhelming impression one has that all clinical pictures are so many mimetic or histrionic demonstrations of certain definite character traits. The pathological problem upon which everything turns has virtually nothing to do with the clinical picture, but is essentially an expression of character.

Psychological Types (1921), CW 6, § 970.

It is not the purpose of a psychological typology to classify human beings into categories—this in itself would be pretty pointless. Its purpose is rather to provide a critical psychology which will make a methodical investigation and presentation of the empirical material possible. First and foremost, it is a critical tool for the research worker, who needs definite points of view and guidelines if he is to reduce the chaotic profusion of individual experiences to any kind of order. In this respect we could compare typology to a trigonometric net or, better still, to a crystallographic axial system. Secondly, a typology is a great help in understanding the wide variations that occur among individuals, and it also furnishes a clue to the fundamental differences in the psychological theories now current. Last but not least, it is an essential means for determining the "personal equation" of the practising psychologist, who, armed with an exact knowledge of his differentiated and inferior functions, can avoid many serious blunders in dealing with his patients.

Psychological Types (1921), CW 6, § 986.

My scheme of typology is only a scheme of orientation. There is such a factor as introversion, there is such a factor as extraversion. The classification of individuals means nothing, nothing at all. It is only the instrumentarium for the practical psychologist to explain, for instance, the husband to a wife or vice versa. It is very often the case—I might say it is almost a rule, but I don't want to make too many rules in order not to be schematic—that an introvert marries an extravert for compensation, or another type marries the countertype to complement himself. For instance, a man who has made a certain amount of money is a good business man, but he has no education. His dream is, of course, a grand piano at home, artists, painters, singers or God knows what, and intellectual people, and accordingly he marries a wife of that type in order to have that too. Of course he has nothing of it. She has it, and she marries him because he has a lot of money.

These compensations go on all the time. When you study marriages, you can see it easily. We alienists have to deal with a lot of marriages, particularly those that go wrong, because the types are too different sometimes and they don't understand each other at all. You see, the main values of the extravert are anathema to the introvert, so he says, "To hell with the world, I *think*!" His wife interprets this as his megalomania. But it is just as if an extravert said to an introvert, "Now look here, fellow, these are the facts, this is reality!" And he's right. And the other type says, "But I think!" and that sounds like nonsense to the extravert because he doesn't realize that the other, without knowing it, is seeing an inner world, an inner reality. And he may be right, as he may be wrong, even if he based himself on God knows what solid facts. Take the interpretation of statistics, you can prove anything with statistics. What is more a fact than a statistic?

"The Houston Films" (1957), *C. G. Jung Speaking*, pp. 305–6.

Through the fact that I worried about my difficulty with Freud, I came to study Adler carefully in order to see what was his case against Freud. I was struck at once by the difference in type. Both were treating neurosis and hysteria, and yet to the one man it looked so, and to the other it was something quite different. I could find no solution. Then it dawned on me that possibly I was dealing with two different types, who were fated to approach the same set of facts from widely differing aspects. I began to see among my patients some who fit Adler's theories, and others who fit Freud's, and thus I came to formulate the theory of extraversion: and introversion.

Introduction to Jungian Psychology: Notes of the Seminar on
Analytical Psychology Given in 1925, pp. 32–33.

[J]ust as the three conscious and differentiated parts of these functions are confronted by a fourth, undifferentiated function which acts as a painfully disturbing factor, so also the superior function seems to have its worst enemy in the unconscious. Nor should we omit to mention one final turn of the screw: like the devil who delights in disguising himself as an angel of light, the inferior function secretly and mischievously influences the superior function most of all, just as the latter represses the former most strongly.

"The Phenomenology of the Spirit in Fairytales" (1945/1948), CW 9i,
§ 431.

The book on types yielded the insight that every judgment made by an individual is conditioned by his personality type and that every point of view is necessarily relative.

Memories, Dreams, Reflections (1962), p. 207.

A type is a specimen or example which reproduces in a characteristic way the character of a species or class. In the narrower sense used in this particular work, a type is a characteristic specimen of a general *attitude* occurring in many individual forms. From a great number of existing or possible attitudes I have singled out four; those, namely, that are primarily oriented by the four basic psychological *functions: thinking, feeling, sensation, intuition.* When any of these attitudes is *habitual,* thus setting a definite stamp on the character of an *individual,* I speak of a psychological type. These *function-types,* which one can call the thinking, feeling, sensation, and intuitive types, may be divided into two classes according to the quality of the basic function, i.e., into the *rational* and the *irrational.* The thinking and feeling types belong to the former class, the sensation and intuitive types to the latter. A further division into two classes is permitted by the predominant trend of the movement of *libido*, namely *introversion* and *extraversion*. All the basic types can belong equally well to one or the other of these classes, according to the predominance of the introverted or extraverted attitude.

Psychological Types (1921), CW 6, § 835.

[T]hese constituents of the personality—which one may call functions, or Mendelian units, or the primitives would call them remnants of ancestral souls—these constituents don't always fit. They may be irregular, perhaps, on account of some inner friction. But through the development of life, in the course of years, these constituents ought to function in such a way that there will be in the end a complete synthesis, the integration of human personality.

Dream Analysis: Notes of the Seminar Given in 1928–1930 (29 January 1930), p. 453.

7
Men and Women

If man and woman were the same, that would be stalemate. The earth would be sterile.

"Men, Women, and God" (1955), *C. G. Jung Speaking*, p. 248.

The more a man or woman is unconsciously influenced by the parental imago, the more surely will the figure of the loved one be chosen as either a positive or a negative substitute for the parents. The far-reaching influence of the parental imago should not be considered abnormal; on the contrary, it is a very normal and therefore very common phenomenon. It is, indeed, very important that this should be so, for otherwise the parents are not reborn in the children, and the parental imago becomes so completely lost that all continuity in the life of the individual ceases. He cannot connect his childhood with his adult life, and therefore remains unconsciously a child—a situation that is the best possible foundation for a neurosis. He will then suffer from all those ills that beset parvenus without a history, be they individuals or social groups.

It is normal that children should in a certain sense marry their parents. This is just as important, psychologically, as the biological necessity to infuse new blood if the ancestral tree is to produce a good breed. It guarantees continuity, a reasonable prolongation of the past into the present. Only too much or too little in this direction is harmful.

So long as a positive or negative resemblance to the parents is the deciding factor in a love choice, the release from the parental imago, and hence from childhood, is not complete. Although childhood has to be brought along for the sake of historical continuity, this should not be at the expense of further development. When, towards middle life, the last gleam of childhood illusion fades—this it must be owned is true only of an almost ideal life, for many go as children to their graves—then the archetype of the mature man or woman emerges from the parental imago: an image of man as woman has known him from the beginning of time, and an image of woman that man carries within him eternally.

"Mind and Earth" (1927/1931), CW 10, § 74.

[W]hen you are concerned with a relationship to another human being, you are in connection with two things really, with the conscious obvious person and the unconscious person at the same time. When you analyze any kind of relationship you find a conscious and an unconscious part, which are quite unlike each other.

Visions: Notes of the Seminar Given in 1930–1934, Vol. I (11 February 1931), p. 206.

Seldom or never does a marriage develop into an individual relationship smoothly and without crises. There is no birth of consciousness without pain.

"Marriage as a Psychological Relationship" (1925), CW 17, § 331.

Most connections in the world are not relationships, they are *participation mystique* [mystical connection]. One is then apparently connected, but of course it is never a real connection, it is never a relationship; but it gives the feeling of being one sheep in a flock at least, which is something. While if you disqualify yourself as a sheep you are necessarily out of the flock and will suffer from a certain loneliness, despite the fact that you then have a chance to reestablish a relationship, and this time a conscious relationship, which is far more satisfactory. *Participation mystique* gives one a peculiar unconsciousness, which is in a way a function of the mother; one is carried in unconsciousness. Sometimes it is nice and sometimes it is not nice at all, but as a rule people prefer it because the average man gets awfully frightened when he has to do something which he cannot share with his world; he is afraid to be alone, to think something which other people don't think, or to feel something which other people don't feel. One is up against man's gregarious instinct as soon as one tries to transcend the ordinary consciousness.

Visions: Notes of the Seminar Given in 1930–1934, Vol. I (9 March 1932), p. 625.

It is an almost regular occurrence for a woman to be wholly contained, spiritually, in her husband, and for a husband to be wholly contained, emotionally, in his wife. One could describe this as the problem of the "contained" and the "container."

"Marriage as a Psychological Relationship" (1925), CW 17, § 331c.

You have experienced in your marriage what is an almost universal fact—that individuals are different from one another. Basically, each remains for the other an unfathomable enigma. There is never complete concord. If you have committed a mistake at all, it consisted in your having striven too hard to understand your wife completely and not reckoning with the fact that in the end people don't want to know what secrets are slumbering in their souls. If you struggle too much to penetrate into another person, you find that you have thrust him into a defensive position, and resistances develop because, through your efforts to penetrate and understand, he feels forced to examine those things in himself which he doesn't want to examine. Everybody has his dark side which—as long as all goes well—he had better not know about. That is no fault of yours. It is a universal human truth which is nevertheless true, even though there are plenty of people who will assure you that they'd be only too glad to know everything about themselves. It is as good as certain that your wife had many thoughts and feelings which made her uneasy and which she wanted to hide even from herself. That is simply human. It is also the reason why so many elderly people withdraw into their own solitude where they won't be disturbed. And it is always about things they would rather not be too clearly conscious of. Certainly *you* are not responsible for the existence of these psychic contents. If nevertheless you are still tormented by guilt feelings, then consider for once what sins you have not committed which you would have liked to commit. This might perhaps cure you of your guilt feelings toward your wife.

Letter to Herr N., 1 November 1951, *Letters, Vol. II*, p. 27.

Hatred is the thing that divides, the force which discriminates. It is so when two people fall in love; they are at first almost identical. There is a great deal of *participation mystique*, so they need hatred in order to separate themselves. After a while the whole thing turns into a wild hatred; they get resistances against one another in order to force each other off—otherwise they remain in a common unconsciousness which they simply cannot stand.

The Psychology of Kundalini Yoga: Notes of the Seminar Given in 1932 (12 October, 1932), p. 5.

Where love reigns, there is no will to power; and where the will to power is paramount, love is lacking. The one is but the shadow of the other.

On the Psychology of the Unconscious (1917/1926/1943), CW 7, § 78.

An unconscious Eros always expresses itself as will to power.

"Psychological Aspects of the Mother Archetype" (1938/1954),
CW 9i, § 167.

[L]ove, in the sense of *concupiscentia* [desire], is the dynamism that most infallibly brings the unconscious to light.

Mysterium Coniunctionis (1955–56), CW 14, § 99.

Great is he who is in love, since love is the present act of the great creator, the present moment of the becoming and lapsing of the world. Mighty is he who loves. But whoever distances himself from love, feels himself powerful.

The Red Book (1915/2009), p. 253.

[N]owadays the sexual question is spoken of as something distinct from love. The two questions should not be separated, for when there is a sexual problem it can be solved only by love. Any other solution would be a harmful substitute. Sexuality dished out as sexuality is brutish; but sexuality as an expression of love is hallowed. Therefore, never ask what a man does, but how he does it. If he does it from love or in the spirit of love, then he serves a god; and whatever he may do is not ours to judge, for it is ennobled.

"The Love Problem of a Student" (1928), CW 10, § 234.

Logos is the principle of discrimination, in contrast to Eros, which is the principle of relatedness. Eros brings things together, establishes dynamic relations between things, while the relations which Logos brings about are perhaps analogies or logical conclusions. It is typical that Logos relationships are devoid of emotional dynamics.

Dream Analysis: Notes of the Seminar Given in 1928–1930 (25 June,
1930), p. 700.

Woman's psychology is founded on the principle of Eros, the great binder and loosener, whereas from ancient times the ruling principle ascribed to man is Logos. The concept of Eros could be expressed in modern terms as psychic relatedness, and that of Logos as objective interest.

"Woman in Europe" (1927), CW 10, § 255.

It is very difficult for a rational man to admit what his Eros really is. A woman has no special difficulty in realizing her Eros principle of relatedness, but it is exceedingly difficult for a man for whom Logos is the principle. Woman has difficulty realizing what her mind is. The Eros in man is inferior, as is the Logos in woman. A man must have a fair amount of the feminine in him to realize his relatedness. Eros is the job of the woman. You can fight with a man half a year before he will admit his feelings, and the same with a woman and her mind. It is so contradictory.

Dream Analysis: Notes of the Seminar Given in 1928–1930 (23 January 1929), p. 87.

Love requires depth of loyalty and feeling; without them it is not love but mere caprice. True love will always commit itself and engage in lasting ties; it needs freedom only to effect its choice, not for its accomplishment. Every true and deep love is a sacrifice. The lover sacrifices all other possibilities, or rather, the illusion that such possibilities exist. If this sacrifice is not made, his illusions prevent the growth of any deep and responsible feeling, so that the very possibility of experiencing real love is denied him.

"The Love Problem of a Student" (1928), CW 10, § 231.

The love problem is part of mankind's heavy toll of suffering, and nobody should be ashamed of having to pay his tribute.

Analytical Psychology and Education (1926/1946), CW 17, § 219.

Love is a force of destiny whose power reaches from heaven to hell.

"The Love Problem of a Student" (1928), CW 10, § 198.

Love has more than one thing in common with religious faith. It demands unconditional trust and expects absolute surrender. Just as nobody but the believer who surrenders himself wholly to God can partake of divine grace, so love reveals its highest mysteries and its wonder only to those who are capable of unqualified devotion and loyalty of feeling. And because this is so difficult, few mortals can boast of such an achievement. But, precisely because the truest and most devoted love is also the most beautiful, let no man seek to make it easy. He is a sorry knight who shrinks from the difficulty of loving his lady. Love is like God: both give themselves only to their bravest knights.

"The Love Problem of a Student" (1928), CW 10, § 232.

The unconscious of a man is always represented by a woman; that of a woman always by a man.

"Diagnosing the Dictators" (1938), *C. G. Jung Speaking*, p. 129.

There is no man who could not exist without a woman—that is, he carries the necessary balance within himself if he be obliged to live his life that way, and the same thing applies to a woman with respect to a man, but if either sex is to have a complete life, it requires the other as a compensatory side.

Introduction to Jungian Psychology: Notes of the Seminar on Analytical Psychology Given in 1925, p. 114.

For two personalities to meet is like mixing two chemical substances: if there is any combination at all, both are transformed.

"Problems of Modern Psychotherapy" (1929), CW 16, § 163.

Woman is world and fate, that is why she is so important to the man.

Letter to Oskar A. H. Schmitz, 21 July 1927, *Letters, Vol. II*, p. xxxii.

The modern woman has become conscious of the undeniable fact that only in the state of love can she attain the highest and best of which she is capable, and this knowledge drives her to the other realization that love is beyond the law.

"Woman in Europe" (1927), CW 10, § 266.

You seek the feminine in women and the masculine in men. And thus there are always only men and women. But where are people?

You, man, should not seek the feminine in women, but seek and recognize it in yourself, as you possess it from the beginning. It pleases you, however, to play at manliness, because it travels on a well-worn track. You, woman, should not seek the masculine in men, but assume the masculine in yourself, since you possess it from the beginning. But it amuses you and is easy to play at femininity, consequently man despises you because he despises his femininity. But humankind is masculine and feminine, not just man or woman. You can hardly say of your soul what sex it is. But if you pay close attention, you will see that the most masculine man has a feminine soul, and the most feminine woman has a masculine soul. The more manly you are, the more remote from you is what woman really is, since the feminine in yourself is alien and contemptuous.

The Red Book (1915/2009), p. 263.

The ensuing split between sexuality and the anima is, by the way, frequently found in men, and often manifests itself as a *neglect of Eros*, which is the essence of the anima. Men are rarely split off from sexuality, because it is too evident for them, but what they lack is Eros, the *relational function*. Men often think they can replace the relational function with reason. They are proud that they don't let themselves be controlled by affect, because this would be womanly, tantamount to weak. No Eros, for God's sake! This lack is what women most complain of in marriage, and is what so disappoints them. For what they seek in a man is the Eros, the capacity to relate.

Children's Dreams: Notes from the Seminar Given in 1936–1940,
p. 313.

A woman possessed by the animus is always in danger of losing her femininity, her adapted feminine persona, just as a man in like circumstances runs the risk of effeminacy. These psychic changes of sex are due entirely to the fact that a function which belongs inside has been turned outside. The reason for this perversion is clearly the failure to give adequate recognition to an inner world which stands autonomously opposed to the outer world, and makes just as serious demands on our capacity for adaptation.

The Relations between the Ego and the Unconscious (1916/1928), CW 7, § 337.

If, therefore, we speak of the *anima* of a man, we must logically speak of the *animus* of a woman, if we are to give the soul of a woman its right name. Whereas logic and objectivity are usually the predominant features of a man's outer attitude, or are at least regarded as ideals, in the case of a woman it is feeling. But in the soul it is the other way round: inwardly it is the man who feels, and the woman who reflects. Hence a man's greater liability to total despair, while a woman can always find comfort and hope; accordingly a man is more likely to put an end to himself than a woman.

Psychological Types (1921), CW 6, § 805.

[T]he "soul" which accrues to ego-consciousness during the *opus* has a feminine character in the man and a masculine character in a woman. His anima wants to reconcile and unite; her animus tries to discern and discriminate.

The Psychology of the Transference (1946), CW 16, § 522.

The anima as a friend or *soror mystica* [mystical sister] has always played a great role in history. In the *cours d'amour* [courts of love] of René d'Anjou she even takes precedence over the wife. The term *maîtresse* actually means mistress or master. In the Middle Ages, for example, the worship of the anima led to courtly love, in which the knight was committed to his lady and was at her service. In later history we know of women such as Madame de Maintenon, Ninon de Lenclos, or Madame de Guyon. The latter was a woman of the highest spiritual eroticism and of a strangely deep wisdom. She deserved being called a saint. It is no sign of culture if a woman is only a daughter, or only a pregnant mother, or only a whore. The primitives and also the apes do act out this one-sidedness. But should she become the *femme inspiratrice* [inspiring woman] oscillating between goddess and whore, representing all the doubtfulness and diversity of life, the highest skills and the highest Eros are called for. Such women are manifestations of a much more developed culture and this was known in the Middle Ages and also in Greece in its heyday.

> *Children's Dreams: Notes from the Seminar Given in 1936–1940,*
> p. 321.

[T]he animus is not created by the conscious, it is a creation of the unconscious, and therefore it is a personification of the unconscious.

> *Visions: Notes of the Seminar Given in 1930–1934, Vol, I* (11 February
> 1931), pp. 208–209.

For the animus when on his way, on his quest, is really a *psychopompos* [mediator between conscious and unconscious], leading the soul to the stars whence it came. On the way back out of the existence in the flesh, the *psychopompos* develops such a cosmic aspect, he wanders among the constellations, he leads the soul over the rainbow bridge into the blossoming fields of the stars.

> *Visions: Notes of the Seminar Given in 1930–1934, Vol. II* (13
> December 1933), p. 1229.

[I]s there any more beautiful love story than the love story of Mary? Wonderfully secret, divine, it is the only love affair of God that we know about. He is the illegitimate divine lover who produces the Redeemer. So these two stages are absolutely parallel; the lover always sees in the beloved something like the Mother of God, and the loving woman sees in her lover the bringer of the divine message. The Hermes stage is the perfect, divine accomplishment, which is again beyond the human grasp.

> *Visions: Notes of the Seminar Given in 1930–1934, Vol. I* (9 December
> 1931), p. 492.

8
Jung and Culture

We always find in the patient a conflict which at a certain point is connected with the great problems of society. Hence, when the analysis is pushed to this point, the apparently individual conflict of the patient is revealed as a universal conflict of his environment and epoch. Neurosis is nothing less than an individual attempt, however unsuccessful, to solve a universal problem; indeed it cannot be otherwise, for a general problem, a "question," is not an *ens per se* [thing in itself], but exists only in the hearts of individuals.

"New Paths in Psychology" (1912), CW 7, § 438.

The machines which we have invented, for instance, are now our masters. Machines are running away with us, they are demons; they are like those huge old saurians that existed when man was a sort of lizard-monkey and deadly afraid of their hooting and tooting. By his will man has invented a Mesozoic world again, monsters that crush thousands by their voice and their weight. The enormous machines in factories, the enormous steamers and trains and automobiles, all that has become so overwhelming that man is the mere victim of it. Look at the city of New York. Nobody can tell me that man feels like a king in New York. He is just an ant on an ant heap and doesn't count at all, he is superfluous there, the ant heap is the thing that counts. It is a town which should be inhabited by giants; then I would believe that those buildings belonged to them. A big city is like a holocaust of humanity, as Zola expressed it. Man has built his own funeral pyre and it is destroying him, and so our whole world is being destroyed. It has taken the bread away from millions, and production is still going on like mad; that is really at the bottom of the actual crisis.

Visions: Notes of the Seminar Given in 1930–1934, Vol. I (9 December 1931), p. 502.

Nowadays we can see as never before that the peril which threatens all of us comes not from nature, but from man, from the psyches of the individual and the mass. The psychic aberration of man is the danger. Everything depends upon whether or not our psyche functions properly. If certain persons lose their head nowadays, a hydrogen bomb will go off.

Memories, Dreams, Reflections (1962), p. 132.

We are awakening a little to the feeling that something is wrong in the world, that our modern prejudice of overestimating the importance of the intellect and the conscious mind might be false. We want simplicity. We are suffering, in our cities, from a need of simple things. We would like to see our great railroad terminals deserted, the streets deserted, a great peace descend upon us.

"Americans Must Say 'No'" (1939), *C. G. Jung Speaking*,
p. 49.

The power of inertia in man is far stronger than his spirit of enterprise; from time to time somebody has a fit of enterprise and does something, but the world in general exists by inertia. So the primordial man personifies the enormous power of inertia in the first place, yet within that is a peculiar kind of longing which causes fits of enterprise at times, bringing about greater or smaller disturbances, and it also causes a certain movement which one prefers to call development or evolution. But it is very questionable whether there is any such thing as improvement in the world; we can only say there is movement, change. Sometimes there is complication, sometimes things get simpler, but whether it is really a movement for the better is most questionable. For the basic predisposition in the human being is that tremendous power of inertia, and the spirit within that inertia is more irrational and fitful; so it is exceedingly difficult to form a definite judgment about it.

Visions: Notes from the Seminar Given in 1930–1934, Vol. II (7 June
1933), p. 1034.

All human control comes to an end when the individual is caught in a mass movement. Then the archetypes begin to function, as happens also in the lives of individuals when they are confronted with situations that cannot be dealt with in any of the familiar ways.

"Wotan" (1936), CW 10, § 395.

It is obvious that a social group consisting of stunted individuals cannot be a healthy and viable institution; only a society that can preserve its internal cohesion and collective values, while at the same time granting the individual the greatest possible freedom, has any prospect of enduring vitality. As the individual is not just a single, separate being, but by his very existence presupposes a collective relationship, it follows that the process of individuation must lead to more intense and broader collective relationships and not to isolation.

Psychological Types (1921), CW 6, § 758.

[I] feel and know myself to be one of many, and what moves the many moves me. In our strength we are independent and isolated, are masters of our own fate; in our weakness we are dependent and bound, and become unwilling instruments of fate, for here it is not the individual will that counts but the will of the species.

"Woman in Europe" (1927), CW 10, § 261.

One of the most baffling facts which has been revealed through analysis, is that when you analyze a person, you have not only that individual on your hands, but it is as if you were analyzing a whole group. It has magic effects in the distance, even in people who are not immediately related to the patient.

Visions: Notes of the Seminar Given in 1930–1934, Vol. I
(25 November 1931), p. 475.

The vast majority of people are quite incapable of putting themselves individually into the mind of another. This is indeed a singularly rare art, and, truth to tell, it does not take us very far. Even the man whom we think we know best and who assures us himself that we understand him through and through is at bottom a stranger to us. He is *different*. The most we can do, and the best, is to have at least some inkling of his otherness, to respect it, and to guard against the outrageous stupidity of wishing to interpret it.

The Relations between the Ego and the Unconscious (1916/1928),
CW 7, § 363.

The sole and natural carrier of life is the individual, and that is so throughout nature.

"Psychotherapy Today" (1945), CW 16, § 224.

Through the shifting of interest from the inner to the outer world our knowledge of nature was increased a thousandfold in comparison with earlier ages, but knowledge and experience of the inner world were correspondingly reduced. The religious interest, which ought normally to be the greatest and most decisive factor, turned away from the inner world, and great figures of dogma dwindled to strange and incomprehensible vestiges, a prey to every sort of criticism.

Symbols of Transformation (1912/1952), CW 5, § 113.

In the last resort it is neither the "eighty-million-strong-nation" nor the State that feels peace and happiness, but the individual. Nobody can ever get round the simple computation that a million noughts in a row do not add up to one, just as the loudest talk can never abolish the simple psychological fact that the larger the mass the more nugatory is the individual.

Mysterium Coniunctionis (1955–56), CW 14, § 196.

The great events of world history are, at bottom, profoundly unimportant. In the last analysis, the essential thing is the life of the individual. This alone makes history, here alone do the great transformations first take place, and the whole future, the whole history of the world, ultimately spring as a gigantic summation from these

hidden sources in individuals. In our most private and most subjective lives we are not only the passive witnesses of our age, and its
sufferers, but also its makers.

"The Meaning of Psychology for Modern Man" (1933/1934), CW 10,

§ 315.

Yet the real carrier of life is the individual. He alone feels happiness,
he alone has virtue and responsibility and any ethics whatsoever.
The masses and the state have nothing of the kind. Only man as an
individual being lives; the state is just a system, a mere machine for
sorting and tabulating the masses. Anyone, therefore, who thinks
in terms of men minus the individual, in huge numbers, atomizes
himself and becomes a thief and a robber to himself. He is infected
with the leprosy of collective thinking and has become an inmate
of that insalubrious stud-farm called the totalitarian State. Our
time contains and produces more than enough of that "crude sulphur" which with "arsenical malignity" prevents man from discov-
ering his true self.

Mysterium Coniunctionis (1955–56), CW 14, § 194.

Collective thinking and feeling and collective effort are far less of a
strain than individual functioning and effort; hence there is always
a great temptation to allow collective functioning to take the place
of individual differentiation of the personality.

The Relations between the Ego and the Unconscious (1928), CW 7,

§ 239.

But the principal and indeed the only thing that is wrong with the
world is man.

"After the Catastrophe" (1945), CW 10, § 441.

Instead of being at the mercy of wild beasts, earthquakes, land-
slides, and inundations, modern man is battered by the elemental
forces of his own psyche. This is the World Power that vastly exceeds all other powers on earth. The Age of Enlightenment, which

stripped nature and human institutions of gods, overlooked the God of Terror who dwells in the human soul.

"The Development of Personality" (1934), CW 17, § 302.

No one can claim to be immune to the spirit of his own epoch or to possess anything like a complete knowledge of it. Regardless of our conscious convictions, we are all without exception, in so far as we are particles in the mass, gnawed at and undermined by the spirit that runs through the masses. Our freedom extends only as far as our consciousness reaches.

"Paracelsus as a Spiritual Phenomenon" (1942), CW 13, § 153.

If man cannot exist without society, neither can he exist without oxygen, water, albumen, fat, and so forth. Like these, society is one of the necessary conditions of his existence. It would be ludicrous to maintain that man lives in order to breathe air. It is equally ludicrous to maintain that the individual exists for society. "Society" is nothing more than a term, a concept for the symbiosis of a group of human beings. A concept is not a carrier of life. The sole and natural carrier of life is the individual, and that is so throughout nature.

"Psychotherapy Today" (1945), CW 16, § 224.

[I]f the individual is not truly regenerated in spirit, society cannot be either, for society is the sum total of individuals in need of redemption.

The Undiscovered Self (1957), CW 10, § 536.

As individuals we are not completely unique, but are like all other men. Hence a dream with a collective meaning is valid in the first place for the dreamer, but it expresses at the same time the fact that his momentary problem is also the problem of other people. This is often of great practical importance, for there are countless people who are inwardly cut off from humanity and oppressed by the thought that nobody else has their problems. Or else they are those all-too-modest souls who, feeling themselves nonentities, have kept their claim to social recognition on too low a level. Moreover, every individual problem is somehow connected with the problem of the age, so that practically every subjective difficulty has to be viewed from the standpoint of the human situation as a whole. But this is permissible only when the dream really is a mythological one and makes use of collective symbols.

"The Meaning of Psychology for Modern Man" (1933/1934), CW 10, § 323.

Our age has shifted all emphasis to the here and now, and thus brought about a daemonization of man and his world. The phenomenon of dictators and all the misery they have wrought springs from the fact that man has been robbed of transcendence by the shortsightedness of the super-intellectuals. Like them, he has fallen a victim to unconsciousness. But man's task is the exact opposite: to become conscious of the contents that press upward from the unconscious. Neither should he persist in his unconsciousness, nor remain identical with the unconscious elements of his being, thus evading his destiny, which is to create more and more consciousness. As far as we can discern, the sole purpose of human existence is to kindle a light in the darkness of mere being. It may even be assumed that just as the unconscious affects us, so the increase in our consciousness affects the unconscious.

Memories, Dreams, Reflections (1962), p. 326.

Every advance, every conceptual achievement of mankind, has been connected with an advance in self-awareness; man differentiated himself from the object and faced Nature as something distinct from her. Any reorientation of psychological attitude will have to follow the same road.

"General Aspects of Dream Psychology" (1916/1928/1948), CW 8, § 523.

On the surface it may look as if the war had no effect at all, as if it had taught man nothing. Governments go on playing the same tricks as before. The world is spending two and a half millions more in preparation than before the war. Human psychology today is as if people had learned absolutely nothing. German psychology remains the same. And look at Italy! It is as if she had not lost half a million young men. They are propagating like rabbits down there, in preparation. It is the psychology of despair. That is what Mussolini is doing. Everywhere it looks as if nothing had been learned. Nevertheless such a thing cannot happen without affecting the processes of our psychology; it has left deep marks, but we are not psychological enough to link up our own individual difficulties with it. The war accounts for the disorientation of the individual in our time. The religious and moral and philosophical confusion, even the confusion in our art, is due to the World War.

Visions: Notes of the Seminar Given in 1930–1934, Vol. I (12 November 1930), p. 77.

When Nietzsche said "God is dead," he uttered a truth which is valid for the greater part of Europe. People were influenced by it not because he said so, but because it stated a widespread psychological fact. The consequences were not long delayed: after the fog of–isms, the catastrophe. Nobody thought of drawing the slightest conclusions from Nietzsche's pronouncement. Yet it has, for some ears, the same eerie sound as that ancient cry which came echoing over the sea to mark the end of the nature gods: "Great Pan is dead."

Psychology and Religion (1938/1940), CW 11, § 145.

The coming new age will be as vastly different from ours as the world of the 19th century was from that of the 20th with its atomic physics and its psychology of the unconscious. Never before has mankind been torn into two halves, and never before was the power of absolute destruction given into the hand of man himself. It is a "godlike" power that has fallen into human hands.

Letter to Pater Lucas Menz, O.S.B., 22 February 1955, *Letters, Vol. II*, p. 225.

The great work of art is a product of the time, of the whole world in which the artist is living, and of the millions of people who surround him, and of the thousands of currents of thought and the myriad streams of activity which flow around him.

"Diagnosing the Dictators" (1938), *C. G. Jung Speaking*, p. 128.

Art is just a particular way of decorating the nest in which you lay your eggs. Well, the biological point of view is that you eat and drink, you propagate your species, you sleep, and you die; that is nature, biological life. And in contrast to nature, or beyond nature is the cultural point of view, our civilization. That is the particular achievement of man, no animal ever dreamt of culture. It is a condition by itself, a creation due to the increase of human consciousness, and this has produced a new and different world. The surface of the world has changed. One sees water where water has never been and should not be, a canal that goes even over the hills, against all those laws of nature. And one sees straight roads, straight lines on the earth, which have never been seen before; the only straight line that ever existed in the earth was the furrow of a meteor.

Visions: Notes of the Seminar Given in 1930–1934, Vol. II (22 February 1933), pp. 913–14.

The criterion of art is that it grips you.

Introduction to Jungian Psychology: Notes of the Seminar on Analytical Psychology Given in 1925, p. 57.

Art is a kind of innate drive that seizes a human being and makes him its instrument. The artist is not a person endowed with free will who seeks his own ends, but one who allows art to realize its purposes through him. As a human being he may have moods and a will and personal aims, but as an artist he is "man" in a higher sense—he is "collective man," a vehicle and moulder of the unconscious psychic life of mankind. That is his office, and it is sometimes so heavy a burden that he is fated to sacrifice happiness and everything that makes life worth living for the ordinary human being.

"Psychology and Literature" (1930/1950), CW 15, § 157.

The true genius nearly always intrudes and disturbs. He speaks to a temporal world out of a world eternal. He says the wrong things at the right time. Eternal truths are never true at any given moment in history. The process of transformation has to make a halt in order to digest and assimilate the utterly impractical things that the genius has produced from the storehouse of eternity. Yet the genius is the healer of his time, because anything he reveals of eternal truth is healing.

"What India Can Teach Us" (1939), CW 10, § 1004.

There can be no doubt that the unconscious comes to the surface in modern art and with its dynamism destroys the orderliness that is characteristic of consciousness. This process is a phenomenon that can be observed in more or less developed form in all epochs, as for instance under primitive conditions where the habitual way of life, regulated by strict laws, is suddenly disrupted, either by outbreaks of panic coupled by wild lawlessness at solar and lunar eclipses, or in the form of religious license as in the Dionysian orgies, or during the Middle Ages in the monasteries with the reversal of the hierarchical order, and today at carnival time. These episodic or regular disruptions of the accustomed order should be regarded as psychohygienic measures since they give vent from time to time to the suppressed forces of chaos.

Letter to Horst Scharschuch, 1 September 1952, *Letters, Vol. II*, p. 81.

It makes no difference whether the artist knows that his work is generated, grows and matures within him, or whether he imagines that it is his own invention. In reality it grows out of him as a child its mother.

"Psychology and Literature" (1930/1950), CW 15, § 159.

It seems to me that a characteristic thing of modern art is that it no longer concerns itself with being merely beautiful. It has passed through and beyond mere conventional beauty, and in this it reflects our changed views of life. Before the war we lived in a beautiful world—or perhaps I would better say in a world that was merely sweet and pretty, a world of sticky sentimentality in which nothing brutal nor ugly was given place. Modern art cares nothing for prettiness; in fact, it would rather have the ugly than the pretty; and sometimes, I think, it seeks a new realization of beauty beyond the pale of what was formerly considered possible—in ugliness itself, even.

> *Introduction to Jungian Psychology*: *Notes of the Seminar on*
> *Analytical Psychology Given in 1925*, p. 58.

The artist's relative lack of adaptation turns out to his advantage; it enables him to follow his own yearnings far from the beaten path, and to discover what it is that would meet the unconscious needs of his age. Thus, just as the one-sidedness of the individual's conscious attitude is corrected by reactions from the unconscious, so art represents a process of self-regulation in the life of nations and epochs.

> "On the Relation of Analytical Psychology to Poetry" (1922), CW 15,
> § 131.

Attainment of consciousness is culture in the broadest sense, and self-knowledge is therefore the heart and essence of this process.

> *Memories, Dreams, Reflections* (1962), pp. 324–25.

9
The Problem of the Opposites

[T]he principal pair of opposites is the conscious world and the unconscious world, and when the two come together, it is as if man and woman were coming together, the union of the male and the female, of the light and the darkness. Then a birth will take place.

Visions: Notes of the Seminar Given in 1930–1934, Vol. I (10 February 1932), p. 574.

I see in all that happens the play of opposites, and derive from this conception my idea of psychic energy. I hold that psychic energy involves the play of opposites in much the same way as physical energy involves a difference of potential, that is to say the existence of opposites such as warm and cold, high and low, etc.

"Freud and Jung: Contrasts" (1929), CW 4, § 779.

[T]here is no energy unless there is a tension of opposites; hence it is necessary to discover the opposite to the attitude of the conscious mind.

On the Psychology of the Unconscious (1917/1926/1943), CW 7, § 78.

Experience of the opposites has nothing whatever to do with intellectual insight or with empathy. It is more what we would call fate.

Psychology and Alchemy (1944), CW 12, § 23.

The psychological rule says that when an inner situation is not made conscious, it happens outside, as fate. That is to say, when the individual remains undivided and does not become conscious of his inner opposite, the world must perforce act out the conflict and be torn into opposing halves.

Aion (1951), CW 9ii, § 126.

It may well be said that the contemporary cultural consciousness has not yet absorbed into its general philosophy the idea of the unconscious and all that it means, despite the fact that modern man has been confronted with this idea for more than half a century. The assimilation of the fundamental insight that psychic life has two poles still remains a task for the future.

Memories, Dreams, Reflections (1962), p. 169.

Every psychological extreme secretly contains its own opposite or stands in some sort of intimate and essential relation to it. Indeed, it is from this tension that it derives its peculiar dynamism. There is no hallowed custom that cannot on occasion turn into its opposite, and the more extreme a position is, the more easily may we expect an enantiodromia, a conversion of something into its opposite. The best is the most threatened with some devilish perversion just because it has done the most to suppress evil.

Symbols of Transformation (1912/1952), CW 5, § 581.

[I]n all chaos there is a cosmos, in all disorder a secret order, in all caprice a fixed law, for everything that works is grounded on its opposite.

"Archetypes of the Collective Unconscious" (1934/1954), CW 9i,

§ 66.

The fact that individual consciousness means separation and opposition is something that man has experienced countless times in his long history.

"The Meaning of Psychology for Modern Man" (1933/1934), CW 10,

§ 290.

The conscious mind is on top, the shadow underneath, and just as high always longs for low and hot for cold, so all consciousness, perhaps without being aware of it, seeks its unconscious opposite, lacking which it is doomed to stagnation, congestion, and ossification. Life is born only of the spark of opposites.

On the Psychology of the Unconscious (1917/1926/1943), CW 7,

§ 78.

There is no consciousness without discrimination of opposites. This is the paternal principle, the Logos, which eternally struggles to extricate itself from the primal warmth and primal darkness of the maternal womb; in a word, from unconsciousness. Divine curiosity yearns to be born and does not shrink from conflict, suffering, or sin. Unconsciousness is the primal sin, evil itself, for the Logos. Therefore its first creative act of liberation is matricide, and the spirit that dared all heights and all depths must, as Synesius says, suffer the divine punishment, enchainment on the rocks of the Caucasus. Nothing can exist without its opposite; the two were one in the beginning and will be one again in the end. Consciousness can only exist through continual recognition of the unconscious, just as everything that lives must pass through many deaths.

"Psychological Aspects of the Mother Archetype" (1938/1954),
CW 9i, § 178.

When I see so much refinement and sentiment as I see in America, I look always for an equal amount of brutality. The pair of opposites—you find them everywhere.

"America Facing Its Most Tragic Moment" (1912), *C. G. Jung Speaking*, p. 13.

Without the experience of the opposites there is no experience of wholeness and hence no inner approach to the sacred figures.

Psychology and Alchemy (1944), CW 12, § 24.

It is, moreover, a very useful thing to experience a conflict of opposites. Nobody can solve this conflict for you, and it is a conflict in your own nature. A man must be able to stand this struggle. This act of courage is essential for the doctor. Anyone who has solved the conflict for you would have got the better of you, for he would rob you of a reward on which all self-respect and manliness are ultimately grounded. You can find in my books all the necessary indications that might make the solution possible on a human and intellectual level. If you need human help, there are enough simple folk who from the simplicity of their hearts could give you the support you need.

Letter to G. Meyer, 20 May 1933, *Letters, Vol. I*, p. 121.

The outer opposition is an image of my inner opposition. Once I realize this, I remain silent and think of the chasm of antagonism in my soul. Outer oppositions are easy to overcome. They indeed exist, but nevertheless you can be united with yourself. They will indeed burn and freeze your soles, but only your soles. It hurts, but you continue and look toward distant goals.

The Red Book (1915/2009), p. 279.

[W]hen pairs of opposites appear together it is like fire and water; it either means an immediate crash, a tremendous catastrophe, or that they merely counteract one another.

Visions: Notes of the Seminar Given in 1930–1934, Vol. I (16 March 1932), p. 647.

[E]verything that exists will turn into its opposite. What lives will become dead, what is dead will live, what is young will become old, the old young, what is awake will sleep, and what sleeps will awake. The flow of creation and destruction never ends.

Children's Dreams: Notes from the Seminar Given in 1936–1940, p. 328.

The ego keeps its integrity only if it does not identify with one of the opposites, and if it understands how to hold the balance between them. This is possible only if it remains conscious of both at once. However, the necessary insight is made exceedingly difficult not by one's social and political leaders alone, but also by one's religious mentors. They all want decision in favour of one thing, and therefore the utter identification of the individual with the necessarily one-sided "truth." Even if it were still a question of some great truth, identification with it would still be a catastrophe, as it arrests all further spiritual development.

"On the Nature of the Psyche" (1947/1954), CW 8, § 425.

All opposites are of God, therefore man must bend to this burden; and in so doing he finds that God in his "oppositeness" has taken possession of him, incarnated himself in him. He becomes a vessel filled with divine conflict.

Answer to Job (1952), CW 11, § 659.

The apparently unendurable conflict is proof of the rightness of your life. A life without inner contradiction is either only half a life or else a life in the Beyond, which is destined only for angels. But God loves human beings more than the angels.

Letter to Olga Fröbe-Kapteyn, Bollingen, 20 August, 1945, *Letters,*
Vol. I, p. 375.

It is quite right, therefore, that fear of God should be considered the beginning of all wisdom. On the other hand, the much-vaunted goodness, love, and justice of God should not be regarded as mere propitiation, but should be recognized as genuine experience, for God is a *coincidentia oppositorum* [unity of the opposites]. Both are justified, the fear of God as well as the love of God.

Answer to Job (1952), CW 11, § 664.

Just as all energy proceeds from opposition, so the psyche too possesses its inner polarity, this being the indispensable prerequisite for its aliveness, as Heraclitus realized long ago. Both theoretically and practically, polarity is inherent in all living things. Set against this overpowering force is the fragile unity of the ego, which has come into being in the course of millennia only with the aid of countless protective measures. That an ego was possible at all appears to spring from the fact that all opposites seek to achieve a state of balance. This happens in the exchange of energy which results from the collision of hot and cold, high and low, and so on. The energy underlying conscious psychic life is pre-existent to it and therefore at first unconscious.

Memories, Dreams, Reflections (1962), p. 346.

The greater the tension, the greater the potential. Great energy springs from a correspondingly great tension of opposites.

"Paracelsus as a Spiritual Phenomenon" (1942), CW 13, § 154.

Out of the collision of opposites the unconscious psyche always creates a third thing of an irrational nature, which the conscious mind neither expects nor understands. It presents itself in a form that is neither a straight "yes" nor a straight "no."

"The Psychology of the Child Archetype" (1940), CW 9i, § 285.

In the center is the individual where the opposites are united, the one peaceful spot in man, the space where nothing moves embedded in a world of chaos. The task is now to bring about order, the alchemistic process must begin, namely, the production of the valuable substance, the transformation into the light. You see this mandala does not represent a normal condition of the collective unconscious; this is a turmoil caused by the appearance of the disturbing element in the center. For we may assume that the collective unconscious is in absolute peace until the individual appears. Therefore individuation is a sin; it is an assertion of one particle against the gods, and when that happens even the world of the gods is upset, then there is turmoil. But in that abstraction, or that union—the coming together of the pair of opposites—there is absolute peace. Otherwise there is only the peace of God in a world in which there is no individual, in other words, no consciousness. Yes, perhaps it exists to metaphysical consciousness, but not to any mortal consciousness because there is none. You see, this chaos is due to the appearance of that center, but that is a center of peace because the pairs of opposites are united.

Visions: Notes of the Seminar Given in 1930–1934, Vol. I (3 March 1931), p. 263.

[O]pposites can be united only in the form of a compromise, or *irrationally*, some new thing arising between them which, although different from both, yet has the power to take up their energies in equal measure as an expression of both and of neither. Such an expression cannot be contrived by reason, it can only be created through living.

Psychological Types (1921), CW 6, § 169.

The transcendent function is not something one does oneself; it comes rather from experiencing the conflict of opposites.

Letter to M. Zarine, 3 May 1939, *Letters, Vol. I*, p. 269.

The sad truth is that man's real life consists of a complex of inexorable opposites—day and night, birth and death, happiness and misery, good and evil. We are not even sure that one will prevail over the other, that good will overcome evil, or joy defeat pain. Life is a battleground. It always has been, and always will be; and if it were not so, existence would come to an end.

"Approaching the Unconscious" (1964), *Man and His Symbols*, p. 85.

When we strive after the good or the beautiful, we thereby forget our own nature, which is distinctiveness, and we are delivered over to the qualities of the pleroma, which are pairs of opposites. We labor to attain to the good and the beautiful, yet at the same time we also lay hold of the evil and the ugly, since in the pleroma these are one with the good and the beautiful. When, however, we remain true to our own nature, which is distinctiveness, we distinguish ourselves from the good and the beautiful, and, therefore, at the same time, from the evil and the ugly. And thus we fall not into the pleroma, namely, into nothingness and dissolution.

Memories, Dreams, Reflections (1962), p. 381.

The tremendous role which the opposites and their union play in alchemy helps us to understand why the alchemists were so fond of paradoxes. In order to attain this union, they tried not only to visualize the opposites together but to express them in the same breath.

Mysterium Coniunctionis (1955–56), CW 14, § 36.

[R]ebirth symbolism always means a new uniting of opposites in the process of transformation. But to bring pairs of opposites together in a static condition is a sort of compromise. One says sadly: "Alas, yes, black is white and white is black," and that causes a sort of indifferent mixture, an apathetic standstill. The union is only correct when the opposites grow together in a living progress.

> *Visions: Notes of the Seminar Given in 1930–1934, Vol. I* (16 March 1932), p. 649.

The self is a union of opposites *par excellence*.

> *Psychology and Alchemy* (1944), CW 12, § 22.

For the conscious mind knows nothing beyond the opposites and, as a result, has no knowledge of the thing that unites them.

> "The Psychology of the Child Archetype" (1940), CW 9i, § 285

The splitting of the Original Man into husband and wife expresses an act of nascent consciousness; it gives birth to the pair of opposites, thereby making consciousness possible.

> *Aion* (1951), CW 9ii, § 320.

[I]dentity of opposites is a characteristic feature of every psychic event in the unconscious state.

> *Psychology and Alchemy* (1944), CW 12, § 398.

Insofar as analytical treatment makes the "shadow" conscious, it causes a cleavage and a tension of the opposites which in their turn seek compensation in unity. The adjustment is achieved through symbols. The conflict between the opposites can strain our psyche to the breaking point, if we take them seriously, or if they take us seriously. The *tertium non datur* [the third that is not given] of logic proves its worth: no solution can be seen. If all goes well, the solution, seemingly of its own accord, appears out of nature. Then and then only is it convincing. It is felt as "grace." Since the solution proceeds out of the confrontation and clash of opposites, it is usually an unfathomable mixture of conscious and unconscious factors, and therefore a symbol, a coin split into two halves which fit together precisely. It represents the result of the joint labors of consciousness and the unconsciousness, and attains the likeness of the God-image in the form of the mandala, which is probably the sim-

plest model of a concept of wholeness, and one which spontaneously arises in the mind as a representation of the struggle and reconciliation of opposites. The clash, which is at first of a purely
personal nature, is soon followed by the insight that the subjective
conflict is only a single instance of the universal conflict of opposites. Our psyche is set up in accord with the structure of the universe, and what happens in the macrocosm likewise happens in the
infinitesimal and most subjective reaches of the psyche. For that
reason the God-image is always a projection of the inner experience of a powerful *vis-à-vis*. This is symbolized by objects from
which the inner experience has taken its initial impulse, and which
from then on preserve numinous significance, or else it is characterized by its numinosity and the overwhelming force of that numinosity. In this way the imagination liberates itself from the con-
cretism of the object and attempts to sketch the image of the
invisible as something which stands behind the phenomenon. I am
thinking here of the simplest basic form of the mandala, the circle,
and the simplest (mental) division of the circle, the quadrant or, as
the case may be, the cross.

Memories, Dreams, Reflections (1962), pp. 335–36.

Once I had a very wealthy patient who on coming to me said, "I
don't know what you are going to do to me, but I hope you are
going to give me something that isn't grey." And that is exactly what
life would be if there were no opposites in it; therefore the pairs of
opposites are not to be understood as mistakes but as the origin of
life. For the same thing holds in nature. If there is no difference in
high and low, no water can come down. Modern physics expresses
the condition that would ensue were the opposites removed from
nature by the term entropy: that is, death in an equitable tepidity. If
you have all your wishes fulfilled, you have what could be called
psychological entropy. I found, then, that what I had thought to be
a pathological phenomenon is in fact a rule of nature.

*Introduction to Jungian Psychology: Notes of the Seminar on
Analytical Psychology Given in 1925*, p. 85.

The division into two was necessary in order to bring the "one" world out of the state of potentiality into reality. Reality consists of a multiplicity of things. But one is not a number; the first number is two, and with it multiplicity and reality begin.

Mysterium Coniunctionis (1955–56), CW 14, § 659.

Since the psychological condition of any unconscious content is one of potential reality, characterized by the polar opposites of "being" and "non-being," it follows that the union of opposites must play a decisive role in the alchemical process. The result is something in the nature of a "uniting symbol," and this usually has a numinous character.

Psychology and Alchemy (1944), CW 12, § 557.

[T]ill Eulenspiegel laughed like mad when he went uphill, and wept when he went downhill. People could not understand it, for wisdom is never understood by ordinary people, but to him it was perfectly clear. In going up he thinks of the descent and that makes him laugh. He rejoices in the idea that soon he will be able to go downhill. But when he goes downhill he foresees that he will soon have to climb again and he weeps therefor. And that is the nature of Zarathustra. So it is the man Nietzsche who discovers that he is at the noon of life. He was born in 1844 so he was just thirty-nine when he started to write *Zarathustra*, and that is the noontide, the beginning of the afternoon. In his case, it was of course particularly important to see that, because he had only six years left before the atrophy of his brain began in 1889.

Nietzsche's Zarathustra: Notes of the Seminar Given in 1934–1939,
Vol. I (7 November 1934), pp. 226–27.

[T]he united personality will never quite lose the painful sense of innate discord. Complete redemption from the sufferings of this world is and must remain an illusion. Christ's earthly life likewise ended, not in complacent bliss, but on the cross.

The Psychology of the Transference (1946), CW 16, § 400.

It is the age-old drama of opposites, no matter what they are called, which is fought out in every human life.

Mysterium Coniunctionis (1955–56), CW 14, § 199.

10
East and West

The book on types yielded the insight that every judgment made by an individual is conditioned by his personality type and that every point of view is necessarily relative. This raised the question of the unity which must compensate this diversity, and it led me directly to the Chinese concept of Tao.

Memories, Dreams, Reflections (1962), pp. 207–8.

The East teaches us another, broader, more profound, and higher understanding—understanding through life.

"Commentary on *The Secret of the Golden Flower*" (1929), CW 13, § 2.

The Western mind can never accept the possibility that the unconscious can do anything but cause a stomach neurosis, or a heart neurosis, or bad dreams, or some other nuisance. People think that anything entrusted to the unconscious is either nonsense or a terrible nuisance. They never assume that the unconscious might behave intelligently. And the East is convinced that the unconscious consists of nothing but sense, which is going a bit too far in the other direction. Therefore they have to work for consciousness, while with us it is just the reverse. For it is really true that if one creates a better relation to the unconscious, it proves to be a helpful power, it then has an activity of its own, it produces helpful dreams, and at times it really produces little miracles.

Visions: Notes of the Seminar Given in 1930–1934, Vol. I (24 February 1932), p. 604.

[W]hen you step out of this world, you withdraw and think you are alone with yourself, but the East says: "You forget the old man that is dwelling in your heart and sees everything." Then, alone, you come to the critical point, to your personal unconscious. Extraverts, and all people who are identified with their persona, hate to be alone because they begin to see themselves. Our own society is always the worst: when we are alone with ourselves things get very disagreeable.

> *Dream Analysis: Notes of the Seminar Given in 1928–1930* (12 December 1928), p. 75.

In India everything spiritual has grown out of nature. The unconscious flows absolutely freely into consciousness. Indians have no thoughts that would prevent consciousness from functioning, no devils that could devastate consciousness.

> *Children's Dreams: Notes from the Seminar Given in 1936–1940*, p. 409.

I was frequently so wrought up that I had to do certain yoga exercises in order to hold my emotions in check. But since it was my purpose to know what was going on within myself, I would do these exercises only until I had calmed myself enough to resume my work with the unconscious. As soon as I had the feeling that I was myself again, I abandoned this restraint upon the emotions and allowed the images and inner voices to speak afresh. The Indian, on the other hand, does yoga exercises in order to obliterate completely the multitude of psychic contents and images.

> *Memories, Dreams, Reflections* (1962), p. 177.

In India I was principally concerned with the question of the psychological nature of evil. I had been very much impressed by the way this problem is integrated in Indian spiritual life, and I saw it in a new light. In a conversation with a cultivated Chinese I was also impressed, again and again, by the fact that these people are able to integrate so-called "evil" without "losing face." In the West we cannot do this. For the Oriental the problem of morality does not appear to take first place, as it does for us. To the Oriental, good and evil are meaningfully contained in nature, and are merely varying degrees of the same thing.

Memories, Dreams, Reflections (1962), pp. 275–76.

[T]he best cure for anybody is when the one who thinks about curing has cured himself; inasmuch as he cures himself it is a cure. If he is in Tao, he has established Tao, and whoever beholds him beholds Tao and enters Tao. This is a very Eastern idea.

Nietzsche's Zarathustra: Notes of the Seminar Given in 1934–1939,
Vol. II (12 February 1936), p. 825.

As I have had the good fortune to go more closely into the psychology of the Orientals, it has become clear to me that anything like a question of the unconscious—a quite notorious question for us—simply doesn't exist for these people. In the case of the Indians and Chinese, for instance, it is overwhelmingly clear that their whole spiritual attitude is based on what with us is profoundly unconscious.

Letter to B. Milt, 8 June 1942, *Letters, Vol. I*, p. 318.

I am alone, but I fill my solitariness with my life. I am man enough. I am noise, conversation, comfort, and help enough unto myself. And so I wander to the far East. Not that I know anything about what my distant goal might be. I see blue horizons before me: they suffice as a goal. I hurry toward the East and my rising—I will my rising.

The Red Book (1915/2009), p. 277.

That tiny thing, that unique individual, that Self, is small as the point of a needle, yet because it is so small it is also greater than great. There again is the Eastern formula, and it is of tremendous importance.

Visions: Notes of the Seminar Given in 1930–1934, Vol. I (21 May 1931), pp. 358–59.

Science is the tool of the Western mind, and with it one can open more doors than with bare hands. It is part and parcel of our understanding, and it obscures our insight only when it claims that the understanding it conveys is the only kind there is. The East teaches us another, broader, more profound, and higher understanding—understanding through life.

"Commentary on *The Secret of the Golden Flower*" (1929), CW 13, § 2.

Even a superficial acquaintance with Eastern thought is sufficient to show that a fundamental difference divides East and West. The East bases itself upon psychic reality, that is, upon the psyche as the main and unique condition of existence. It seems as if this Eastern recognition were a psychological or temperamental fact rather than a result of philosophical reasoning. It is a typically introverted point of view, contrasted with the equally typical extraverted point of view of the West.

"Psychological Commentary on *The Tibetan Book of the Great Liberation*" (1939/1954), CW 11, § 770.

The experience of Tao can happen at any time. If you are in the psychology of the first part of life—it is not necessarily a matter of years—if you fulfill the personal ends of your existence and it is the right moment, you may have such an experience. For it is quite understood that a young animal still in the process of maturation is just as much a fulfillment of the totality of nature as one that is dying, who, if dying properly, is also fulfilling life because the idea of life includes death, it is a cycle. There is the same possibility at any moment of life. You probably experienced Tao when you were a child, when you woke up in your little bed in the morning with the sun shining into your room. That would be an experience of Tao inasmuch as your parents had not twisted you. But it is quite possible that your parents put dirt on your nose, and then, even as a child, you could only experience a twisted feeling. Or you might experience it at fifteen or twenty if you fulfill your own personal and individual expectations which are then valid. And you can experience the same when you are fading away, dying, if you do it properly, as that fulfillment which is in accordance with the laws of nature. Just that is demanded and nothing else. Many people have never in their whole lives felt such a natural fulfillment because they were completely twisted. But they would experience it in the moment when they were able to liberate themselves from the twist—in that moment they would experience Tao.

> *Visions: Notes of the Seminar Given in 1930–1934, Vol. II* (22 June, 1932), p. 761.

The West is always seeking uplift, but the East seeks a sinking or deepening. Outer reality, with its bodiliness and weight, appears to make a much stronger and sharper impression on the European than it does on the Indian. The European seeks to raise himself above this world, while the Indian likes to turn back into the maternal depths of Nature.

> "The Psychology of Eastern Meditation" (1943), CW 11, § 936.

The fact that the East can dispose so easily of the ego seems to point to a mind that is not to be identified with our "mind." Certainly the ego does not play the same role in Eastern thought as it does with us. It seems as if the Eastern mind were less egocentric, as if its contents were more loosely connected with the subject, and as if greater stress were laid on mental states which include a depotentiated ego.

> "Psychological Commentary on *The Tibetan Book of the Great Liberation*" (1939/1954), CW 11, § 775.

A growing familiarity with the spirit of the East should be taken merely as a sign that we are beginning to relate to the alien elements within ourselves. Denial of our historical foundations would be sheer folly and would be the best way to bring about another uprooting of consciousness. Only by standing firmly on our own soil can we assimilate the spirit of the East.

"Commentary on *The Secret of the Golden Flower*" (1938), CW 13, § 72.

[T]he day comes when you are outgrown and then you are approaching the void, which seems to me to be the most desirable thing, the thing which contains the most meaning. And you end where you started. This is the philosophy of the East.

Visions: Notes of a Seminar Given in 1930–1934, Vol. II (31 May 1933), p. 1026.

In the East philosophy is not an intellectual business at all; it is not an attempt at producing a logical system consisting of many concepts. The Eastern philosophy is a sort of yoga, it is alive, it is an art, the art of making something of oneself.

Visions: Notes of a Seminar Given in 1930–1934, Vol. II (31 May 1933), p. 1024.

The great asset of the East is that they are based on instinct.

Visions: Notes of the Seminar Given in 1930–1934, Vol. II (21 June 1933), p. 1066.

[W]e must have a concept that covers both functions, consciousness and unconsciousness, and we call this the Self. You can choose any other name if you please, it does not matter. I have chosen the term which has been used since time immemorial in Eastern philosophy to designate this fact, the union of our psychological system; it is the term by which the total of the phenomenon, man, has been expressed.

Visions: Notes of the Seminar Given in 1930–1934, Vol. II (31 January 1934), p. 1270.

In the East the idea prevails that life is only relatively valuable, and if destroyed not much has been lost; so they lose their lives more easily than we do.

Visions: *Notes of the Seminar Given in 1930–1934, Vol. II* (14 June 1933), p. 1058.

It is also the Eastern idea that through understanding one finds the roots of suffering.

Visions: *Notes of the Seminar Given in 1930–1934, Vol. I* (20 January 1932), p. 524.

My God, I love you as a mother loves the unborn whom she carries in her heart. Grow in the egg of the East, nourish yourself from my love, drink the juice of my life so that you will become a radiant God. We need your light, Oh Child. Since we go in darkness, light up our paths. May your light shine before us, may your fire warm the coldness of our life. We do not need your power but life.

The Red Book (1915/2009), p. 286.

[E]astern yoga is based upon man as he really is.

Letter to Mr. N., 5 July 1932, *Letters, Vol. I*, p. 97.

[N]owadays far too many Europeans are inclined to accept Oriental ideas and methods uncritically and to translate them into the mental language of the Occident. In my view this is detrimental both to ourselves and to those ideas. The products of the Oriental mind are based on its own peculiar history, which is radically different from ours. Those peoples have gone through an uninterrupted development from the primitive state of natural polydemonism to polytheism at its most splendid, and beyond that to a religion of ideas within which the originally magical practices could evolve into a method of self-improvement. These antecedents do not apply to us.

Letter to Oskar A. H. Schmitz, 26 May 1923, *Letters, Vol. I*, p. 39.

[T]he patient knows that the main idea in Chinese philosophy is the union of the pairs of opposites.

> Visions: Notes of a Seminar Given in 1930–1934, Vol. I (16 March
> 1932), p. 647.

Among the great religious problems of the present is one which has received scant attention, but which is in fact the main problem of our day: the evolution of the religious spirit. If we are to discuss it, we must emphasize the difference between East and West in their treatment of the "jewel," the central symbol. The West lays stress on the human incarnation, and even on the personality and historicity of Christ, whereas the East says: "Without beginning, without end, without past, without future." The Christian subordinates himself to the superior divine person in expectation of his grace; but the Oriental knows that redemption depends on the work he does on himself. The Tao grows out of the individual.

> "Commentary on The Secret of the Golden Flower" (1929), CW 13,
> § 80.

Western psychology knows the mind as the mental functioning of a psyche. It is the "mentality" of an individual. An impersonal Universal Mind is still to be met with in the sphere of philosophy, where it seems to be a relic of the original human "soul." This picture of our Western outlook may seem a little drastic, but I do not think it is far from the truth. At all events, something of the kind presents itself as soon as we are confronted with the Eastern mentality. In the East, mind is a cosmic factor, the very essence of existence; while in the West we have just begun to understand that it is the essential condition of cognition, and hence of the cognitive existence of the world. There is no conflict between religion and science in the East, because no science is there based upon the passion for facts, and no religion upon mere faith; there is religious cognition and cognitive religion. With us, man is incommensurably small and the grace of

God is everything; but in the East, man is God and he redeems himself.

"Psychological Commentary on *The Tibetan Book of the Great Liberation*" (1954), CW 11, § 768.

As long as the opposites are apart there is desire, the longing of the separated heart, but when they are together there is rest, there is perfection. Therefore the East always represents the perfect condition by the union of opposites. That is *nirvana*, the void, absolute peace.

Visions: Notes of the Seminar Given in 1930–1934, Vol. I (3 March 1931), p. 261.

Everything requires for its existence its own opposite, or else it fades into nothingness. The ego needs the self and vice versa. The changing relations between these two entities constitute a field of experience which Eastern introspection has exploited to a degree almost unattainable to Western man. The philosophy of the East, although so vastly different from ours, could be an inestimable treasure for us too; but, in order to process it, we must first earn it.

"The Holy Men of India" (1944), CW 11, § 961.

I no longer think that you come from the blessed Western lands. Your country must be desolate, full of paralysis and renunciation. I yearn for the East, where the pure source of our live-giving wisdom flows.

The Red Book (1915/2009), p. 279.

[A]ny Eastern philosophy—or Yoga, rather, for it is not philosophy in the Western sense—begins with the question, "Who am I? Who are you?" That is the philosophic question *par excellence* which the Yogin asks his disciples. For the goal, and the purpose of Eastern philosophy is that complete realization of the thing which lives, the thing which *is*. And they have that idea because they are aware of the fact that man's consciousness is always behind the facts; it never keeps up with the flux of life. Life is in a way too rich, too quick, to be realized fully, and they know that one only lives completely when one's mind really accompanies one's life, when one lives no more than one can reflect upon with one's thought, and when one thinks no further than one is able to live. If one could say that of oneself, it would be a guarantee that one really was living.

Nietzsche's Zarathustra: Notes of the Seminar Given in 1934–1939,
Vol. II (30 November 1938), pp. 1425–26.

Observations made in my practical work have opened out to me a quite new and unexpected approach to Eastern wisdom. In saying this I should like to emphasize that I did not have any knowledge, however inadequate, of Chinese philosophy as a starting point. On the contrary, when I began my career as a psychiatrist and psychotherapist, I was completely ignorant of Chinese philosophy, and only later did my professional experience show me that in my technique I had been unconsciously following that secret way which for centuries had been the preoccupation of the best minds of the East. This could be taken for a subjective fancy—which was one reason for my previous reluctance to publish anything on the subject—but Richard Wilhelm, that great interpreter of the soul of China, enthusiastically confirmed the parallel and thus gave me the courage to write about a Chinese text that belongs entirely to the mysterious shadowland of the Eastern mind. At the same time—and this is the extraordinary thing—its content forms a living parallel to what takes place in the psychic development of my patients, none of whom is Chinese.

"Commentary on *The Secret of the Golden Flower*" (1929), CW 13,
§ 10.

If I understand anything of the *I Ching*, then I should say it is *the* book that teaches you your own way and the all-importance of it. Not in vain has the book been the secret treasure of the sages.

Letter to Mr. N., 25 October 1935, *Letters, Vol. I,* p. 201.

It may be said in passing that Chinese science is based on the principle of synchronicity, or parallelism in time, which is naturally regarded by us as superstition. The standard work on this subject is the *I Ching*, of which Richard Wilhelm brought out a translation with an excellent commentary.

Letter to Pascual Jordan, 10 November 1934, *Letters, Vol. I*, p. 178.

The *I Ching* does not offer itself with proofs and results; it does not vaunt itself, nor is it easy to approach. Like a part of nature, it waits until it is discovered. It offers neither facts nor power, but for lovers of self-knowledge, of wisdom—if there be such—it seems to be the right book. To one person its spirit appears as clear as day; to another, shadowy as twilight; to a third, dark as night. He who is not pleased by it does not have to use it, and he who is against it is not obliged to find it true. Let it go forth into the world for the benefit of those who can discern its meaning.

"Foreword to the *I Ching*" (1950), CW 11, § 1018.

The manner in which the *I Ching* tends to look upon reality seems to disfavor our causal procedures. The moment under actual observation appears to the ancient Chinese view more of a chance hit than a clearly defined result of concurrent causal chains. The matter of interest seems to be the configuration formed by chance events at the moment of observation, and not at all the hypothetical reasons that seemingly account for the coincidence. While the Western mind carefully sifts, weighs, selects, classifies, isolates, the Chinese picture of the moment encompasses everything down to the minutest nonsensical detail, because all of the ingredients make up the observed moment.

"Foreword to the *I Ching*" (1950), CW 11, § 969.

The strange antithesis between East and West is expressed most clearly in religious practice. We speak of religious uplift and exaltation; for us God is the Lord of the universe, we have a religion of brotherly love, and in our heaven-aspiring churches there is a *high altar*. The Indian, on the other hand, speaks of *dhyana*, of self-immersion, and of *sinking* into meditation; God is within all things and especially within man, and one turns away from the outer world to the inner. In the old Indian temples the altar is sunk six to eight feet deep in the earth, and what we hide most shame-facedly is the holiest symbol to the Indian. We believe in *doing*, the Indian in impassive *being*. Our religious exercises consist of prayer, worship, and singing hymns. The Indian's most important exercise is yoga, an immersion in what we would call an uncon-scious state, but which he praises as the highest consciousness. Yoga is the most eloquent expression of the Indian mind and at the same time the instrument continually used to produce this pe-culiar attitude of mind.

"The Psychology of Eastern Meditation" (1943), CW 11, § 911.

The goal of Eastern religious practice is the same as that of Western mysticism: the shifting of the center of gravity from the ego to the self, from man to God. This means that the ego disappears in the self, and man in God.

"The Holy Men of India" (1944), CW 11, § 958.

That an atheist is particularly concerned with God is not under-stood with us because we are still unspeakably barbarous in that respect, but the East is a bit more differentiated in such matters. They have the saying that a man who loves God needs seven re-births in order to be redeemed or to reach Nirvana, but a man who hates God needs only three. And why? Because a man who hates God will think of him much oftener than a man who loves God. So the atheist hates God, but he is in a way a better Christian than the man who loves him.

Nietzsche's Zarathustra: Notes of the Seminar Given in 1934–1939,
Vol. I (6 June 1934), pp. 72–73.

11
Religious Experience and God

The decisive question for man is: Is he related to something infinite or not? That is the telling question of his life. Only if we know that the thing which truly matters is the infinite can we avoid fixing our interest upon futilities, and upon all kinds of goals which are not of real importance.

Memories, Dreams, Reflections (1962), p. 325.

The religious attitude, it is quite different, and above all it is not conscious. You can profess whatever you like consciously while your unconscious attitude is totally different.

Visions: Notes of the Seminar Given in 1930–1934, Vol. I (29 October 1930), p. 41.

It is the role of religious symbols to give a meaning to the life of man. The Pueblo Indians believe that they are the sons of Father Sun, and this belief endows their life with a perspective (and a goal) that goes far beyond their limited existence. It gives them ample space for the unfolding of personality and permits them a full life as complete persons. Their plight is infinitely more satisfactory than that of a man in our own civilization who knows that he is (and will remain) nothing more than an underdog with no inner meaning to his life.

"Approaching the Unconscious" (1964), *Man and His Symbols*, p. 89.

"Called or uncalled, God is present!" It is a Delphic oracle. The translation is by Erasmus. You ask whether the oracle is my motto. In a way, you see, it contains the entire reality of the psyche. "Oh God!" is what we say, irrespective of whether we say it by way of a curse or by way of love.

"On Creative Achievement" (1946), *C. G. Jung Speaking*, p. 164.

[I]f I can help it, I never preach my belief. If asked I shall certainly stand by my convictions, but these do not go beyond what I consider to be my actual knowledge. I believe only what I *know*. Everything else is hypothesis and beyond that I can leave a lot of things to the Unknown. They do not bother me. But they would begin to bother me, I am sure, if I felt that I *ought* to know about them.

Psychology and Religion (1938/1940), CW 11, § 79.

I am very grateful for the spiritual help you extend to me. I am in need of it with this gigantic misunderstanding which surrounds me. All the riches I seem to possess are also my poverty, my lonesomeness in the world. The more I seem to possess, the more I stand to lose, when I get ready to approach the dark gate. I did not seek my life with its failures and accomplishments. It came on me with a power not my own. Whatever I have acquired serves a purpose I have not foreseen. Everything has to be shed and nothing remains my own. I quite agree with you: it is not easy to reach utmost poverty and simplicity. But it meets you, unbidden, on the way to the end of this existence.

To the Mother Prioress of a Contemplative Order, September 1959, *Letters, Vol. II*, p. 516.

All that I have learned has led me step by step to an unshakeable conviction of the existence of God. I only believe in what I know. And that eliminates believing. Therefore I do not take His existence on belief—I *know* that He exists.

"Men, Women, and God" (1955), *C. G. Jung Speaking*, p. 251.

I don't *believe* [in a personal God], but I do *know* of a power of a very personal nature and an irresistible influence. I call it "God." I use this term because it has been used for this kind of experience since time immemorial. From this point of view, any gods, Zeus, Wotan, Allah, Yahweh, the Summum Bonum [the Highest Good], etc., have their intrinsic truth. They are different and more or less differentiated expressions or aspects of one ineffable truth.

Letter to Palmer A. Hilty, 25 October 1955, *Letters, Vol. II*,
pp. 274–75.

Happy am I who can recognize the multiplicity and diversity of the Gods. But woe unto you, who replace this incompatible multiplicity with a single God. In so doing you produce the torment of incomprehension, and mutilate the creation whose nature and aim is differentiation. How can you be true to your own nature when you try to turn the many into one? What you do unto the Gods is done likewise unto you. You all become equal and thus your nature is maimed.

The Red Book (1915/2009), p. 351.

The real purpose of the religious ceremonial is to revivify. It was created to lift man out of the ordinary, to disturb his habitual ways, that he may become aware of things outside.

Dream Analysis: Notes from the Seminar Given in 1928–1930 (20
November 1929), p. 399.

The majority of my patients consisted not of believers but of those who had lost their faith. The ones who came to me were the lost sheep. Even in this day and age the believer has the opportunity, in his church, to live the "symbolic life." We need only think of the experience of the Mass, of baptism, of the *imitatio Christi* [the imitation of Christ], and many other aspects of religion. But to live and experience symbols presupposes a vital participation on the part of the believer, and only too often this is lacking in people today. In the neurotic it is practically always lacking. In such cases we have to observe whether the unconscious will not spontaneously bring up symbols to replace what is lacking. But then the question remains of whether a person who has symbolic dreams or visions will also be able to understand their meaning and take the consequences upon himself.

Memories, Dreams, Reflections (1962), p. 140.

[R]eligious statements without exception have to do with the reality of the *psyche*.

Answer to Job (1952), CW 11, § 752.

It is only through the psyche that we can establish that God acts upon us, but we are unable to distinguish whether these actions emanate from God or from the unconscious. We cannot tell whether God and the unconscious are two different entities. Both are border-line concepts for transcendental contents. But empirically it can be established, with a sufficient degree of probability, that there is in the unconscious an archetype of wholeness which manifests itself spontaneously in dreams, etc., and a tendency, independent of the conscious will, to relate other archetypes to this centre. Consequently, it does not seem improbable that the archetype of wholeness occupies as such a central position which approximates it to the God-image.

Answer to Job (1952), CW 11, § 757.

John Freeman: "Do you now believe in God?" Jung: "Now? [Pause] Difficult to answer. I *know*. I don't need to believe. I know."

"The 'Face-to-Face' Interview" (1959), *C. G. Jung Speaking*, p.383.

I did not say in the broadcast, "There is a God." I said, "I do not need to believe in a God; I *know*." Which does not mean: I do know a certain God (Zeus, Jahwe, Allah, the Trinitarian God, etc.) but rather I do know that I am obviously confronted with a factor unknown in itself, which I call "God" in *consensium omnium* [by common consensus] (*"quod semper, quod ubique, quod omnibus creditor"* [what is always believed everywhere and by everyone]). I remember Him, I evoke Him, whenever I use His name overcome by anger, or by fear, whenever I involuntarily say: "Oh God." That happens when I meet somebody or something stronger than myself. It is an apt name given to all overpowering emotions in my own psychical system subduing my conscious will and usurping control over myself. This is the name by which I designate all things which cross my willful path violently and recklessly, all things which upset my subjective views, plans, and intentions and change the course of my life for better or for worse. In accordance with tradition I call the power of fate in this a positive as well as negative aspect, and inasmuch as its origin is out of my control, "God," a "personal god," since my fate means very much myself, particularly when it approaches me in the form of conscience as *vox dei* [the voice of God], with which I can even converse and argue. (We do and, at the same time, we know that we do. One is subject as well as object.)

Jung's response to many letters, *The Listener* (21 January 1960), in
Bennet, *What Jung Really Said*, pp. 167–68.

[I] understood religion as something that God did to me; it was an act on His part, to which I must simply yield, for He was the stronger. My "religion" recognized no human relationship to God, for how could anyone relate to something so little known as God? I must know more about God in order to establish a relationship to him.

Memories, Dreams, Reflections (1962), p. 57.

[A] true religion is exceedingly simple. It is a revelation, a new light.

Dream Analysis: Notes of the Seminar Given in 1928–1930 (4
December 1929), p. 419.

From the psychological standpoint religion is a psychic phenomenon which irrationally exists, like the fact of our physiology or anatomy. If this function is lacking, man as an individual lacks balance, because religious experience is an expression of the existence and function of the unconscious. It is not true that we can manage with reason and will alone. We are on the contrary continually under the influence of disturbing forces that thwart our reason and our will because they are stronger. Hence it is that highly rational people suffer most of all from disturbances which they cannot get at either with their reason or their will. From time immemorial man has called anything he feels or experiences as stronger than he is "divine" or "daemonic." God is the Stronger in him. This psychological definition of God has nothing to do with Christian dogma, but it does describe the experience of the Other, often a very uncanny opponent, which coincides in the most impressive way with the historical "experiences of God."

Letter to Piero Cogo, 21 September 1955, *Letters, Vol. II*, pp. 271–72.

Religion gives us a rich application for our feelings. It gives meaning to life.

"The World on the Verge of Spiritual Rebirth" (1934), *C. G. Jung Speaking*, p. 69.

The great difficulty of course is the "Will of God." Psychologically the "Will of God" appears in your inner experience in the form of a superior deciding power, to which you may give various names like instinct, fate, unconscious, faith, etc. The psychological criterion of the "Will of God" is forever the dynamic superiority. It is the factor that finally decides when all is said and done. It is essentially something you cannot know beforehand. You only know it after the fact. You only learn it slowly in the course of your life. You have to live thoroughly and very consciously for many years in order to understand what your will is and what Its will is. If you learn about yourself and if eventually you discover more or less who you are, you also learn about God, and who He is.

Letter to William Kinney, 26 May 1956, *Letters, Vol. II*, p. 301.

There is no escape. So it is that you come to know what a real God is. Now you'll think up clever truisms, preventive measures, secret escape routes, excuses, potions capable of inducing forgetfulness, but it's all useless. The fire burns right through you. That which guides forces you onto the way.

The Red Book (1915/2009), p. 291.

His craving for alcohol was the equivalent on a low level of the spiritual thirst of our being for wholeness, expressed in medieval language: the union with God.

How could one formulate such an insight in a language that is not misunderstood in our days?

The only right and legitimate way to such an experience is that it happens to you in reality, and it can only happen to you when you walk on a path which leads you to higher understanding. You might be led to that goal by an act of grace or through a personal and honest contact with friends or through a high education of the mind beyond the confines of mere rationalism. I see from your letter that Roland H. has chosen the second way, which was, under the circumstances, obviously the best one.

I am strongly convinced that the evil principle prevailing in this world leads the unrecognized spiritual need into perdition, if it is not counteracted either by a real religious insight or by the protective wall of human community. An ordinary man, not protected by an action from above, and isolated in society, cannot resist the power of evil, which is called very aptly the Devil. But the use of such words arouses so many mistakes that one can only keep aloof from them as much as possible.

These are the reasons why I could not give a full and sufficient explanation to Roland H. But I am risking it with you because I conclude from your very decent and honest letter that you have acquired a point of view about the misleading platitudes one usually hears about alcoholism.

You see, alcohol in Latin is *spiritus* and you use the same word for the highest religious experience as well as for the most depraving poison. The helpful formula therefore is: *spiritus contra spiritum* [spirit against spirit].

Letter to William G. Wilson, 30 January 1961, *Letters, Vol. II*,
pp. 624–25.

The divine voice, as I said, is simply a mana value—a powerful voice, a sort of superior fact which takes possession of one. That is the way in which the gods or any superior spiritual facts have always worked; they took possession of man. And where there is a demonstration of divine power, it does not come under the category of natural phenomena but it is a psychological fact. When human life is inferior, when conscious intentions are disturbed, there one sees divine intercession, intercession through the unconscious, through powerful fact. Naturally one has to dismiss moral categories altogether. The idea that God is necessarily good and spiritual is simply a prejudice made by man. We wish it were so, we wish that the good and spiritual might be supreme, but it is not. To arrive again at a primordial religious phenomenon, man must return to a condition where that functioning is absolutely unprejudiced, where one cannot say that it is good or that it is evil, where one has to give up all bias as to the nature of religion; for as long as there is any kind of bias, there is no submission.

Dream Analysis: Notes of the Seminar Given in 1928–1930 (5 March 1930), pp. 512–13.

[B]elief or faith is your own activity, as what you touch and see, what you experience, is all your own making. You are entirely in the world of known things, even if you approach God, which is the strangest thing you can imagine. You discover that you believe in God and if you did not he would not be. God would be nowhere, he could do nothing. You must believe and then he begins to operate.

Nietzsche's Zarathustra: Notes of the Seminar Given in 1934–1939, Vol. I (5 December 1934), p. 294.

"Legitimate" faith must always rest on experience.

Symbols of Transformation (1912/1952), CW 5, § 345.

[T]he soul must contain in itself the faculty of relationship to God, i.e., a correspondence, otherwise a connection could never come about. *This correspondence is, in psychological terms, the archetype of the God-image.*

Psychology and Alchemy (1944), CW 12, § 11.

With our human knowledge we always move in the human sphere, but in the things of God we should keep quiet and not make any arrogant assertions about what is greater than ourselves. Belief as a religious phenomenon cannot be discussed. It seems to me, however, that when belief enters into practical life we are entitled to the opinion that it should be coupled with the Christian virtue of modesty, which does not brag about absoluteness but brings itself to admit the unfathomable ways of God which have nothing to do with the Christian revelation.

Letter to Paul Maag, 12 June 1933, *Letters, Vol. I*, p. 125.

The human psyche and the psychic background are boundlessly underestimated, as though God spoke to man exclusively through the radio, the newspapers, or through sermons. God has never spoken to man except in and through the psyche, and the psyche understands it and we experience it as something psychic.

Letter to Pastor Damour, 15 August 1932, *Letters, Vol. I*, p. 98.

I believe we have the choice: I preferred the living wonders of the God. I daily weigh up my whole life and I continue to regard the fiery brilliance of the God as a higher and fuller life than the ashes of rationality. The ashes are suicide to me. I could perhaps put out the fire but I cannot deny to myself the experience of the God. Nor can I cut myself off from this experience. I also do not want to, since I want to live. My life wants itself whole.

The Red Book (1915/2009), p. 339.

Without knowing it man is always concerned with God.

"Men, Women, and God," (1955), *C. G. Jung Speaking*, p. 249.

This symbolic process within us, or that need to express unknown, unknowable, inexpressible facts, culminates in religion. Religion is a symbolic system by which we try to express our most important impressions of unknown things, say, the concept of God. Perhaps something overwhelming happens to us; we cannot say that an animal has jumped on us, or that a house has collapsed on us, but something has happened, we don't know what, and we are over-whelmed and call it God. So when something overwhelming happens, we exclaim, "God!"

Visions: Notes of the Seminar Given in 1930–1934, Vol. II (15 June 1932), pp. 742–43.

The primordial experience is not concerned with the historical bases of Christianity but consists in an immediate experience of God (as it was had by Moses, Job, Hosea, Ezekiel among others) which "convinces" because it is "over-powering." But this is something you can't easily talk about. One can only say that somehow one has to reach the rim of the world or get to the end of one's tether in order to partake of the terror or grace of such an experience at all. Its nature is such that it is really understandable why the Church is actually a place of refuge or protection for those who cannot endure the fire of the divine presence.

Letter to Herr N., 13 March 1958, *Letters, Vol. II*, p. 424.

God is not human, I thought; that is His greatness, that nothing human impinges on Him. He is kind and terrible—both at once—and is therefore a great peril from which everyone naturally tries to save himself.

Memories, Dreams, Reflections (1962), pp. 55–56.

[T]he unconscious is the only available source of religious experience. This is certainly not to say that what we call the unconscious is identical with God or is set up in his place. It is simply the medium from which religious experience seems to flow. As to what the further cause of such experience might be, the answer to this lies beyond the range of human knowledge. Knowledge of God is a transcendental problem.

The Undiscovered Self (1957), CW 10, § 565.

Religion means dependence on and submission to the irrational facts of experience.

The Undiscovered Self (1957), CW 10, § 505.

You may have, say, a religious attitude, which means an attitude of great totality, so that you receive the next leaf that falls from the tree as a message from God, and it works.

Visions: Notes of the Seminar Given in 1930–1934, Vol. II (22 February 1933), p. 919.

The unconscious is ambivalent; it can produce both good and evil effects. So the image of God also has two sides, like YHWH or the God of Clement of Rome with two hands; the right is Christ, the left Satan, and it is with these two hands that he rules the world.

"Letter to Père Lachat" (27 March 1954), CW 18, § 1537.

Like God, then, the unconscious has two aspects; one good, favourable, beneficient, the other evil, malevolent, disastrous. The unconscious is the immediate source of our religious experiences.

"Letter to Père Lachat" (27 March 1954), CW 18, § 1538.

[W]hen you are just one with a thing you are completely identical—you cannot compare it, you cannot discriminate, you cannot recognize it. You must always have a point outside if you want to understand. So people who have problematical natures with many conflicts are the people who can produce the greatest understanding, because from their own problematic natures they are enabled to see other sides and to judge by comparison. We could not possibly judge this world if we had not also a standpoint outside, and that is given by the symbolism of religious experiences.

The Psychology of Kundalini Yoga: Notes of the Seminar Given in 1932 (19 October, 1932), p. 27.

[T]he spirit of the depths opened my vision and let me become aware of the birth of the new God.

The divine child approached me out of the terrible ambiguity, the hateful-beautiful, the evil-good, the laughable-serious, the sick-healthy, the inhuman-human and the ungodly-godly.

I understood that the God whom we seek in the absolute was not to be found in absolute beauty and goodness, how should he encompass the fullness of life, which is beautiful and hateful, good and evil, laughable and serious, human and inhuman? How can man live in the womb of the God if the Godhead himself attends only to one-half of him?

The Red Book (1915/2009), p. 243.

[O]ne can never know in what form a man will experience God.

"Brother Klaus" (1933), CW 11, § 482.

The idea of God originated with the experience of the *numinosum*. It was a psychical experience, with moments when man felt overcome. Rudolf Otto has designated this moment in his *Psychology of Religion* as the *numinosum*, which is derived from the Latin *numen*, meaning hint, or sign.

Nietzsche's Zarathustra: Notes of the Seminar Given in 1934–1939,

Vol. II (5 May 1937), p. 1038.

Religions are not necessarily lovely or good. They are powerful manifestations of the spirit and we have no power to check the spirit. Surely great catastrophes such as earthquakes or fires are no longer convincing to the modern mind, but we don't need them. There are things much more gruesome, namely man's insanity, the great mental contagions from which we actually suffer most indubitably.

Letter to Leslie Hollingsworth, 21 April 1934, *Letters, Vol. I*, p. 159.

Religion appears to me to be a peculiar attitude of mind which could be formulated in accordance with the original use of the word *religio*, which means a careful consideration and observation of certain dynamic factors that are conceived as "powers": spirits, daemons, gods, laws, ideas, ideals, or whatever name man has given to such factors in his world as he has found powerful, dangerous, or helpful enough to be taken into careful consideration, or grand, beautiful, and meaningful enough to be devoutly worshipped and loved.

Psychology and Religion (1938/1940), CW 11, § 8.

I profess no "belief." I *know* that there are experiences one *must* pay "religious" attention to. There are many varieties of such experiences. At first glance the only thing they have in common is their *numinosity*, that is to say their gripping emotionality. But on closer inspection one also discovers a *common meaning*. The word *religio* comes from *religere*, according to the ancient view, and not from the patristic *religare*. The former means "to consider or observe carefully." This derivation gives *religio* the right empirical basis, namely, the religious *conduct of life*, as distinct from mere credulity and imitation, which are either religion at second hand or substitutes for religion.

Letter to Günther Wittwer, 10 October 1959, *Letters, Vol. II*, p. 517.

Numinosity, however, is wholly outside conscious volition, for it transports the subject into the state of rapture, which is a state of will-less surrender.

"On the Nature of the Psyche" (1947/1954), CW 8, § 383.

[I]n the least the greatest will appear—such is your expectation. And that is the *numen*, the hint of the god.

Visions: Notes of the Seminar Given in 1933–1934, Vol. II (22 February 1933), p. 919.

Religion, as the Latin word [*religio*] denotes, is a careful and scrupulous observation of what Rudolph Otto aptly termed the *numinosum*, that is, a dynamic agency or effect not caused by an arbitrary act of will. On the contrary, it seizes and controls the human subject, who is always rather its victim than its creator. The *numinosum*, whatever its cause may be, is an experience of the subject independent of his will. At all events, religious teaching as well as the *consensus gentium* [general consensus] always and everywhere explain this experience as being due to a cause external to the individual. The *numinosum* is either a quality belonging to a visible object or the influence of an invisible presence that causes a peculiar alteration of consciousness.

Psychology and Religion (1938/1940), CW 11, § 6.

"Holiness" means that an idea or thing possesses the highest value, and that in the presence of this value men are, so to speak, struck dumb. Holiness is also revelatory: it is the illuminative power emanating from an archetypal figure. Nobody ever feels himself as the subject of such a process, but always as its object. *He* does not perceive holiness, *it* takes him captive and overwhelms him; nor does *he* behold it in a revelation, *it* reveals itself to him, and he cannot even boast that he has understood it properly. Everything happens apparently outside the sphere of his will, and these happenings are contents of the unconscious. Science is unable to say anything more than this, for it cannot, by an act of faith, overstep the limits appropriate to its nature.

"A Psychological Approach to the Dogma of the Trinity,"
(1942/1948), CW 11, § 225.

But, fortunately, the man [Wolfgang Pauli] had *religio*, that is, he "carefully took account of" his experiences and he had enough *pistis,* or loyalty to his experience, to enable him to hang on to it and continue it. He had the *great advantage of being neurotic* and so, whenever he tried to be disloyal to his experience or to deny the voice, the neurotic condition instantly came back. He simply could not "quench the fire" and finally he had to admit the incomprehensibly numinous character of his experience. He had to confess that the unquenchable fire [in a dream] was holy. This was the *sine qua non* of his cure.

Psychology and Religion (1938/1940), CW 11, § 74.

Deviation from the numen seems to be universally understood as being the worst and the most original sin.

> Letter to the Rev. H. L. Philp, 11 June 1957, *Letters, Vol. II*, p. 370.

There is religious sentimentality instead of the *numinosum* of divine experience. This is the well-known characteristic of a religion that has lost its living mystery. It is readily understandable that such a religion is incapable of giving help or of having any other moral effect.

> *Psychology and Religion* (1938/1940), CW 11, § 52.

You are quite right, the main interest of my work is not concerned with the treatment of neuroses but rather with the approach to the numinous. But the fact is that the approach to the numinous is the real therapy and in as much as you attain to the numinous experiences you are released from the curse of pathology. Even the very disease takes on a numinous character.

> Letter to P. W. Martin, 20 August 1945, *Letters, Vol. I*, p. 377.

Healing may be called a religious problem.

> "Psychotherapists or the Clergy" (1932), CW 11, § 523.

[R]eligion is the fruit and culmination of the completeness of life, that is, of a life which contains both sides.

> *Psychology and Religion* (1938/1940), CW 11, § 71.

It seems to me to be the Holy Spirit's task and charge to reconcile and unite the opposites in the human individual through a special development of the human soul. The soul is paradoxical like the Father; it is black and white, divine and demon-like, in its primitive and natural state. By the discriminative function of its conscious side it separates opposites of every kind, and especially those of the moral order personified in Christ and the Devil. Thereby the soul's spiritual development creates an enormous tension, from which man can only suffer.

> "Letter to Père Lachat" (27 March 1954), CW 18, § 1553.

A religious conversation is inevitable with the devil, since he demands it, if one does not want to surrender to him unconditionally. Because religion is precisely what the devil and I cannot agree about. I must have it out with him, as I cannot expect that he as an independent personality would accept my standpoint without further ado.

The Red Book (1915/2009), 261.

She [an assimilated young Jewish woman] had no mythological ideas, and therefore the most essential feature of her nature could find no way to express itself. All her conscious activity was directed toward flirtation, clothes, and sex, because she knew of nothing else. She knew only the intellect and lived a meaningless life. In reality she was a child of God whose destiny was to fulfill His secret will. I had to awaken mythological and religious ideas in her, for she belonged to that class of human beings of whom spiritual activity is demanded. Thus her life took on a meaning, and no trace of the neurosis was left.

In this case I had applied no "method," but had sensed the presence of the numen. My explaining this to her had accomplished the cure. Method did not matter here; what mattered was the "fear of God."

Memories, Dreams, Reflections (1962), pp. 139–40.

Since neurosis is an attitudinal problem, and the attitude depends on, or is grounded in, certain "dominants," i.e., the ultimate and highest ideas and principles, the problem of attitude can fairly be characterized as a religious one. This is supported by the fact that religious motifs appear in dreams and fantasies for the obvious purpose of regulating the attitude and restoring the disturbed equilibrium. These experiences compelled me to come to grips with religious questions, or rather to examine the psychology of religious statements more closely. My aim is to unearth the psychic facts to which religious statements refer. I have found that, as a rule, when "archetypal" contents spontaneously appear in dreams, etc., numinous and healing effects emanate from them. They are *primordial psychic experiences* which very often give patients access again to blocked religious truths. I have also had this experience myself.

Letter to Vera von Lier-Schmidt Ernsthausen, 25 April 1952, *Letters, Vol. II*, pp. 56–57.

Among all my patients in the second half of life—that is to say, over 35—there has been not one whose problem in the last resort was not that of finding a religious outlook on life. It is safe to say that every one of them fell ill because he had lost what the living religions of every age have given to their followers, and none of them has been really healed who did not regain his religious outlook. This of course has nothing to with a particular creed or membership of a church.

"Psychotherapists or the Clergy" (1932), CW 11, § 509.

As a neurosis starts from a fragmentary state of human consciousness, it can only be cured by an approximate totality of the human being. Religious ideas and convictions from the beginning of history have the aspect of the mental *pharmakon* [pharmacy]. They represent the world of wholeness in which fragments can be gathered and put together again. Such a cure cannot be effected by pills and injections.

Letter to Father David, 11 February 1961, *Letters, Vol. II*, p. 625.

It is also a fact that under the influence of a so-called scientific enlightenment great masses of educated people have either left the Church or become profoundly indifferent to it. If they were all dull rationalists or neurotic intellectuals the loss would not be regrettable. But many of them are religious people, only incapable of agreeing with the existing forms of belief.

Psychology and Religion (1938/1940), CW 11, § 34.

I am not, however, addressing myself to the happy possessors of faith, but to those many people for whom the light has gone out, the mystery has faded, and God is dead. For most of them there is no going back, and one does not know either whether going back is always the better way. To gain an understanding of religious matters, probably all that is left us today is the psychological approach. That is why I take these thought-forms that have become historically fixed, try to melt them down again, and pour them into moulds of immediate experience. It is certainly a difficult undertaking to discover connecting links between dogma and immediate experience of psychological archetypes, but a study of natural symbols of the unconscious gives us the necessary raw material.

Psychology and Religion (1938/1940), CW 11, § 148.

Religion is a very apt instrument to express the unconscious. The main significance of any religion is that its forms and rites express the peculiar life of the unconscious. The relationship between religion and the unconscious is everywhere obvious: all religions are full of figures from the unconscious.

Nietzsche's Zarathustra: Notes of the Seminar Given in 1934–1939,
Vol. II (19 October 1938), p. 1351.

Religions are psychotherapeutic systems in the truest sense of the word, and on the grandest scale. They express the whole range of the psychic problem in mighty images; they are the avowal and recognition of the soul, and at the same time the revelation of the soul's nature.

"The State of Psychotherapy Today" (1934), CW 10, § 367.

I find I am incapable of knowing the infinite and eternal or paradoxical; it is beyond my powers. *I may say* that I know what is infinite and eternal; I may even assert that I have experienced it; but that one could actually *know* it is impossible because man is neither an infinite nor an eternal being. He can know only the part but not the whole, not the infinite and eternal. So when the believer assures me that I do not possess the organ he possesses, he makes me aware of my humanity, of my limitation which he allegedly does not have. He is the superior one, who regretfully points out my deformity or mutilation. Therefore I speak of the *beati possidentes* [those blessed with being able to believe] of belief, and this is what I reproach them with: that they exalt themselves above our human stature and our human limitation and won't admit to pluming themselves on a possession which distinguishes them from the ordinary mortal. I confess with the confession of not knowing and not being able to know; believers start with the assertion of knowing and being able to know. There is now only one truth, and when we ask the believers what this truth is they give us a number of very different answers with regard to which the one sure thing is that each believer announces his own particular truth. Instead of saying: To me personally it seems so, he says: It is so, thus putting everybody else automatically in the wrong.

Letter to Bernhard Lang, June 1957, *Letters, Vol. II*, pp. 375–76.

Only the mystics bring creativity into religion. That is probably why they can feel the presence and the workings of the Holy Ghost, and why they are nearer to the experience of the brotherhood in Christ.

Mysterium Coniunctionis (1955–56), CW 14, § 530.

The teaching of the past, for example, of St. Paul or Jesus, can be edifying, but *in itself* does nothing, Paul himself had a sudden revelation. Unless there is a personal religious experience—realizing from the inside what it means—nothing happens. Such an experience can take many forms, for instance falling in love; anything which is really lived.

Conversation with E. A. Bennet, 7 July 1959, *Meetings with Jung*,

pp. 92–93.

Only those people who can really touch bottom can be human. Therefore Meister Eckhart says that one should not repent too much of one's sins because it might keep one away from grace. One is only confronted with the spiritual experience when one is absolutely human.

Visions: Notes of the Seminar Given in 1930–1934, Vol. I (3 June 1931), p. 394.

Christians often ask why God does not speak to them, as he is believed to have done in former days. When I hear such questions, it always makes me think of the rabbi who was asked how it could be that God often showed himself to people in the olden days while nowadays nobody ever sees him. The rabbi replied: "Nowadays there is no longer anybody who can bow low enough."

"Approaching the Unconscious" (1964), Man and His Symbols, p. 102.

GEORGES DUPLAIN: How can you speak of the grace of God?

JUNG: And why not? A good dream, for example, that's grace. The dream is in essence a gift. The collective unconscious, it's not for you, or me, it's the invisible world, it's the great spirit. It makes little difference what I call it: God, Tao, the Great Voice, the Great Spirit. But for people of our time God is the most comprehensible name with which to designate the Power beyond us.

"On the Frontiers of Knowledge" (1959), C. G. Jung Speaking, p. 419.

The "relativity of God," as I understand it, denotes a point of view that does not conceive of God as "absolute," i.e., wholly "cut off" from man and existing outside and beyond all human conditions, but as in a certain sense dependent on him; it also implies a reciprocal and essential relation between man and God, whereby man can be understood as a function of God, and God as a psychological function of man. From the empirical standpoint of analytical psychology, the God-image is the symbolic expression of a particular psychic state, or function, which is characterized by its absolute ascendancy over the will of the subject, and can therefore bring about or enforce actions and achievements that could never be done by conscious effort. This overpowering impetus to action (so far as the God-function manifests itself in acts), or this inspiration that transcends conscious understanding, has its source in an accumulation of energy in the unconscious. The accumulated libido activates images lying dormant in the collective unconscious, among them the God-image, that engram or imprint which from the beginning of time has been the collective expression of the most overwhelmingly powerful influences exerted on the conscious mind by unconscious concentrations of libido.

Psychological Types (1921), CW 6, § 412.

I know people who feel that the strange power in their own psyche is something divine, for the very simple reason that it has given them an understanding of what is meant by religious experience.

"The Meaning of Psychology for Modern Man" (1933/1934), CW 10,

§ 312.

The religious myth is one of man's greatest and most significant achievements, giving him the security and inner strength not to be crushed by the monstrousness of the universe.

Symbols of Transformation (1912/1952), CW 5, § 343.

[M]yth is not fiction: it consists of facts that are continually repeated and can be observed over and over again. It is something that happens to man, and men have mythical fates just as much as the Greek heroes do.

Answer to Job (1952), CW 11, § 648.

Religious observances, i.e., the retelling and ritual repetition of the mythical event, consequently serve the purpose of bringing the image of childhood, and everything connected with it, again and again before the eyes of the conscious mind so that the link with the original condition may not be broken.

"The Psychology of the Child Archetype" (1940), CW 9i, § 275.

A revelation always means a revealing will, a will to manifest which is not identical with your own will and which is not your activity. You may be overcome by it; it falls upon you.

Nietzsche's Zarathustra: Notes of the Seminar Given in 1934–1939,
Vol. II (4 March 1936), p. 876.

All these yoga methods, and practices similar to them, will bring about the desired condition, but only if God be willing, so to speak; that is to say, there is another factor involved which is necessary, but the nature of which we do not know. All kinds of primitive practices are to be understood as an effort on the part of man to make himself receptive to a revelation from nature.

Introduction to Jungian Psychology: Notes from the Seminar on
Analytical Psychology Given in 1925, p. 88.

Whereas a true religion is exceedingly simple. It is a revelation, a new light.

Dream Analysis: Notes of the Seminar Given in 1928–1930 (4
December 1929), p. 419.

That is what comes to the man who is outside the church: he has to learn to feed himself, with no longer a mother to push the spoon into his mouth. There is no human being who can provide what is provided by the church. The church provides for all that naturally; inasmuch as you are a member of the church you get the *panis super substantialis* [the most substantial bread]; in partaking of the communion, you receive the spiritual food and are spiritually transformed. Do you think that any father or mother or godmother or aunt or any book can produce the miracle of transubstantiation? If you yourself can provide for it, then you are the whole mystery of the church: you *are* the transubstantiation. If you understand that, you can have the spiritual food every day; then you know what it costs and you understand what the church costs and what the church means.

Nietzsche's Zarathustra: Notes of the Seminar Given in 1934–1939,
Vol. II (17 June 1936), pp. 1012–13.

Christianity, like every closed system of religion, has an undoubted tendency to suppress the unconscious in the individual as much as possible, thus paralyzing his fantasy activity. Instead, religion offers stereotyped symbolic concepts that are meant to take the place of his unconscious once and for all. The symbolic concepts of all religions are recreations of unconscious processes in a typical, universally binding form. Religious teaching supplies, as it were, the final information about the "last things" and the world beyond human consciousness. Wherever we can observe a religion being born, we see how the doctrinal figures flow into the founder himself as revelations, in other words, as concretizations of his unconscious fantasy. The forms welling up from his unconscious are declared to be universally valid and thus replace the individual fantasies of others.

Psychological Types (1921), CW 6, § 80.

Religion is a "revealed" way of salvation. Its ideas are products of a pre-conscious knowledge which, always and everywhere, expresses itself in symbols. Even if our intellect does not grasp them, they still work, because our unconscious acknowledges them as exponents of universal psychic facts. For this reason faith is enough—if it is there. Every extension and intensification of rational consciousness, however, leads us further away from the sources of the symbols and, by its ascendancy, prevents us from understanding them. That is the situation today.

"A Psychological Approach to the Dogma of the Trinity"

(1942/1948), CW 11, § 293.

The fact of God's "unconsciousness" throws a peculiar light on the doctrine of salvation. Man is not so much delivered from his sins, even if he is baptized in the prescribed manner and thus washed clean, as delivered from fear of the consequences of sin, that is, from the wrath of God. Consequently, the work of salvation is intended to save man from the fear of God.

Answer to Job (1952), CW 11, § 659.

Religious rites and their stock of symbols must have developed in much the same way from beginnings now lost to us, and not just in one place only, but in many places at once, and also at different periods. They have grown spontaneously out of the basic conditions of human nature, which are never invented but are everywhere the same.

"Transformation Symbolism in the Mass" (1942/1954), CW 11,
§ 339.

To the degree that the modern mind is passionately concerned with anything and everything rather than religion, religion and its prime object—original sin—have mostly vanished into the unconscious. That is why, today, nobody believes in either. People accuse psychology of dealing in squalid fantasies, and yet even a cursory glance at ancient religions and the history of morals should be sufficient to convince them of the demons hidden in the human soul. This disbelief in the devilishness of human nature goes hand in hand with the blank incomprehension of religion and its meaning. The *unconscious* conversion of instinctual impulses into religious activity is ethically worthless, and often no more than an hysterical outburst, even though its products may be aesthetically valuable. Ethical decision is possible only when one is conscious of the conflict in all its aspects. The same is true of the religious attitude: it must be fully conscious of itself and of its foundations if it is to signify anything more than unconscious imitation.

Symbols of Transformation (1912/1952), CW 5, § 106.

It is my practical experience that psychological understanding immediately revivifies the essential Christian ideas and fills them with the breath of life. This is because our worldly light, i.e., scientific knowledge and understanding, coincides with the symbolic statement of the myth, whereas previously we were unable to bridge the gulf between knowing and believing.

"Jung and Religious Belief" (1958), CW 18, § 1666.

I want to make clear that by the term "religion" I do not mean a creed. It is, however, true that every creed is originally based, on the one hand, upon the experience of the *numinosum* and, on the other hand, upon *pistis*, that is to say, trust or loyalty, faith and confidence in a certain experience of a numinous nature and in the change of consciousness that ensues. The conversion of Paul is a striking example of this. We might say, then, that the term religion designates the attitude peculiar to a consciousness which has been changed by experience of the *numinosum*.

Psychology and Religion (1938/1940), CW 11, § 9.

What is ordinarily called "religion" is a substitute to such an amazing degree that I ask myself seriously whether this kind of "religion," which I prefer to call a creed, may not after all have an important function in human society. The substitute has the obvious purpose of replacing *immediate experience* by a choice of suitable symbols tricked out with an organized dogma and ritual.

Psychology and Religion (1938/1940), CW 11, § 75.

In my profession I have encountered many people who have had immediate experience and who would not and could not submit to the authority of ecclesiastical decision. I had to go with them through the crises of passionate conflicts, through the panics of madness, through desperate confusions and depressions which were grotesque and terrible at the same time, so that I am fully aware of the extraordinary importance of dogma and ritual, at least as methods of mental hygiene.

Psychology and Religion (1938/1940), CW 11, § 76.

A creed gives expression to a definite collective belief, whereas the word *religion* expresses a subjective relationship to certain metaphysical, extra-mundane factors. A creed is a confession of faith intended chiefly for the world at large and is thus an intra-mundane affair, while the meaning and purpose of religion lie in the relationship of the individual to God (Christianity, Judaism,

Islam) or to the path of salvation and liberation (Buddhism). From this basic fact all ethics are derived, which without the individual's responsibility before God can be nothing more than conventional morality.

The Undiscovered Self (1957), CW 10, § 507.

A creed coincides with the established Church or, at any rate, forms a public institution whose members include not only true believers but vast numbers of people who can only be described as "indifferent" in matters of religion and who belong to it simply by force of habit. Here the difference between a creed and a religion becomes palpable.

The Undiscovered Self (1957), CW 10, § 508.

Creeds are codified and dogmatized forms of religious experience. The contents of the experience have become sanctified and are usually congealed in a rigid, often elaborate structure of ideas. The practice and repetition of the original experience have become a ritual and an unchangeable institution. This does not necessarily mean lifeless petrification. On the contrary, it may prove to be a valid form of religious experience for millions of people for thousands of years, without there arising any vital necessity to alter it. Although the Catholic Church has often been accused of particular rigidity, she nevertheless admits that dogma is a living thing and that its formulation is therefore capable of change and development. Even the number of dogmas is not limited and can be multiplied in the course of time. The same holds true of the ritual.

Psychology and Religion (1938/1940), CW 11, § 10.

If I find myself in a critical or doubtful situation, I always ask myself, whether there is not something in it, explaining the need of my presence, before I make a plan of how to escape. If I should find nothing hopeful or meaningful in it, I think I would not hesitate to jump out of it as quick as possible. Well, I may be all wrong, but the fact that you find yourself in the Church does not impress me as being wholly nonsensical. Of course huge sacrifices are expected of you, but I wonder whether there is any vocation or any kind of meaningful life that does not demand sacrifices of a sort. There is no place where those striving after consciousness could find absolute safety. Doubt and insecurity are indispensable components of a complete life. Only those who can lose this life *really*, can gain it really. A "complete" life does not consist in a theoretical completeness, but in the fact, that one accepts the particular fatal tissue in which one finds oneself embedded without reservation, and that one tries to make sense of it or to create a Kosmos from the chaotic mess into which one is born. If one lives properly and completely, time and again one will be confronted with a situation, of which one will say: "This is too much. I cannot bear it any more." Then the question must be answered: "Can one really not bear it?"

Letter to Father Victor White, 10 April 1954, *The Jung-White Letters*, p. 240.

This woman is seeking an attitude which will help her to meet the problems of her life. She has not found the conviction or the attitude which would help her to accept life as it is—one cannot say life in general, but her own individual fate; for that she needs a sort of religious attitude which she can find nowhere else.

Visions: Notes of the Seminar Given in 1930–1934, Vol. I (27 May 1931), p. 372.

The renewed God signifies a regenerated attitude, a renewed possibility of life, a recovery of vitality, because, psychologically speaking, God always denotes the highest value, the maximum sum of libido, the fullest intensity of life, the optimum of psychological vitality.

Psychological Types (1921), CW 6, § 301.

I want to love my God, the defenseless and hopeless one. I want to care for him, like a child.

The Red Book (1915/2009), p. 286.

"What does God want? To act or not to act? I must find out what God wants with Me, and I must find out right away."

Memories, Dreams, Reflections (1962), p. 38.

From the beginning I had a sense of destiny, as though my life was assigned to me by fate and had to be fulfilled. This gave me an inner security, and although I could never prove it to myself, it proved itself to me. I did not have the certainty, it had me. Nobody could rob me of the conviction that it was enjoined upon me to do what God wanted and not what I wanted. That gave me the strength to go my own way. Often I had the feeling that in all decisive matters I was no longer among men, but was alone with God. And when I was "there," where I was no longer alone, I was outside time; I belonged to the centuries; and He who then gave answer was He who had always been, who had been before my birth. He who always is was there.

Memories, Dreams, Reflections (1962), p. 48.

It is of the *highest importance* that the educated and "enlightened" public should know religious truth as a thing living in the human soul and not as an abstruse and unreasonable relic of the past.

Letter to Father Victor White, 5 October, 1945, *The Jung-White Letters*, p. 10.

[T]he soul possesses by nature a religious function.

Psychology and Alchemy (1944), CW 12, § 14.

So long as religion is only faith and outward form, and the religious function is not experienced in our own souls, nothing of any importance has happened. It has yet to be understood that the *mysterium magnum* [the great mystery] is not only an actuality but is first and foremost rooted in the human psyche. The man who does not know this from his own experience may be a most learned theologian, but he has no idea of religion and still less of education.

Psychology and Alchemy, (1944), CW 12, § 13.

If you try to be literal about the doctrine, you are putting yourself aside until there is nobody left that would represent it, but corpses. If, on the other hand, you truly assimilate the doctrine, you will alter it creatively, by your individual understanding and thus give life to it. The life of most ideas consists in their controversial nature, i.e., that you can disagree with them, even if you recognize their importance for a majority. If you fully agree with them, you could replace yourself just as well by a gramophone record.

> Letter to Father Victor White, 10 April 1954, *The Jung-White Letters*,
> p. 238.

By removing yourself from the dogma you get into the world which is increasingly chaotic and primitive, in which you must find or create a new orientation. You must create a new cosmos out of the chaos into which you fall when you leave the Christian church. The church has been a cosmos, but it is no longer, we are living in chaos; therefore the general confusion and disorientation. We are profoundly bewildered through this experience which we cannot put into the frame of things that we have hitherto known.

> *Visions: Notes of the Seminar Given in 1930–1934, Vol. II* (1 February
> 1933), p. 905

Nietzsche's idea is that out of that lack of order, a dancing star should be born.

> *Nietzsche's Zarathustra: Notes of the Seminar Given in 1934–1939,*
> *Vol. I* (13 June 1934), p. 106.

If one fulfills the will of God one can be sure of going the right way.

> *Memories, Dreams, Reflections* (1962), p. 40.

[I]t is tremendously important that people should be able to accept themselves; otherwise the will of God cannot be lived. They are sort of cramped or blighted, they don't really produce themselves as the whole of the creative will which is in them, they assume a better judgment than God himself, assuming that man ought to be so-and-so. In that way they exclude many of their real qualities, with the result that they are like the apple tree that produces carrots, or the famous good tiger that eats apples, which surely is not the original meaning of God. Now to bring forth what the original will intended is really the task of a whole lifetime, a very serious undertaking.

Visions: Notes of the Seminar Given in 1930–1934, Vol. I (3 June 1931), p. 391.

[T]he paradox is one of our most valuable spiritual possessions, while uniformity of meaning is a sign of weakness. Hence a religion becomes inwardly impoverished when it loses or waters down its paradoxes; but their multiplication enriches because only the paradox comes anywhere near to comprehending the fullness of life. Non-ambiguity and non-contradiction are one-sided and thus unsuited to express the incomprehensible.

Psychology and Alchemy (1944), CW 12, § 18.

A dogma is always the result and fruit of many minds and many centuries, purified of all the oddities, shortcomings, and flaws of individual experience. But for all that, the individual experience, by its very poverty, is immediate life, the warm red blood pulsating today. It is more convincing to a seeker after truth than the best tradition.

Psychology and Religion (1938/1940), CW 11, § 88.

When, through mass rule, the individual becomes social unit No. so-and-so and the State is elevated to the supreme principle, it is only to be expected that the religious function too will be sucked into the maelstrom. Religion, as the careful observation and taking account of certain invisible and uncontrollable factors, is an *instinctive* attitude peculiar to man, and its manifestations can be followed all through human history. Its evident purpose is to maintain the psychic balance, for the natural man has an equally natural "knowledge" of the fact that his conscious functions may at any time be thwarted by uncontrollable happenings coming from inside as well as outside. For this reason he has always taken care that any difficult decisions likely to have consequences for himself and others shall be rendered safe by suitable measures of a religious nature. Offerings are made to the invisible powers, formidable blessings are pronounced, and all kinds of solemn rites are performed.

The Undiscovered Self (1957), CW 10, § 512.

Here each of us must ask: Have I any religious experience and immediate relation to God, and hence that certainty which will keep me, as an individual, from dissolving in the crowd?

The Undiscovered Self (1957), CW 10, § 564.

It was obedience which brought me grace, and after that experience I knew what God's grace was. One must be utterly abandoned to God; nothing matters but fulfilling His will. Otherwise all is folly and meaninglessness.

Memories, Dreams, Reflections (1962), p. 40.

[T]he creation of a God is a creative act of highest love.

The Red Book (1915/2009), p. 291.

Surrender to God is a formidable adventure, and as "simple" as any situation over which man has no control. He who can risk himself wholly to it finds himself directly in the hands of God, and is there confronted with a situation which makes "simple faith" a vital necessity; in other words, the situation becomes so full of risk or overtly dangerous that the deepest instincts are aroused. An experience of this kind is always numinous, for it unites all aspects of totality.

"Letter to Père Lachat" (27 March 1954), CW 18, § 1539.

When, therefore, we make use of a concept of a God we are simply formulating a definite psychological fact, namely the independence and sovereignty of certain psychic contents which express themselves by their power to thwart our will, to obsess our consciousness and to influence our moods and actions. We may be outraged at the idea of an inexplicable mood, a nervous disorder, or an un-controllable vice being, so to speak, a manifestation of God. But it would be an irreparable loss for religious experience if such things, perhaps even evil things, were artificially segregated from the sum of autonomous psychic contents.

The Relations between the Ego and the Unconscious (1916/1928), CW 7, § 400.

God has a terrible double aspect: a sea of grace is met by a seething lake of fire, and the light of love glows with a fierce dark heat which it is said, '*ardet non lucet*'—it burns but gives no light. That is the eternal, as distinct from the temporal, gospel: *one can love God but must fear him.*

Answer to Job (1952), CW 11, § 733.

The paradoxical nature of God has a like effect on man: it tears him asunder into opposites and delivers him over to a seemingly insol-uble conflict. What happens in such a condition? Here we must let psychology speak, for psychology represents the sum of all the ob-servations and insights it has gained from the empirical study of severe states of conflict. There are, for example, conflicts of duty no one knows how to solve.

Answer to Job (1952), CW 11, § 738.

Suffering that is not understood is hard to bear, while on the other hand it is often astounding to see how much a person can endure when he understands the why and the wherefore. A philosophical or religious view of the world enables him to do this, and such views prove to be, at the very least, psychic methods of healing if not of salvation.

"On the Discourses of the Buddha" (1956), CW 18, § 1578.

What does man possess that God does not have? Because of his littleness, puniness, and defenselessness against the Almighty, he possesses, as we have already suggested, a somewhat keener con-sciousness based on self-reflection; he must, in order to survive, always be mindful of his impotence. God has no need of this circumspection, for nowhere does he come up against an insuperable obstacle that would force him to hesitate and hence make him reflect on himself.

Answer to Job (1952), CW 11, § 579.

Job realizes God's inner antinomy, and in the light of this realization his knowledge attains a divine numinosity.

Answer to Job (1952), CW 11, § 584.

Although the divine incarnation is a cosmic and absolute event, it only manifests empirically in those relatively few individuals capable of enough consciousness to make ethical decisions, that is, to decide for the Good. Therefore God can be called good only inasmuch as He is able to manifest His goodness in individuals. His moral quality depends upon individuals. That is why He incarnates. Individuation and individual existence are indispensable for the transformation of God the Creator.

Letter to Elined Kotschnig, 30 June 1956, *Letters, Vol. II*, p. 314.

Yahweh's decision to become man is a symbol of the development that had to supervene when man becomes conscious of the sort of God-image he is confronted with. God acts out of the unconscious of man and forces him to harmonize and unite the opposing influences to which his mind is exposed from the unconscious. The unconscious wants both: to divide and to unite. In his striving for unity, therefore, man may always count on the help of a metaphysical advocate, as Job clearly recognized. The unconscious wants to flow into consciousness in order to reach the light, but at the same time it continually thwarts itself, because it would rather remain unconscious. That is to say, God wants to become man, but not quite. The conflict in his nature is so great that the incarnation can only be bought by an expiatory self-sacrifice offered up to the wrath of God's dark side.

Answer to Job (1952), CW 11, § 740.

We can, of course, hope for the undeserved grace of God, who hears our prayers. But God, who also does *not* hear our prayers, wants to become man, and for that purpose he has chosen, through the Holy Ghost, the creaturely man filled with darkness—the natural man who is tainted with original sin and who learnt the divine arts and sciences from the fallen angels.

Answer to Job (1952), CW 11, § 746.

I don't know what Job is supposed to have seen. But it seems possible that he unconsciously anticipated the historical future, namely, the evolution of the God-image. God had to become man. Man's suffering does not derive from his sins but from the maker of his imperfections, the paradoxical God. The righteous man is the instrument into which God enters in order to attain self-reflection and thus consciousness and rebirth as a divine child trusted to the care of adult man.

"Jung and Religious Belief" (1958), CW 18, § 1681.

In the experience of the self it is no longer the opposites "God" and "man" that are reconciled, as it was before, but rather the opposites within the God-image itself. That is the meaning of divine service, of the service which man can render to God, that light may emerge from the darkness, that the Creator may become conscious of His creation, and man conscious of himself.

Memories, Dreams, Reflections (1962), p. 338.

Since the Apocalypse we now know again that God is not only to be loved, but also to be feared. He fills us with evil as well as with good, otherwise he would not need to be feared; and because he wants to become man, the uniting of his antinomy must take place in man. This involves man in a new responsibility. He can no longer wriggle out of it on the plea of his littleness and nothingness, for the dark God has slipped the atom bomb and chemical weapons into his hands and given him the power to empty out the apocalyptic vials of wrath on his fellow creatures. Since he has been granted an almost godlike power, he can no longer remain blind and unconscious. He must know something of God's nature and of metaphysical processes if he is to understand himself and thereby achieve gnosis of the Divine.

Answer to Job (1952), CW 11, § 747.

God wants to be born in the flame of man's consciousness, leaping ever higher. And what if this has no roots in the earth? If it is not a house of stone where the fire of God can dwell, but a wretched straw hut that flares up and vanishes? Could God then be born? One must be able to suffer God. That is the supreme task for the carrier of ideas. He must be the advocate of the earth. God will take care of himself. My inner principle is: Deus *et* homo. God and man. God needs man in order to become conscious, just as he needs limitation in time and space. Let us therefore be for him limitation in time and space, an earthly tabernacle.

Letter to Walter Robert Corti, 30 April 1929, *Letters, Vol. I*, pp. 65–66.

One should make clear to oneself what it means when God becomes man. It means more or less what Creation meant in the beginning, namely an objectivation of God. At the time of the Creation he revealed himself in Nature; now he wants to be more specific and become man. It must be admitted, however, that there was a tendency in this direction right from the start. For, when those other human beings, who had evidently been created before Adam, appeared on the scene along with the higher mammals, Yahweh created on the following day, by a special act of creation, a man who was the image of God. This was the first prefiguration of his becoming man. He took Adam's descendants, especially the people of Israel, into his personal possession, and from time to time he filled this people's prophets with his spirit. All these things were preparatory events and symptoms of a tendency within God to become man. But in omniscience there had existed from all eternity a knowledge of the human nature of God or of the divine nature of man. That is why, long before Genesis was written, we find corresponding testimonies in the ancient Egyptian records. These intimations and prefigurations of the Incarnation must strike one as either completely incomprehensible or superfluous, since all creation *ex nihilo* [from nothing] is God's and consists of nothing but God, with the result that man, like the rest of creation, is simply God become concrete. Prefigurations, however, are not in themselves creative events, but are only stages in the process of becoming conscious. It was only quite late that we realized (or rather, that we are beginning to realize) that God is Reality itself and therefore—last but not least—man. This realization is a millennial process.

Answer to Job (1952), CW 11, § 631.

Man's relation to God probably has to undergo a certain important change. Instead of the propitiating praise to an unpredictable king or the child's prayer to a loving father, the responsible living and fulfilling of the divine will in us will be our form of worship and commerce with God. His goodness means grace and light and His dark side the terrible temptation of power. Man has already received so much knowledge that he can destroy his own planet. Let us hope that God's good spirit will guide him in his decisions, because it will depend upon man's decision whether God's creation will continue. Nothing shows more drastically than this possibility how much of divine power has come within the reach of man.

Letter to Elined Kotschnig, 30 June 1956, *Letters, Vol. II*, p. 316.

[E]ven the enlightened person remains what he is, and is never more than his own limited ego before the One who dwells within him, whose form has no knowable boundaries, who encompasses him on all sides, fathomless as the abysms of the earth and vast as the sky.

Answer to Job (1952), CW 11, § 758.

12
Good and Evil

Human nature is capable of an infinite amount of evil, and the evil deeds are as real as the good ones so far as human experience goes and so far as the psyche judges and differentiates between them. Only unconsciousness makes no difference between good and evil. Inside the psychological realm one honestly does not know which of them predominates in the world. We hope, merely, that good does, i.e., what seems suitable to us. No one could possibly say what the general good might be. No amount of insight into the relativity and fallibility of our moral judgment can deliver us from these defects, and those who deem themselves beyond good and evil are usually the worst tormentors of mankind, because they are twisted with the pain and fear of their own sickness.

Aion (1951), CW 9ii, § 97.

One must be positively blind not to see the colossal role that evil plays in the world. Indeed, it took the intervention of God himself to deliver humanity from the curse of evil, for without his intervention man would have been lost.

Aion (1951), CW 9ii, § 114.

Only an infantile person can pretend that evil is not at work everywhere, and the more unconscious he is, the more the devil drives him. It is just because of this inner connection with the black side of things that it is so incredibly easy for the mass man to commit the most appalling crimes without thinking. Only ruthless self-knowledge on the widest scale, which sees good and evil in correct perspective and can weigh up the motives of human action, offers some guarantee that the end-result will not turn out too badly.

Aion (1951), CW 9ii, § 255.

It should never be forgotten—and of this the Freudian school must be reminded—that morality was not brought down on tables of stone from Sinai and imposed on the people, but is a function of the human soul, as old as humanity itself. Morality is not imposed from outside; we have it in ourselves from the start—not the law, but our moral nature without which the collective life of human society would be impossible. That is why morality is found at all levels of society. It is the instinctive regulator of action which also governs the collective life of the herd. But moral laws are valid only within a compact human group. Beyond that, they cease. There the old truth runs: *Homo homini lupus* [man is a wolf of man]. With the growth of civilization we have succeeded in subjecting ever larger human groups to the rule of the same morality, without, however, having yet brought the moral code to prevail beyond the social frontiers, that is, in the free space between mutually independent societies. There, as of old, reign lawlessness and licence and mad immorality—though of course it is only the enemy who dares to say it out loud.

On the Psychology of the Unconscious (1917/1926), CW 7, § 30.

Of course I am unable, as anybody is, to define what evil is in itself. There is nothing which at times cannot be called evil. It is a subjective qualification supported by a more or less general consent. Deviation from the numen seems to be universally understood as being the worst and the most original sin.

Letter to the Rev. H. L. Philp, 11 June 1957, *Letters, Vol. II*, p. 370.

Today as never before it is important that human beings should not overlook the danger of the evil lurking within them. It is unfortunately only too real, which is why psychology must insist on the reality of evil and must reject any definition that regards it as insignificant or actually non-existent. Psychology is an empirical science and deals with realities.

Aion (1951), CW 9ii, § 98.

[W]hen you study carefully the true biography of the individual—of course no written biography is really true, I mean the biography as the doctor sees it—you come to the conclusion that if there had not been a certain evil, a certain good would also not have been. Without mistakes or sins, the best moral qualities would never have developed. For what is morality without freedom? Where there is no freedom, there is no morality. The thief in jail is not moral just because for the moment he cannot steal, he is a caged animal. Let him be made cashier of a big bank where he has the opportunity to steal every day, and then if he doesn't steal, you can say he is all right, he is no thief any longer. If there is no freedom to do wrong, there is never the choice between good and evil, so a specifically moral action is simply prohibited by a sort of moral cage. If there is freedom, there is the chance of choice, there is the ultimate fight between good and evil. And sometimes it is a much greater moral achievement if one chooses to lie than to tell the truth. It is often the case that a thing which would be wrong, looked at from the standpoint of the four hundred million people, is the only right thing in the individual case. When it comes to the individual, it is exactly like going into the interior of the atom, where the natural law doesn't count any longer. The moral laws that are good for the four hundred millions come to an end, just as the natural law in the interior of the atom comes to an end; it is irrational. And so the human individual in the zone of his moral ethical freedom is irrational. There you simply cannot judge. The mistake is that we believe (and it is not the worst and most stupid people who believe it) that this general moral law is absolutely valid throughout the whole universe—as we used to suppose that natural laws applied to the interior of the atom. It is a great discovery of recent years that these natural laws have not a universal application; they do not apply to the facts in the interior of the atom.

Visions: Notes of the Seminar Given in 1930–1934, Vol. I (3 December 1930), p. 137.

[I]n the self good and evil are indeed closer than identical twins!

Psychology and Alchemy (1944), CW 12, § 24.

[W]here is a height without depth, and how can there be light that throws no shadow? There is no good that is not opposed by evil.

"Woman in Europe" (1927), CW 10, § 271.

You can never deny your knowledge of good and evil to yourself, so that you could betray your good in order to live evil. For as soon as you separate good and evil, you recognize them. They are united only in growth. But you grow if you stand still in the greatest doubt, and therefore steadfastness in great doubt is a veritable flower of life.

The Red Book (1915/2009), p. 301.

If, as many are fain to believe, the unconscious were only nefarious, only evil, then the situation would be simple and the path clear: to do good and to eschew evil. But what is "good" and what is "evil"? The unconscious is not just evil by nature, it is also the source of the highest good: not only dark but also light, not only bestial, semi-human and demonic but superhuman, spiritual, and, in the classical sense of the word, "divine."

The Psychology of the Transference (1946), CW 16, § 389.

In dealing with darkness you have got to cling to the Good, otherwise the devil devours you. You need every bit of your goodness in dealing with Evil and just there. To keep the light alive in the darkness, that's the point, and only there your candle makes sense.

Letter to Victor White, 24 November 1953, *The Jung-White Letters*,
p. 219.

The fact that *deity and devil belong together* also plays a great role in alchemy.

Children's Dreams: Notes from the Seminar Given in 1936–1940,
p. 373.

[T]he devil is a preliminary stage of individuation, in the negative it has the same goal as the divine quaternity, namely, wholeness.

Although it is still darkness, it already carries the germ of light within itself. Its activities are still dangerous and deadly, but at the same time it is like the darkness of earth in which the seed germinates.

Children's Dreams: Notes from the Seminar Given in 1936–1940,
p. 372.

If you take the pairs of opposites you are almost supposing two parties at war with one another—this is a dualistic conception. Ambivalence is a monistic conception; there the opposites do not appear as split apart, but as contrasting aspects of one and the same thing. Take for instance a man who has good and bad sides—such a man is ambivalent. We say about him that he is weak, that he is torn between God and the Devil—all the good is in God, all the bad in the Devil; and he is an atom swaying between the two, and you can never tell what he is going to do; his character has never established itself, but remains ambivalent. On the other hand, we can have a son who stands in between conflicting parents—nothing said of his character, he is the victim of these opposites; and so he can remain indefinitely. One had to invent the term "image" to meet this situation. Such a person can make no progress until he realizes that he has only stated half the case when he thinks himself victimized between the pairs of opposites, father and mother. He must know that he carries the images of the two within himself, and that within his own mind such a conflict is going on—in other words, that he is ambivalent. Until he comes to this realization, he can use the actual parents or their images as weapons with which to protect himself against meeting life. If he admits that the conflicting parties are parts of himself, he assumes responsibility for the problem they represent. In the same way I can see no sense in our blaming the war for things that have happened to us. Each of us carried within himself the elements that brought on the war.

*Introduction to Jungian Psychology: Notes of the Seminar on
Analytical Psychology Given in 1925,* p. 92.

You suffer from evil because you love it secretly and are unaware of your love. You wish to escape your predicament, and you begin to hate evil. And once more you are bound to evil through your hate, since whether you love or hate it, it makes no difference: you are bound to evil. Evil is to be accepted. What we want remains in our hands. What we do not want, and yet is stronger than us, sweeps us away and we cannot stop it without damaging ourselves, for our force remains in evil. Thus we probably have to accept our evil without love and hate, recognizing that it exists and must have its share in life. In doing so, we can deprive it of the power it has to overwhelm us.

The Red Book (1915/2009), p. 288.

Evil cannot be eradicated once and for all; it is an inevitable component of life and is not to be had without paying for it. The thief whom the police do not catch has, nonetheless, robbed himself, and the murderer is his own executioner.

Mysterium Coniunctionis (1955–56), CW 14, § 202.

It is, however, true that much of the evil in the world comes from the fact that man in general is hopelessly unconscious, as it is also true that with increasing insight we can combat this evil at its source in ourselves, in the same way that science enables us to deal effectively with injuries inflicted from without.

"The Spiritual Problem of Modern Man" (1928/1931), CW 10, § 166.

For where is a height without depth, and how can there be light that throws no shadow? There is no good that is not opposed by evil.

"Woman in Europe" (1927), CW 10, § 271.

It is obviously a moment of supreme possibilities both for good and for evil. Usually, however, it is first one and then the other: the good man succumbs to evil, the sinner is converted to good, and that, to an uncritical eye, is the end of the matter. But those endowed with a finer moral sense or deeper insight cannot deny that this seeming one-after-another is in reality a happening of events side-by-side, and perhaps no one has realized this more clearly than St. Paul, who knew that he bore a thorn in the flesh and that the messenger of Satan smote him in the face lest he be "exalted above measure." The one-after-another is a bearable prelude to the deeper knowledge of the side-by-side, for this is an incomparably more difficult problem. Again, the view that good and evil are spiritual forces outside us, and that man is caught in the conflict between them, is more bearable by far than the insight that the opposites are the ineradicable and indispensable preconditions of all psychic life, so much so that life itself is guilt. Even a life dedicated to God is still lived by an ego, which speaks of an ego and asserts an ego in God's despite, which does not instantly merge itself with God but reserves for itself a freedom and a will which it sets up outside God and against him. How *can* it do this against the overwhelming might of God? Only through self-assertion, which is as sure of its free will as Lucifer. All distinction from God is separation, estrangement, a falling away. The Fall was inevitable even in paradise. Therefore Christ is "without the stain of sin," because he stands for the whole of the Godhead and is not distinct from it by reason of his manhood. Man, however, is branded by the stain of separation from God. This state of things would be insupportable if there were nothing to set against evil but the law and the Decalogue, as in pre-Christian Judaism—until the reformer and rabbi Jesus tried to introduce the more advanced and psychologically more correct view that not fidelity to the law but love and kindness are the antithesis of evil.

Mysterium Coniunctionis (1955–56), CW 14, § 206.

It is indeed no small matter of know of one's guilt and one's own evil, and there is certainly nothing to be gained by losing sight of one's shadow. When we are conscious of our guilt we are in a more favourable position—we can at least hope to change and improve ourselves. As we know, anything that remains in the unconscious is incorrigible; psychological corrections can be made only in consciousness. Consciousness of guilt can therefore act as a powerful moral stimulus. In every treatment of neurosis the discovery of the shadow is indispensable, otherwise nothing changes. In this respect, I rely on those parts of the German body-politic which have remained sound to draw conclusions from the facts. Without guilt, unfortunately, there can be no psychic maturation and no widening of the spiritual horizon. Was it not Meister Eckhart who said: "For this reason God is willing to bear the brunt of sins and often winks at them, mostly sending them to people for whom he has prepared some high destiny. See! Who was dearer to our Lord or more intimate with him than his apostles? Not one of them but fell into mortal sin, and all were mortal sinners."

"After the Catastrophe" (1945), CW 10, § 440.

Did you ever think of the evil in you? Oh, you spoke of it, you mentioned it, and you confessed it smilingly, as a generally human vice, or a recurring misunderstanding. But did you know what evil is, and that it stands precisely right behind your virtues, that it is also your virtues themselves, as their inevitable substance? You locked Satan in the abyss for a millennium, and when the millennium had passed, you laughed at him, since he had become a children's fairy tale. But if the dreadful great one raises his head, the world winces. The most extreme coldness draws near.

The Red Book (1915/2009), p. 274.

[T]he grand plan on which the unconscious life of the psyche is constructed is so inaccessible to our understanding that we can never know what evil may not be necessary in order to produce good by enantiodromia, and what good may very possibly lead to evil.

"The Phenomenology of the Spirit in Fairytales" (1945/1948), CW 9i, § 397.

In the Christ symbol the conquest of evil is suggested by the descent into hell and the breaking open of its gates. But nobody has ever heard that the devil departed this life afterwards; on the contrary, the authentic New Testament view is that after the thousand-year reign of Christ he shall be loosed again on earth in all his youthful freshness, in the form of Antichrist. Also, as you rightly point out, a strong light is the best shadow-projector, provided that there is something to cast a shadow. Even the saints cast a shadow. We do not know whether there is more good than evil or whether the good is stronger. We can only hope that the good will predominate. If good is identified with constructiveness, there is some probability that life will go on in a more or less endurable form; but if destructiveness were to prevail, the world would surely have done itself to death long ago. As that hasn't happened yet, we may suppose that the positive exceeds the negative. Hence the optimistic assumption of psychotherapy that conscious realization accentuates the good more than the overshadowing evil. Becoming conscious reconciles the opposites and thus creates a higher third.

Letter to Helen Kiener, 14 May 1955, *Letters, Vol. II*, pp. 253–54.

I understood that the God whom we seek in the absolute was not to be found in absolute beauty, goodness, seriousness, elevation, humanity or even in godliness. Once the God was there.

I understood that the new God would be in the relative. If the God is absolute beauty and goodness, how should he encompass the fullness of life, which is beautiful and hateful, good and evil, laughable and serious, human and inhuman? How can man live in the womb of the God if the Godhead himself attests only to one-half of him?

If we have risen near the heights of good and evil, then our badness and hatefulness lie in the most extreme torment. Man's torment is so great and the air of the heights so weak that he can hardly live anymore.

The Red Book (1915/2009), p. 243.

You cannot keep on the white side only, you have to admit that the spirit of life will at times take on the aspect of evil. Life consists of night and day, and the night is just as long as the day; so evil and good are pairs of opposites without which there is no energy and no life. They are the Yang and the Yin and they are necessary. Even the Holy Ghost has to turn into a bird of prey in order to snatch the germ of life. The content of life is not always above, sometimes it is below. That is the important truth.

> *Visions: Notes of the Seminar Given in 1930–1934, Vol. I* (3 December 1930), p. 140.

We *can* act differently, if we want to.

> *Aion* (1951), CW 9ii, § 114.

Touching evil brings with it the grave peril of succumbing to it. We must, therefore, no longer succumb to anything at all, not even to good. A so-called good to which we succumb loses its ethical character. Not that there is anything bad in it on that score, but to have succumbed to it may breed trouble. Every form of addiction is bad, no matter whether the narcotic be alcohol or morphine or idealism. We must beware of thinking of good and evil as absolute opposites. The criterion of ethical action can no longer consist in the simple view that good has the force of a categorical imperative, while so-called evil can resolutely be shunned. Recognition of the reality of evil necessarily relativizes the good, and the evil likewise, converting both into halves of a paradoxical whole.

In practical terms, this means that good and evil are no longer so self-evident. We have to realize that each represents a *judgment*. In view of the fallibility of all human judgment, we cannot believe that we will always judge rightly. We might so easily be the victims of misjudgment. The ethical problem is affected by this principle only to the extent that we become somewhat uncertain about moral evaluations. Nevertheless we have to make ethical decisions. The relativity of "good" and "evil" by no means signifies that these categories are invalid, or do not exist. Moral judgment is always present and carries with it characteristic psychological consequences. I have pointed out many times that as in the past, so in the future the wrong we have done, thought, or intended will wreak its vengeance on our souls. Only the contents of judgment are subject to the differing conditions of time and place and, therefore, take correspondingly different forms. For moral evaluation is always founded upon the apparent certitudes of a moral code which pretends to know precisely what is good and what evil. But once we know how uncertain the foundation is, ethical decision becomes a subjective, creative act. We can convince ourselves of its validity only *Deo concendente* [by the grace of God]—that is, there must be a spontaneous and decisive impulse on the part of the unconscious. Ethics itself, the decision between good and evil, is not affected by this impulse, only made more difficult for us. Nothing can spare us the torment of ethical decision. Nevertheless, harsh as it may sound, we must have the freedom in some circumstances to avoid the known moral good and do what is considered to be evil, if our ethical decision so requires. In other words, again: we must not succumb to either of the opposites.

Memories, Dreams, Reflections (1962), pp. 329–30.

A religious conversation is inevitable with the devil, since he demands it, if one does not want to surrender to him unconditionally. Because religion is precisely what the devil and I cannot agree about. I must have it out with him, as I cannot expect that he as an independent personality would accept my standpoint without further ado.

I would be fleeing if I did not try to come to an understanding with him. If ever you have the rare opportunity to speak with the devil, then do not forget to confront him in all seriousness. He is your devil after all. The devil as the adversary is your own other standpoint; he tempts you and sets a stone in your path where you least want it. Taking the devil seriously does not mean going over to his side, or else one becomes the devil. Rather it means coming to an understanding. Thereby you accept your other standpoint. With that the devil fundamentally loses ground, and so do you. And that may be well and good.

Although the devil very much abhors religion for its particular solemnity and candor, it has become apparent, however, that it is precisely through religion that the devil can be brought to an understanding.

The Red Book (1915/2009), p. 261.

[T]he individual who wishes to have an answer to the problem of evil, as it is posed today, has need, first and foremost, of *self-knowledge*, that is, the utmost possible knowledge of his own wholeness. He must know relentlessly how much good he can do, and what crimes he is capable of, and must beware of regarding the one as real and the other as illusion. Both are elements within his nature, and both are bound to come to light in him, should he wish—as he ought—to live without self-deception or self-delusion.

Memories, Dreams, Reflections (1962), p. 330.

13
Body and Soul

Since psyche and matter are contained in one and the same world, and moreover are in continuous contact with one another and ultimately rest on irrepresentable, transcendental factors, it is not only possible but fairly probable, even, that psyche and matter are two different aspects of one and the same thing. The synchronicity phenomena point, it seems to me, in this direction, for they show that the nonpsychic can behave like the psychic, and vice versa, without there being any causal connection between them. Our present knowledge does not allow us to do much more than compare the relation of the psychic to the material world with two cones, whose apices, meeting in a point without extension—a real zeropoint—touch and do not touch.

"On the Nature of the Psyche" (1947/1954), CW 8, § 418.

Psyche cannot be totally different from matter, for how otherwise could it move matter? And matter cannot be alien to psyche, for how else could matter produce psyche? Psyche and matter exist in one and the same world, and each partakes of the other, otherwise any reciprocal action would be impossible. If research could only advance far enough, therefore, we should arrive at an ultimate agreement between physical and psychological concepts. Our present attempts may be bold, but I believe they are on the right lines.

Aion (1951), CW 9ii, § 413.

One cannot say that every symptom is a challenge and that every cure takes place in the intermediate realm between psyche and physis. One can only say that it is advisable to approach every illness from the psychological side as well, because this may be extraordinarily important for the healing process. When these two aspects work together, it may easily happen that the cure takes place in the intermediate realm, in other words that it consists of a *complexio oppositorum* [complexity of the opposites], like the *lapis*.[5] In this case the illness is in the fullest sense a stage of the individuation process.

Letter to Joachim Knopp, 10 July 1946, *Letters, Vol. I*, p. 429.

Probably in absolute reality there is no such thing as body and mind, but body and mind or soul are the same, the same life, subject to the same laws, and what the body does is happening in the mind.

Dream Analysis: Notes of the Seminar Given in 1928–1930 (14 November 1928), p. 20.

[5] See section 15, "Alchemical Transformation."

[W]e suffer very much from the fact that we consist of mind and have lost the body.

Nietzsche's Zarathustra: Notes of the Seminar Given in 1934–1939,
Vol. I (21 November 1934), p. 251.

Not infrequently the dreams show that there is a remarkable inner symbolical connection between an undoubted physical illness and a definite psychic problem, so that the physical disorder appears as a direct mimetic expression of the psychic situation. I mention this curious fact more for the sake of completeness than to lay any particular stress on this problematic phenomenon. It seems to me, however, that a definite connection does exist between physical and psychic disturbances and that its significance is generally underrated, though on the other hand it is boundlessly exaggerated owing to certain tendencies to regard physical disturbances merely as an expression of psychic disturbances, as is particularly the case with Christian Science. Dreams throw very interesting sidelights on the inter-functioning of body and psyche.

"General Aspects of Dream Psychology," (1916/1948), CW 8, § 502.

The materialistic premise is that the physical process causally determines the psychic process. The spiritualistic premise is the reverse of this. I think of this relationship in the physical sense as a reciprocal one, in which now one side and now the other acts as a cause. One could also say that under certain conditions the physical process reflects itself in the psychic, just as the psychic does in the physical.

Letter to Markus Fierz, 7 May 1945, *Letters, Vol. I*, p. 366.

[T]he body is a terribly awkward thing and so it is omitted; we can deal with things spiritually so much more easily without the despicable body.

Nietzsche's Zarathustra: Notes of the Seminar Given in 1934–1939,
Vol. I (23 May 1934), p. 63.

We are entangled in the roots, and we ourselves are the roots. We make roots, we cause roots to be, we are rooted in the soil, and there is no getting away for us, because we must be there as long as we live. That idea, that we can sublimate ourselves and become entirely spiritual and no hair left, is an inflation. I am sorry, that is impossible; it makes no sense.

The Psychology of Kundalini Yoga: Notes of the Seminar Given in 1932
(19 October, 1932), p. 29.

[T]he symptomatology of an illness is at the same time a natural attempt at healing.

"The Structure of the Psyche" (1927/1931), CW 8, §312.

Regarding organic illness (accidents, injuries, etc.) it can be stated with certainty that these things do at least have psychological syndromes, i.e., there is a concomitant psychic process which can sometimes also have an aetiological significance, so that it looks as though the illness were a psychic arrangement. At any rate there are numerous cases where the symptoms exhibit, in a positively remarkable way, a symbolic meaning even if no psychological pathogenesis is present.

Letter to Joachim Knopp, 10 July 1946, *Letters, Vol. I*, p. 429.

Even a ghost, if he wants to make an effect on this earth, always needs a body, a medium; otherwise he cannot ring bells or lift tables or anything that ghosts are supposed to do.

Nietzsche's Zarathustra: Notes of the Seminar Given in 1934–1939,
Vol. I (17 October 1934), p. 168.

Anything experienced outside of the body has the quality of being without body; so you must experience the whole thing over again, it must come in a new way. Then whatever you learn in analysis will happen to you in reality. It must be like that, because you are the point of identity, you are the one that experiences analysis and the one that experiences life. Whatever you experience outside of the body, in a dream for instance, is not experienced unless you take it into the body, because the body means the here and now. If you just have a dream and let it pass by you, nothing has happened at all, even if it is the most amazing dream; but if you look at it with the purpose of trying to understand it, and succeed in understanding it, then you have taken it into the here and now, the body being a visible expression of the here and now. For instance, if you had not taken your body into this room, nobody would know you were here; though even if you seem to be in the body, it is by no means sure that you are, because your mind might be wandering without your realizing it. Then whatever is going on here would not be realized; it would be like a vague dream that floats in and out, and nothing has happened.

> *Visions: Notes of the Seminar Given in 1930–1934, Vol. II* (21
> February 1934), p. 1316.

People who are not consciously aware of the body suffer from a certain unreality of life in that inter-relatedness through *participation mystique*; they don't know when they are hungry, and they neglect the simple functions of the body. I had a case, a girl of twenty-eight, who no longer heard her steps when she walked out in the street. That frightened her and she came to me. She dreamt that she was riding in a balloon—not in the basket but on top, high up in the air—and there she saw me with a rifle shooting at her from below. I finally shot her down. She was that girl I have told you about who never had seen her body. I suggested that she must bathe once in a while, and then she told me she had been brought up in a nunnery where the nuns taught her that the sight of the body was sin, that she should always cover her bath tub with a linen, so she never saw herself. I said: "Now go home and undress and stand before your long mirror and look at yourself." And when she came back, she said: "It was not so bad after all, only I think my legs are a bit too hairy!" That is the truth, that is the way people think and feel when they have such symptoms.

> *Nietzsche's Zarathustra: Notes of the Seminar Given in 1934–1939.*
> *Vol. I* (23 May 1934), p. 65.

Zarathustra says to go back to the body, go into the body, and then everything will be right, for there the greatest intelligence is hidden.

Nietzsche's Zarathustra: Notes of the Seminar Given in 1934–1939,
Vol. I (6 February 1935), p. 370.

[J]ust as there is a relationship of mind to body, so there is a relationship of body to earth.

"The Role of the Unconscious" (1918), CW 10, § 19.

For what is the body? The body is merely the visibility of the soul, the psyche; and the soul is the psychological experience of the body.

Nietzsche's Zarathustra: Notes of the Seminar Given in 1934–1939,
Vol. I (30 January 1935), p. 355.

[S]oul and body are not two things. They are one.

Nietzsche's Zarathustra: Notes of the Seminar Given in 1934–1939,
Vol. I (30 January 1935), p. 355.

The body is the past, our earth, the world of heretofore, but out of it rises a new light which is not identical with the body.

Visions: Notes of the Seminar Given in 1930–1934, Vol. I (27 May 1931), p. 374.

[I]nasmuch as the living body contains the secret of life, it is an intelligence. It is also a plurality which is gathered up in one mind, for the body is extended in space, and the here and the there are two things; what is in your toes is not in your fingers, and what is in your fingers is not in your ears or your stomach or your knees or anywhere else in your body. Each part is always something in itself. The different forms and localizations are all represented in your mind as more or less different facts, so there is a plurality. What you think with your head doesn't necessarily coincide with what you feel in your heart, and what your belly thinks is not what your mind thinks. The extension in space, therefore, creates a pluralistic quality in the mind. That is probably the reason why consciousness is possible.

Nietzsche's Zarathustra: Notes of the Seminar Given in 1934–1939,
Vol. I (6 February 1935), p. 360.

The synchronicity principle possesses properties that may help to clear up the body-soul problem. Above all it is a fact of causeless order, or rather, of meaningful orderedness, that may throw light on psychophysical parallelism. The "absolute knowledge" which is characteristic of synchronistic phenomena, a knowledge not mediated by the sense organs, supports the hypothesis of a self-subsistent meaning, or even expresses its existence. Such a form of existence can only be transcendental, since, as the knowledge of future or spatially distant events shows, it is contained in a psychically relative space and time, that is to say in an irrepresentable space-time continuum.

"Synchronicity: An Acausal Connecting Principle" (1952), CW 8,
§ 948.

You can be anything if you are a spirit, because you have no form, no shape, you are just gas. You can assume any form; you can be this or that; you can transform at will quite arbitrarily into God knows what. "But you should not think like that," or: "You should believe something, that will save you." Believe if you can! You see, that is just the trouble. And why can't you? Because you have a body. If you were a spirit you could be anywhere, but the damnable fact is that you are rooted just here, and you cannot jump out of your skin; you have definite necessities. You cannot get away from the fact of your sex, for instance, or of the color of your eyes, or the health or the sickness of your body, your physical endurance. Those are definite facts which make you an individual, a self that is just yourself and nobody else. If you were a spirit you could exchange your form every minute for another one—but being in the body you are caught; therefore, the body is such an awkward thing: it is a definite nuisance. All people who claim to be spiritual try to get away from the fact of the body; they want to destroy it in order to be something imaginary, but they never will be that, because the body denies them; the body says otherwise. They think they can live without sex or feeding, without the ordinary human conditions; and it is a mistake, a lie, and the body denies their convictions.

Nietzsche's Zarathustra: Notes of the Seminar Given in 1934–1939,
Vol. I (23 May 1934), pp. 63–64.

Asthma is a suffocation phobia, and the more the fear increases, the more actual the suffocation, darkness, and unconsciousness.

Dream Analysis: Notes of the Seminar Given in 1928–1930 (6 March 1929), p. 154.

When you see that a certain spark of life has gone from the eye, the physical functioning of the body somewhere has gone wrong.

Dream Analysis: Notes of the Seminar Given in 1928–1930 (23 January 1929), p. 91.

We should return to the body in order to create spirit again; without body there is no spirit because spirit is a volatile substance of the body. The body is the alembic, the retort, in which materials are cooked, and out of that process develops the spirit, the effervescent thing that rises.

Nietzsche's Zarathustra: Notes of the Seminar Given in 1934–1939,
Vol. I (6 February 1935), p. 368.

I take his cancer to be a spontaneous growth, which originated in the part of the psyche that is not identical with consciousness. It appears as an autonomous function intruding upon consciousness.

Psychology and Religion (1938/1940), CW 11, § 21.

The spirit consists of possibilities—one could say the world of possibilities was the world of the spirit. The spirit can easily be anything, but the earth can only be something definite. So remaining true to the earth would mean maintaining your conscious relationship to the body. Don't run away and make yourself unconscious of bodily facts, for they keep you in real life and help you not to lose your real way in the world of mere possibilities where you are simply blindfolded. This is of course a somewhat one-sided teaching, and to a person who is nothing but the body, it is all wrong. You must not forget that by far the majority of people are nothing but body. This teaching, therefore, is only valid for those who have lost it, who have been deceived by the spirit.

Nietzsche's Zarathustra: Notes of the Seminar Given in 1934–1939,
(23 May 1934), p. 66.

Those who are able to express the unconscious by means of bodily movements are rather rare. The disadvantage that movements cannot easily be fixed in the mind must be met by making careful drawings of movements afterwards, so that they shall not be lost to the memory. Still rarer, but equally valuable, is automatic writing, direct or with the planchette [a device for writing under supposed spirit guidance]. This, too, yields useful results.

"The Transcendent Function" ([1916]/1958), CW 8, § 171.

There is little difference between Nietzsche's life and the life of a saint; he forsook his ordinary life, and went into the woods. The woods were called Rapallo, the Engadine, Nice, and so on, but he was alone, a hermit. He lived entirely in his books. He devoted himself to spiritual practices, one could say, and he lost the connection with the world of the flesh. He really became a sort of modern saint; the spiritual side got hold of him more than was good for the solution of his moral problem. For to solve the problem one must give equal value. We cannot say the side of the spirit is twice as good as the other side; we must bring the pairs of opposites together in an altogether different way, where the rights of the body are just as much recognized as the rights of the spirit.

Nietzsche's Zarathustra: Notes of the Seminar Given in 1934–1939,
Vol. I (7 November 1934), p. 235.

[I]t had become clear to me, in a flash of illumination, that for me the only possible goal was psychiatry. Here alone the two currents of my interest could flow together and in a united stream dig their own bed. Here was the empirical field common to biological and spiritual facts, which I had everywhere sought and nowhere found. Here at last was the place where the collision of nature and spirit became a reality.

Memories, Dreams, Reflections (1962), pp. 108–9.

14
Creativity and the Imagination

The definiteness and directedness of the conscious mind are extremely important acquisitions which humanity has bought at a very heavy sacrifice, and which in turn have rendered humanity the highest service. Without them science, technology, and civilization would be impossible, for they all presuppose the reliable continuity and directedness of the conscious process. For the statesman, doctor, and engineer as well as for the simplest labourer, these qualities are absolutely indispensable. We may say in general that social worthlessness increases to a degree that these qualities are impaired by the unconscious. Great artists and others distinguished by creative gifts are, of course, exceptions to this rule. The very advantage that such individuals enjoy consists precisely in the permeability of the partition separating the conscious and the unconscious. But, for those professions and social activities which require just this continuity and reliability, these exceptional human beings are as a rule of little value.

"The Transcendent Function" ([1916]/1958), CW 8, § 135.

The creative process, so far as we are able to follow it at all, consists in the unconscious activation of an archetypal image, and in elaborating and shaping this image into the finished work. By giving it shape, the artist translates it into the language of the present, and so makes it possible for us to find our way back to the deepest springs of life. Therein lies the social significance of art: it is constantly at work educating the spirit of the age, conjuring up the forms in which the age is most lacking. The unsatisfied yearning of the artist reaches back to the primordial image in the unconscious which is best fitted to compensate the inadequacy and one-sidedness of the present. The artist seizes on this image, and in raising it from deepest unconsciousness he brings it into relation with conscious values, thereby transforming it until it can be accepted by the minds of his contemporaries according to their powers.

"On the Relation of Analytical Psychology to Poetry" (1922), CW 15, § 130.

I am indeed convinced that creative imagination is the only primordial phenomenon accessible to us, the real Ground of the psyche, the only immediate reality.

Letter to Kurt Plachte, 10 January 1929, *Letters, Vol. I*, p. 60.

To give birth to the ancient in a new time is creation. This is the creation of the new, and that redeems me. Salvation is the resolution of the task. The task is to give birth to the old in a new time.

The Red Book (1915/2009), p. 311.

It is to this unconscious that all those who do creative work must turn. All new ideas and combinations of ideas are premeditated by the unconscious.

"Cryptomnesia" (1905), CW 1, § 172.

[I]nasmuch as you say these creative forces are in Nietzsche or in me or anywhere else, you cause an inflation, because man does not possess creative powers, he is possessed by them. That is the truth. If he allows himself to be thoroughly possessed by them without questioning, without looking at them, there is no inflation, but the moment he splits off, when he thinks, "I am the fellow," an inflation follows.

> *Nietzsche's Zarathustra*: Notes of the Seminar Given in 1934–1939,
> *Vol. I* (23 May 1934), p. 57.

In order to do anything creative, we must be unhistorical. Creation begins today, it has no history and no cause, creation is always creation from nothing.

> *Visions*: Notes of the Seminar Given in 1930–1934, Vol. II (7 June
> 1933), p. 1035.

The daimon of creativity has ruthlessly had its way with me.

> *Memories, Dreams, Reflections* (1962), p. 358.

Only in our creative acts do we step forth into the light and see ourselves whole and complete.

> "Analytical Psychology and *Weltanschauung*" (1928/1931), CW 8,
> § 737.

Through being creative one creates the thing that has come into existence at this moment, that was in a potential existence before.

> *Nietzsche's Zarathustra*: Notes of the Seminar Given in 1934–1939,
> *Vol. I* (6 June 1934), p. 73.

By the "creative element" you probably mean a person's faculty. Your question as to whether this faculty is present from the beginning is not easy to answer. There are undoubtedly cases where one can take it as certain that it was present from the start, but in other cases it seems to develop in the course of life. I personally incline to the view that this faculty, like everything else, was present from the start.

> Letter to D. Tochtermann, 13 January 1940, *Letters, Vol. I*, p. 281.

Creative life always stands outside convention. That is why, when the mere routine of life predominates in the form of convention and tradition, there is bound to be a destructive outbreak of creative energy. This outbreak is a catastrophe only when it is a mass phenomenon, but never in the individual who consciously submits to these higher powers and serves them with all his strength.

"The Development of Personality" (1934), CW 17, § 305.

Art is a kind of innate drive that seizes a human being and makes him his instrument. The artist is not a person endowed with free will who seeks his own ends, but one who allows art to realize its purposes through him. As a human being he may have moods and a will and personal aims, but as an artist he is "man" in a higher sense—he is "collective man," a vehicle and moulder of the unconscious psychic life of mankind. That is his office, and it is sometimes so heavy a burden that he is fated to sacrifice happiness and everything that makes life worth living for the ordinary human being.

"Psychology and Literature" (1930/1950), CW 15, § 157.

We cannot, therefore, afford to be indifferent to the poets, since in their principal works and deepest inspirations they create from the very depths of the collective unconscious, voicing aloud what others only dream.

Psychological Types (1921), CW 6, § 323.

[T]he fight against the paralysing grip of the unconscious calls forth man's creative powers. That is the source of all creativity, but it needs heroic courage to do battle with these forces and to wrest from them the treasure hard to attain. Whoever succeeds in this has triumphed indeed.

Symbols of Transformation (1912/1952), CW 5, § 523.

[N]othing can be created without destruction. There is an old Latin sentence that expresses it very nicely: *Creatio unius est corruptio alterius*, "The creation of the one is the corruption of the other."

Nietzsche Seminars: Notes of the Seminar Given in 1934–1939, Vol. II
(5 February 1936), p. 818.

You cannot put something on a table which is already laden; you must first clear those things away in order to put new ones in their place. And to build a house where an old house stands, you must first destroy the old house. We must go a bit deeper and realize that with the instinct of creation is always connected a destructive something; the creation in its own essence is also destructive. You see that quite clearly in the moment when you check the creative impulse; nothing is more poisonous to the nervous system than a disregarded or checked creative impulse. It even destroys people's organic health. It is dangerous because there is that extraordinary destructive quality in the creative thing. Just because it is the deepest instinct, the deeper power in man, a power which is beyond conscious control, and because it is on the other side the function which creates the greatest value, it is most dangerous to interfere with it.

Nietzsche's Zarathustra: Notes of the Seminar Given in 1934–1939,
Vol. I (30 October 1935), p. 654.

[Y]ou experience that great relief when you realize that you are not identical with the creative power. For instance, if Nietzsche could have realized that he was not identical with Zarathustra, I don't know what it might not have done for his brain. To feel that you are the creator is a terrible burden, hellish anguish, provided of course that you are creator enough to feel it consciously. The creator is usually like a child that just plays with the gods and can produce the most awful monster without seeing it. Many artists can only produce because they don't know what they are producing; the moment they know, the creation is completely stopped. For then they begin to reflect; then they feel responsible and cannot play like the gods, unless they fulfil the psychological demand that they dissociate themselves from the creation, from the archetype, from the creative impulse itself. If they can do that, they can go on creating; then they can allow the god to play. It needs a certain faculty, the art to live amorally; if any kind of morality is caught up with the creative impulse, it simply cannot work and it will destroy you. On the other hand, if you destroy the creative impulse, you will destroy the intrinsic value of the individual at the same time. But you can still live on as a wall decoration.

Nietzsche's Zarathustra: Notes of the Seminar Given in 1934–1939,
Vol. I (30 October 1935), pp. 654–55.

[T]he creative impulse has always been the maker of the individual. You see, creative impulse does not appear in everybody in the same strength: certain individuals are picked, they have a particular gift. They create something which is striking and they are then the innovators, and stick out like old man Prometheus, that great sinner against the gods. He was an individual and he was punished for it, but he was made to stand out through his creative impulse. Naturally, the creative impulse is forever the maker of personality and uses that individual form, that distinction. Therefore it is absolutely necessary that, in the process of individuation, everybody should become aware of his creative instinct, no matter how small it is.

Nietzsche's Zarathustra: Notes of the Seminar Given in 1934–1939,
Vol. I (6 November 1935), p. 667.

A person must pay dearly for the divine gift of creative fire. It is as though each of us were born with a limited store of energy. In the artist, the strongest force in his makeup, that is, his creativeness, will seize and all but monopolize this energy, leaving so little left over that nothing of value can come of it. The creative impulse can drain him of his humanity to such a degree that the personal ego can exist only on a primitive or inferior level and is driven to develop all sort of defects—ruthlessness, selfishness ("autoeroticism"), vanity, and other infantile traits. These inferiorities are the only means by which it can maintain its vitality and prevent itself from being wholly depleted.

"Psychology and Literature" (1930/1950), CW 15, § 158.

[T]he more the creation is significant the less you are capable of reducing it to the personal psychology. Freud tried it, for instance—tried to reduce a very perfect work of art to the very imperfect personal psychology of the artist. But nothing comes out of the destruction of a work of art.

Nietzsche's Zarathustra: Notes of the Seminar Given in 1934–1939,
Vol. I (6 November 1935), p. 667.

[W]e know that every good idea and all creative work are the offspring of the imagination, and have their source in what one is pleased to call infantile fantasy. Not the artist alone, but every creative individual whatsoever owes all that is greatest in his life to fantasy. The dynamic principle of fantasy is *play*, a characteristic also of the child, and as such it appears inconsistent with the principle of serious work. But without this playing with fantasy no creative work has ever yet come to birth. The debt we owe to the play of imagination is incalculable. It is therefore short-sighted to treat fantasy, on account of its risky or unacceptable nature, as a thing of little worth. It must not be forgotten that it is just in the imagination that a man's highest value may lie.

Psychological Types (1921), CW 6, § 93.

Besides the obvious personal sources, creative fantasy also draws upon the forgotten and long buried primitive mind with its host of images, which are to be found in the mythologies of all ages and all peoples. The sum of these images constitutes the collective unconscious, a heritage which is potentially present in every individual. It is the psychic correlate of the differentiation of the human brain. This is the reason why mythological images are able to arise spontaneously over and over again, and to agree with one another not only in all the corners of the wide earth, but at all times. As they are present always and everywhere, it is an entirely natural proceeding to relate mythologems, which may be very far apart both temporally and ethnically, to an individual fantasy system. The creative substratum is everywhere this same human psyche and this same human brain, which, with relatively minor variations, functions everywhere in the same way.

Symbols of Transformation (1912/1952), CW 5, p. xxix.

You can dismiss a thing entirely, but you have to search for its symbolic meaning, and the symbolic meaning is the thing that has to be accepted. The best way of dealing with the unconscious is the creative way. Create for instance a fantasy. Work it out with all the means at your disposal. Work it out as if you were it or in it, as you would work out a real situation in life which you cannot escape. All the difficulties you overcome in such a fantasy are symbolic expressions of psychological difficulties in yourself, and inasmuch as you overcome them in your imagination you also overcome them in your psyche.

Letter to Mrs. N., 25 November 1932, *Letters, Vol. I*, p. 109.

When you observe the world you see people, you see houses, you see the sky, you see tangible objects. But when you observe yourself within, you see moving images, a world of images, generally known as fantasies. Yet these fantasies are facts.

"The Houston Films" (1957), *C. G. Jung Speaking*, p. 302.

Take the unconscious in one of its handiest forms, say a spontaneous fantasy, a dream, an irrational mood, an affect, or something of the kind, and operate with it. Give it your special attention, concentrate on it, and observe its alterations objectively. Spare no effort to devote yourself to this task, follow the subsequent transformations of the spontaneous fantasy attentively and carefully. Above all, don't let anything from outside, that does not belong to it, get into it, for the fantasy-image has "everything it needs." In this way one is certain of not interfering by conscious caprice and of giving the unconscious a free hand. In short, the alchemical operation seems to us the equivalent of the psychological process of active imagination.

Mysterium Coniunctionis (1955–56), CW 14, § 749.

The capacity for inner dialogue is a touchstone for outer objectivity.

"The Transcendent Function" ([1916]/1958), CW 8, § 187.

The art of letting things happen, action through non-action, letting go of oneself as taught by Meister Eckhart, became the key that opens the door to the way. We must be able to let things happen in the psyche. For us, this is an art of which most people know nothing. Consciousness is forever interfering, helping, correcting, and negating, never leaving the psychic processes to grow in peace. It would be simple enough, if only simplicity were not the most difficult of all things. To begin with, the task consists solely in observing objectively how a fragment of fantasy develops. Nothing could be simpler, and yet right here the difficulties begin. Apparently one has no fantasy fragments—or yes, there's one, but it is too stupid! Dozens of good reasons are brought against it. One cannot concentrate on it—it is too boring—what would come of it anyway—it is "nothing but" this or that, and so on. The conscious mind raises innumerable objections, in fact it often seems bent on blotting out the spontaneous fantasy activity in spite of real insight and in spite of the firm determination to allow the psychic process to go forward without interference.

"Commentary on *The Secret of the Golden Flower*" (1929), CW 13, § 20.

It is probable that passive fantasies always have their origin in an unconscious process that is antithetical to consciousness, but invested with approximately the same amount of energy as the conscious attitude, and therefore capable of breaking through the latter's resistance. Active fantasies, on the other hand, owe their existence not so much to this unconscious process as to a conscious propensity to assimilate hints or fragments of lightly-toned unconscious complexes and, by associating them with parallel elements, to elaborate them in clearly visual form. It is not necessarily a question of a dissociated psychic state, but rather of a positive participation of consciousness.

Whereas passive fantasy not infrequently bears a morbid stamp or at least shows some trace of abnormality, active fantasy is one of the highest forms of psychic activity. For here the conscious and the unconscious personality of the subject flow together into a common product in which both are united. Such a fantasy can be the highest expression of the unity of a man's *individuality*, and it may even create that individuality by giving perfect expression to its unity. As a general rule, passive fantasy is never the expression of a unified individuality since, as already observed, it presupposes a considerable degree of dissociation based in turn on a marked conscious/unconscious opposition. Hence the fantasy that irrupts into consciousness from such a state can never be the perfect expression of a unified individuality, but will represent mainly the standpoint of the unconscious personality. The life of St. Paul affords a good example of this: his conversion to Christianity signified an acceptance of the hitherto unconscious standpoint and a repression of the hitherto anti-Christian one, which then made itself felt in his hysterical attacks. Passive fantasy, therefore, is always in need of conscious *criticism*, lest it merely reinforce the standpoint of the unconscious opposite. Whereas active fantasy, as the product of a conscious attitude *not* opposed to the unconscious, and of unconscious processes not opposed but merely compensatory to consciousness, does not require criticism so much as *understanding*.

Psychological Types (1921), CW 6, §§ 713–14.

By means of "active imagination" we are put in a position of advantage, for we can then make the discovery of the archetype without sinking back into the instinctual sphere, which would only lead to blank unconsciousness or, worse still, to some kind of intellectual substitute for instinct.

"On the Nature of the Psyche" (1947/1954), CW 8, § 414.

From the beginning I had conceived my voluntary confrontation with the unconscious as a scientific experiment which I myself was conducting and in whose outcome I was vitally interested. Today I might equally well say that it was an experiment which was being conducted on *me*. One of the greatest difficulties for me lay in dealing with my negative feelings. I was voluntarily submitting myself to emotions of which I could not really approve, and I was writing down fantasies which often struck me as nonsense, and toward which I had strong resistances. For as long as we do not understand their meaning, such fantasies are a diabolical mixture of the sublime and the ridiculous. It cost me a great deal to undergo them, but I had been challenged by fate. Only by extreme effort was I finally able to escape from the labyrinth.

In order to grasp the fantasies which were stirring in me "underground," I knew that I had to let myself plummet down into them, as it were. I felt not only violent resistance to this, but a distinct fear. For I was afraid of losing command of myself and becoming a prey to the fantasies—and as a psychiatrist I realized only too well what that meant. After prolonged hesitation, however, I saw that there was no other way out. I had to take the chance, had to try to gain power over them; for I realized that if I did not do so, I ran the risk of their gaining power over me. A cogent motive for my making the attempt was the conviction that I could not expect of my patients something I did not dare to do myself. The excuse that a helper stood at their side would not pass muster, for I was well aware that the so-called helper—that is, myself—could not help them unless he knew their fantasy material from his own direct experience, and that at present all he possessed were a few theoretical prejudices of dubious value. This idea—that I was committing myself to a dangerous enterprise not for myself alone, but also for the sake of my patients—helped me over several critical phases.

Memories, Dreams, Reflections (1962), pp. 178–79.

Perhaps my unconscious is forming a personality that is not me, but which is insisting on coming through to expression.

Introduction to Jungian Psychology: Notes of the Seminar on Analytical Psychology Given in 1925, p. 45.

[I]t is a principle in analysis that we always try to dissociate from the unconscious, to make a difference between ourselves and the voice, or the influence, or the mana, or the archetype—whatever you like to call it. And you can make that difference by criticizing carefully whatever your experience may be. But if you take it for granted in a general way that of course your thoughts, for instance, are all your own, such an obscurity prevails that you can discern nothing. Make the simple experiment of criticizing your own thoughts.

Nietzsche's Zarathustra: Notes of the Seminar Given in 1934–1939,
Vol. I (5 December 1934), p. 295.

Philemon and other figures of my fantasies brought home to me the crucial insight that there are things in the psyche which I do not produce, but which produce themselves and have their own life. Philemon represented a force which was not myself. In my fantasies I held conversations with him, and he said things which I had not consciously thought. For I observed clearly that it was he who spoke, not I. He said I treated thoughts as if I generated them myself, but in his view thoughts were like animals in the forest, or people in a room, or birds in the air, and added, "If you should see people in a room, you would not think that you had made those people, or that you were responsible for them." It was he who taught me psychic objectivity, the reality of the psyche. Through him the distinction was clarified between myself and the object of my thought. He confronted me in an objective manner, and I understood that there is something in me which can say things that I do not know and do not intend, things which may even be directed against me. Psychologically, Philemon represented superior insight. He was a mysterious figure to me. At times he seemed to me quite real, as if he were a living personality. I went walking up and down the garden with him, and to me he was what the Indians call a guru.

Memories, Dreams, Reflections (1962), p. 183.

The essential thing is to differentiate oneself from these unconscious contents by personifying them, and at the same time to bring them into relationship with consciousness. That is the technique for stripping them of their power. It is not too difficult to personify them, as they always possess a certain degree of autonomy, a separate identity of their own. Their autonomy is a most uncomfortable thing to reconcile oneself to, and yet the very fact that the unconscious presents itself in that way gives us the best means of handling it.

Memories, Dreams, Reflections (1962), p. 187.

When I was writing down these fantasies, I once asked myself, "What am I really doing? Certainly this has nothing to do with science. But then what is it?" Whereupon a voice within me said, "It is art." I was astonished. It had never entered my head that what I was writing had any connection with art. Then I thought, "Perhaps my unconscious is forming a personality that is not me, but which is insisting on coming through to expression." I knew for a certainty that the voice had come from a woman. I recognized it as the voice of a patient, a talented psychopath who had a strong transference to me. She had become a living figure within my mind.

Memories, Dreams, Reflections (1962), p. 185.

In many cases it may be quite important for the patient to have some idea of the meaning of the fantasies produced. But it is of vital importance that he should experience them to the full and, in so far as intellectual understanding belongs to the totality of experience, also understand them. Yet I would not give priority to understanding. Naturally the doctor must be able to assist the patient in his understanding, but, since he will not and indeed cannot understand everything, the doctor should assiduously guard against clever feats of interpretation. For the important thing is not to interpret and understand the fantasies, but primarily to experience them.

The Relations between the Ego and the Unconscious (1916/1928),
CW 7, § 342.

[T]he fantasy, to be completely experienced, demands not just perception and passivity, but active participation. The patient would comply with this demand if he conducted himself in the fantasy as he would doubtless conduct himself in reality. He would never remain an idle spectator while his fiancée tried to drown herself; he would leap up and stop her. This should also happen in the fantasy. If he succeeds in behaving in the fantasy as he would behave in a similar situation in reality, he would prove that he was taking the fantasy seriously, i.e., assigning absolute reality value to the unconscious. In this way he would have won a victory over his one-sided intellectualism and, indirectly, would have asserted the validity of the irrational standpoint of the unconscious.

The Relations between the Ego and the Unconscious (1916/1928),
CW 7, § 350.

Fantasy is the creative function—the living form is a result of fantasy. Fantasy is a pre-stage of the symbol, but it is an essential characteristic of the symbol that it is not mere fantasy. We count upon fantasy to take us out of the impasse; for though people are not always eager to recognize the conflicts that are upsetting their lives, the dreams are always at work trying to tell on the one hand of the conflict, and on the other hand of the creative fantasy that will lead the way out. Then it becomes a matter of bringing the material into consciousness. One admits that one is in an impasse and gives free rein to the fantasy, but at the same time, the conscious must keep control in order to have a check on the tendency of nature to experiment. That is to say, one has to keep in mind that the unconscious can produce something disastrous to us. But on the other hand, one must be careful not to prescribe to the unconscious—it may be that a new way is required, and even one beset with disaster. Life often demands the trying out of new ways that are entirely unacceptable to the time in which we live, but we cannot shrink from undertaking a new way for that reason.

*Introduction to Jungian Psychology: Notes of the Seminar on
Analytical Psychology Given in 1925*, p. 11.

[S]witch off your noisy consciousness and listen quietly inwards and look at the images that appear before your inner eye, or hearken to the words which the muscles of your speech apparatus are trying to form. Write down what then comes without criticism. Images should be drawn or painted assiduously no matter whether you can do it or not.

Once you have got at least fragments of these contents, then you may meditate on them *afterwards*. Don't criticize anything away! If any questions arise, put them to the unconscious again the next day. Don't be content with your own explanations no matter how intelligent they are. Remember that your health is seriously at stake, and that the unconscious has an unknown and far-reaching control over it.

Treat any drawings the same way. Meditate on them afterwards and every day go on developing what is unsatisfactory about them. The important thing is to let the unconscious take the lead. You must always be convinced that you have mere after-knowledge and nothing else. In this case the unconscious really does know better.

Letter to Count Hermann Keyserling, 23 April 1931, *Letters, Vol. I*, p. 82.

The light that gradually dawns on him consists in his understanding that his fantasy is a real psychic process which is happening to him personally. Although, to a certain extent, he looks on from outside, impartially, he is also an acting and suffering figure in the drama of the psyche. This recognition is absolutely necessary and marks an important advance. So long as he simply looks at the pictures he is like the foolish Parsifal, who forgot to ask the vital question because he was not aware of his participation in the action. Then, if the flow of images ceases, next to nothing has happened even though the process is repeated a thousand times. But if you recognize your own involvement you yourself must enter into the process with your personal reactions, just as if you were one of the fantasy figures, or rather, as if the drama being enacted before your eyes were real. It is a psychic fact that this fantasy is happening, and it is as real as you—as a psychic entity—are real. If this crucial operation is not carried out, all the changes are left to the flow of images, and you yourself remain unchanged. As Dorn says, you will never make the One unless you become one yourself. It is, however, possible that if you have a dramatic fantasy you will enter the interior world of images as a *fictitious personality* and thereby prevent any real participation; it may even endanger consciousness because you then become the victim of your own fantasy and succumb to the powers of the unconscious, whose dangers the analyst knows all too well. But if you place yourself in the drama as you really are, not only does it gain in actuality but you also create, by your criticism of the fantasy, an effective counterbalance to its tendency to get out of hand. For what is now happening is the decisive rapprochement with the unconscious. This is where insight, the *unio mentalis* [mental union], begins to become real. What you are now creating is the beginning of individuation, whose immediate goal is the experience and production of the symbol of totality.

Mysterium Coniunctionis (1955–56), CW 14, § 753.

Continual conscious realization of unconscious fantasies, together with active participation in the fantastic events, has, as I have witnessed in a very large number of cases, the effect firstly of extending the conscious horizon by the inclusion of numerous unconscious contents; secondly of gradually diminishing the dominant influence of the unconscious; and thirdly of bringing about a change of personality.

The Relations between the Ego and the Unconscious (1916/1928), CW 7, § 358.

[A] fantasy needs to be understood both causally and purposively. Causally interpreted, it seems like a *symptom* of a physiological or personal state, the outcome of antecedent events. Purposively interpreted, it seems like a *symbol*, seeking to characterize a definite goal with the help of the material at hand, or trace out a line of future psychological development.

Psychological Types (1921), CW 6, § 720.

[T]here was a demonic strength in me, and from the beginning there was no doubt in my mind that I must find the meaning of what I was experiencing in these fantasies. When I endured the assaults of the unconscious I had an unswerving conviction that I was obeying a higher will, and that feeling continued to uphold me until I had mastered the task.

Memories, Dreams, Reflections (1962), p. 177.

[S]ince I did not know what was going on, I had no choice but to write everything down in the style selected by the unconscious itself. Sometimes it was as if I were hearing it with my ears, sometimes feeling it with my mouth, as if my tongue were formulating words; now and then I heard myself whispering aloud. Below the threshold of consciousness everything was seething with life.

Memories, Dreams, Reflections (1962), p. 178.

As the process of coming to terms with the counter-position has a total character, nothing is excluded. Everything takes part in the discussion, even if only fragments become conscious. Consciousness is continually widened through the confrontation with previously unconscious contents, or—to be more accurate—could be widened if it took the trouble to integrate them. That is naturally not always the case. Even if there is sufficient intelligence to understand the procedure, there may yet be a lack of courage and self-confidence, or one is too lazy, mentally and morally, or too cowardly, to make an effort. But where the necessary premises exist, the transcendent function not only forms a valuable addition to the psychotherapeutic treatment, but gives the patient the inestimable advantage of assisting the analyst on his own resources, and of breaking a dependence which is often felt as humiliating. It is a way of attaining liberation by one's own efforts and of finding the courage to be oneself.

Memories, Dreams, Reflections (1962), p. 193.

[Y]ou choose a dream, or some other fantasy-image, and concentrate on it by simply catching hold of it and looking at it. You can also use a bad mood as a starting-point, and then try to find out what sort of fantasy-image it will produce, or what image expresses this mood. You then fix this image in the mind by concentrating your attention. Usually it will alter, as the mere fact of contemplating it animates it. The alterations must be carefully noted down all the time, for they reflect the psychic processes in the unconscious background, which appear in the form of images consisting of conscious memory material. In this way conscious and unconscious are united, just as a waterfall connects above and below.

Mysterium Coniunctionis (1955–56), CW 14, § 706.

The art of it consists only in allowing our invisible partner to make herself heard, in putting the mechanism of expression momentarily at her disposal, without being overcome by the distaste one naturally feels at playing such an apparently ludicrous game with oneself, or by doubts as to the genuineness of the voice of one's interlocutor.

The Relations between the Ego and the Unconscious (1916/1928),
CW 7, § 323.

You are not only informed enough but also intelligent enough to go on for a long stretch on the assumption that I'm buried and that there is no analyst for you under the changing moon except the one that is in your own heart. As you will understand, this does not mean at all that you analyse and interpret your dreams according to the rules of the thumb, but that you do what we call in the German language, the "Auseinandersetzung mit dem Unbewusstsein" [Confrontation with the Unconscious], which is a dialectical procedure you carry through with yourself with the aid of active imagination. This is the best means I know to reduce an inordinate production of the unconscious. It doesn't seem right that a man like yourself is still dependent upon analysts. It is also not good for you, because it produces again and again a most unwholesome dissociation of your opposites, namely pride and humility. It will be good for your humility if you can accept the gifts of your unconscious guide that dwells in yourself, and it is good for your pride to humiliate itself to such an extent that you can accept what you receive. I don't intend to behave as if I were a corpse already. I'm therefore quite willing to help in your attempt in this direction, but I refuse in your own interest to plague myself with your material which is only helpful when you acquire its understanding by your own effort. Pride is a wonderful thing when you know how to fulfill its expectations. Did you never ask yourself who my analyst is? Yet, when it comes to the last issue, we must be able to stand alone *vis à vis* the unconscious for better or worse.

Letter to Mr. O., 30 April 1947, *Letters, Vol. I*, p. 459.

It not infrequently happens that the patient simply continues to observe his own images without considering what they mean to him. He can and he should understand their meaning, but this is of practical value only so long as he is not sufficiently convinced that the unconscious can give him valuable insights. But once he has recognized this fact, he should also know that he then has in his hands an opportunity to win, by his knowledge, independence of the analyst.

Mysterium Coniunctionis (1955–56), CW 14, § 754.

When I look back upon it all today and consider what happened to me during the period of my work on the fantasies, it seems as though a message had come to me with overwhelming force. There were things in the images which concerned not only myself but many others also. It was then that I ceased to belong to myself alone, ceased to have the right to do so. From then on, my life belonged to the generality. The knowledge I was concerned with, or was seeking, still could not be found in the science of those days. I myself had to undergo the original experience, and, moreover, try to plant the results of my experience in the soil of reality; otherwise they would have remained subjective assumptions without validity. It was then that I dedicated myself to service of the psyche. I loved it and hated it, but it was my greatest wealth. My delivering myself over to it, as it were, was the only way by which I could endure my existence and live it as fully as possible.

Memories, Dreams, Reflections (1962), p. 192.

Today I can say that I have never lost touch with my initial experiences. All my works, all my creative activity, has come from those initial fantasies and dreams which began in 1912, almost fifty years ago. Everything that I accomplished in later life was already contained in them, although at first only in the form of emotions and images.

My science was the only way I had of extricating myself from that chaos. Otherwise the material would have trapped me in its thicket, strangled me like jungle creepers. I took great care to try to understand every single image, every item of my psychic inventory, and to classify them scientifically—so far as this was possible—and, above all, to realize them in actual life. That is what we usually neglect to do. We allow the images to rise up, and maybe we wonder about them, but that is all. We do not take the trouble to understand them, let alone draw ethical conclusions from them. This stopping-short conjures up the negative effects of the unconscious.

It is equally a grave mistake to think that it is enough to gain some understanding of the images and that knowledge can here make a halt. Insight into them must be converted into an ethical obligation. Not to do so is to fall prey to the power principle, and this produces dangerous effects which are destructive not only to others but even to the knower. The images of the unconscious place a great responsibility upon a man. Failure to understand them, or a shirking of ethical responsibility, deprives him of his wholeness and imposes a painful fragmentariness on his life.

Memories, Dreams, Reflections (1962), pp. 192–193.

Particularly at this time, when I was working on the fantasies, I needed a point of support in "this world," and I may say that my family and my professional work were that to me. It was most essential for me to have a normal life in the real world as a counterpoise to that strange inner world. My family and my profession remained the base to which I could always return, assuring me that I was an actually existing, ordinary person. The unconscious contents could have driven me out of my wits. But my family, and the knowledge: I have a medical diploma from a Swiss university, I must help my patients, I have a wife and five children, I live at 228 Seestrasse in Küsnacht—these were actualities which made demands upon me and proved to me again and again that I really existed, that I was not a blank page whirling about in the winds of the spirit, like Nietzsche. Nietzsche had lost the ground under his feet because he possessed nothing more than the inner world of his thoughts which incidentally possessed him more than he it. He was uprooted and hovered above the earth, and therefore he succumbed to exaggeration and irreality. For me, such irreality was the quintessence of horror, for I aimed, after all, at *this* world and *this* life. No matter how deeply absorbed or how blown about I was, I always knew that everything I was experiencing was ultimately directed at this real life of mine.

Memories, Dreams, Reflections (1962), p. 189.

15
Alchemical Transformation

It must now be sufficiently clear that from its earliest days alchemy had a double face: on the one hand the practical chemical work in the laboratory, on the other a psychological process, in part consciously psychic, in part unconsciously projected and seen in the various transformations of matter.

Psychology and Alchemy (1944), CW 12, § 380.

The alchemist saw the union of opposites under the symbol of the tree, and it is therefore not surprising that the unconscious of present-day man, who no longer feels at home in his world and can base his existence neither on the past that is no more nor on the future that is yet to be, should hark back to the symbol of the cosmic tree rooted in this world and growing up to heaven—the tree that is also man. In the history of symbols this tree is described as the way of life itself, a growing into that which eternally is and does not change; which springs from the union of opposites and, by its eternal presence, also makes that union possible. It seems as if it were only through an experience of symbolic reality that man, vainly seeking his own "existence" and making a philosophy out of it, can find his way back to a world in which he is no longer a stranger.

"Psychological Aspects of the Mother Archetype" (1938/1954),
CW 9i, § 198.

[W]e can see how effectively alchemy prepared the ground for the psychology of the unconscious, firstly by leaving behind, in its treasury of symbols, illustrative material of the utmost value for modern interpretations in this field, and secondly by indicating symbolic procedures for synthesis which we can rediscover in the dreams of our patients.

Mysterium Coniunctionis (1955–56), CW 14, § 792.

For the principal pair of opposites is the conscious world and the unconscious world, and when the two come together, it is as if man and woman were coming together, the union of the male and the female, of the light and the darkness. Then a birth will take place. Therefore in alchemy the *Lapis philosophorum* [the Philosopher's Stone], which is the reconciling symbol, is often characterized by the union of male and female.

Visions: Notes of the Seminar Given in 1930–1934, Vol. I (10 February 1932), p. 574.

For the alchemists the process of individuation represented by the *opus* was an analogy of the creation of the world, and the *opus* itself an analogy of God's work of creation. Man was seen as a micro-cosm, a complete equivalent of the world in miniature.

"A Study in the Process of Individuation" (1934/1950), CW 9i, § 550.

The alchemical idea of transformation is rooted in a spiritual con-cept of value which takes the "transformed" as being *more* valuable, better, higher, more spiritual, etc., and the empirical psychologist has nothing to set against this.

Mysterium Coniunctionis (1955–56), CW 14, § 613.

The state of imperfect transformation, merely hoped for and waited for, does not seem to be one of torment only, but of positive, if hid-den, happiness. It is the state of someone who, in his wanderings among the mazes of his psychic transformation, comes upon a se-cret happiness which reconciles him to his apparent loneliness. In communing with himself he finds not deadly boredom and melan-choly but an inner partner; more than that, a relationship that seems like the happiness of a secret love, or like a hidden spring-time, when the green seed sprouts from the barren earth, holding out the promise of future harvests.

Mysterium Coniunctionis (1955–56), CW 14, § 623.

[W]e have to sacrifice the past in order to illumine the future; we would be immovable, caught, if we could not sacrifice the past. So in every important stage of history, in the actual moment, the destruction of the past became almost inevitable, spiritually and materially. If we can make that change, if we can destroy the body of the father, if we can cut off the paws of the lion, we can produce the medicine of life eternal; that is, we have helped life to go on, we have severed our lives from the past and so we can live again. Now that is a piece of alchemistic philosophy.

Visions: Notes of the Seminar Given in 1930–1934, Vol. I (9 December 1931),

The idea of the alchemists in the Middle Ages was that it was possible to transform chemical matter by "real imagination." This was brought about by intense concentration which impregnated the material with the round image of the soul which is in man. The materia thus received the round form, the perfect thing, and thus impressed it must turn to gold. The gold is a figure of speech, for the alchemists mean the philosopher's gold, not ordinary gold. This is difficult to understand but the alchemists often say that only the hopelessly stupid think that their gold is ordinary gold. The whole process, however, took place in the materia, they saw their soul, not in themselves, but in chemical matter.[6]

Modern Psychology, Notes on Lectures Given at the ETH Zürich by Prof. Dr. C. G. Jung, 1933–40, Vol. III (28 October 1938), p. 14.

[T]he alchemist related himself not only to the unconscious but directly to the very substance which he hoped to transform through the power of imagination.

Psychology and Alchemy (1944), CW 12, § 394.

Investigation of alchemical symbolism, like a preoccupation with mythology, does not lead one away from life any more than a study of comparative anatomy leads away from the anatomy of the living

---

[6] This is not a translation of the verbatim German original but taken from an English summary based on participants' stenographic notes. They were neither checked nor authorized by Jung himself before being circulated privately as *Modern Psychology, Notes on Lectures Given at the ETH Zürich by Prof. Dr. C. G. Jung, 1933–40.*

man. On the contrary, alchemy affords us a veritable treasure-house of symbols, knowledge of which is extremely helpful for an understanding of neurotic and psychotic processes. This, in turn, enables us to apply the psychology of the unconscious to those regions in the history of the human mind which are concerned with symbolism.

Mysterium Coniunctionis (1955–56), CW 14, p. xviii.

However remote alchemy may seem to us today, we should not underestimate its cultural importance for the Middle Ages. Today is the child of the Middle Ages and it cannot disown its parents.

Psychology and Alchemy (1944), CW 12, § 432.

[T]he alchemical opus consisted of two parts: the work in the laboratory, with all its emotional and daemonic hazards, and the *scientia* or *theoria*, the guiding principle of the opus by which its results were interpreted and given their proper place. The whole process, which today we understand as psychological development, was designated the "philosophical tree," a "poetic" comparison that draws an apt analogy between the natural growth of the psyche and that of a plant. For this reason it seemed to me desirable to discuss in some detail the processes which underlie both alchemy and the modern psychology of the unconscious. I am aware, and hope I have also made it clear to the reader, that merely intellectual understanding is not sufficient. It supplies us only with verbal concepts, but it does not give us their true content, which is to be found in the living experience of the process as applied to ourselves. We would do well to harbour no illusions in this respect: no understanding by means of words and no imitation can replace actual experience.

"The Philosophical Tree" (1945/1954), CW 13, § 482.

[T]he alchemists thought of their opus as a continuation and perfection of creation.

"Jung and Religious Belief" (1958), CW 18, § 1631.

We can therefore understand why the *nuptiae chymicae*, the royal marriage, occupies such an important place in alchemy as a symbol of the supreme and ultimate union, since it represents the magic-by-analogy which is supposed to bring the work to its final consummation and bind the opposites by love, for "love is stronger than death."

The Psychology of the Transference (1946), CW 16, § 398.

When a patient begins to feel the inescapable nature of his inner development, he may easily be overcome by a panic fear that he is slipping helplessly into some kind of madness that he can no longer understand. More than once I have had to reach for a book on my shelves, bring down an old alchemist, and show my patient his terrifying fantasy in the form in which it appeared four hundred years ago. This has a calming effect, because the patient then sees that he is not alone in a strange world which nobody understands, but is part of the great stream of human history, which has experienced countless times the very things that he regards as a pathological proof of his craziness.

"The Philosophical Tree" (1945/1954), CW 13, § 325.

Medieval alchemy prepared the way for the greatest intervention in the divine world that man has ever attempted: alchemy was the dawn of the scientific age, when the daemon of the scientific spirit compelled the forces of nature to serve man to an extent that had never been known before. It was from the spirit of alchemy that Goethe wrought the figure of the "superman" Faust, and this superman led Nietzsche's Zarathustra to declare that God was dead and to proclaim the will to give birth to the superman, to "create a god for yourself out of your seven devils." Here we find the true roots, the preparatory processes deep in the psyche, which unleashed the forces at work in the world today. Science and technology have indeed conquered the world, but whether the psyche has gained anything is another matter.

"Paracelsus as a Spiritual Phenomenon" (1942), CW 13, § 163.

It is clear enough from this material what the ultimate aim of alchemy really was: it was trying to produce a *corpus subtile*, a transfigured and resurrected body, i.e., a body that was at the same time spirit. In this it finds common ground with Chinese alchemy, as we have learned from the text of *The Secret of the Golden Flower*. There the main concern is the "diamond body," in other words, the attainment of immortality through the transformation of the body. The diamond is an excellent symbol because it is hard, fiery, and translucent.

Psychology and Alchemy (1944), CW 12, § 511.

As is shown by the texts and their symbolism, the alchemist projected what I have called the process of individuation into the phenomena of chemical change. A scientific term like "individuation" does not mean that we are dealing with something known and finally cleared up, on which there is no more to be said. It merely indicates an as yet very obscure field of research much in need of exploration: the centralizing processes in the unconscious that go to form the personality. We are dealing with life-processes which, on account of their numinous character, have from time immemorial provided the strongest incentive to the formation of symbols. These processes are steeped in mystery; they pose riddles with which the human mind will long wrestle for a solution, and perhaps in vain. For, in the last analysis, it is exceedingly doubtful whether human reason is a suitable instrument for this purpose. Not for nothing did alchemy style itself an "art," feeling—and rightly so—that it was concerned with creative processes that can be truly grasped only by experience, though intellect may give them a name. The alchemists themselves warned us: "Rumpite libros, ne corda vestra rumpantur" (Rend the books, lest your hearts be rent asunder), and this despite their insistence on study. Experience, not books, is what leads to understanding.

Psychology and Alchemy (1944), CW 12, § 564.

Not, this time, in the cheap, unseemly substance, which, rejected by all, could be picked up anywhere in the street, but rather in the distressing darkness of the human psyche, which meanwhile had become accessible to clinical observation. There alone could be found all those contradictions, those grotesque phantasms and scurrilous symbols which had fascinated the mind of the alchemists and confused them as much as illuminated them. And the same problem presented itself to the psychologist that had kept the alchemists in suspense for seventeen hundred years.

Mysterium Coniunctionis (1955), CW 14, § 791.

We need to find our way back to the original, living spirit which, because of its ambivalence, is also a mediator and uniter of opposites, an idea that preoccupied the alchemists for many centuries.

Aion (1951), CW 9ii, § 141.

To most people alchemy simply means a lot of old men who tried to make gold. But that was not the truth at all. If people would only take the trouble to turn up the actual writings of the ancient alchemists, they would find a deep treasure-trove of wisdom, much of which is perfectly applicable to the very events which are happening in the world today. After all, what can possibly be more important than the study of how men's minds work, and have worked in the past?

"The Art of Living" (1960), *C. G. Jung Speaking*, p. 444.

Luckily for us, symbols mean very much more than can be known at first glance. Their meaning resides in the fact that they compensate an unadapted attitude of consciousness, an attitude that does not fulfil its purpose, and that they would enable it to do this if they were understood. But it becomes impossible to interpret their meaning if they are reduced to something else. That is why some of the later alchemists, particularly in the sixteenth century, abhorred all vulgar substances and replaced them by "symbolic" ones which allowed the nature of the archetype to glimmer through. This does not mean that the adept ceased to work in the laboratory, only that he kept an eye on the symbolic aspect of his transmutations. This corresponds exactly to the situation in the modern psychology of the unconscious: while personal problems are not overlooked (the patient himself takes very good care of that!), the analyst keeps an eye on their symbolic aspects, for healing comes only from what leads the patient beyond himself and beyond his entanglement in the ego.

"The Philosophical Tree" (1945/1954), CW 13, § 397.

"Know," says Ripley, "that your beginning should be made towards sunset, and from there you should turn towards midnight, when the lights cease altogether to shine, and you should remain ninety nights in the dark fire of purgatory without light. Then turn your course towards the east, and you will pass through many different colours," etc. The alchemical work starts with the descent into darkness (*nigredo*), i.e., the unconscious.

Aion (1951), CW 9ii, § 231.

[T]he curious personifications characteristic not only of these visions [of Zosimos] but of alchemical literature in general shows in the plainest possible terms that we are dealing with a psychic process that takes place mainly in the unconscious and therefore can come into consciousness only in the form of a dream or vision. At that time and until very much later no one had any idea of the unconscious; consequently all unconscious contents were projected onto the object, or rather were found in nature as apparent objects or properties of matter and were not recognized as purely internal psychic events.

"Transformation Symbolism in the Mass" (1942/1954), CW 11,
§ 375.

[F]or alchemy is the mother of the essential substance as well as the concreteness of modern scientific thinking, and not scholasticism, which was responsible in the main only for the discipline and training of the intellect.

Aion (1951), CW 9ii, § 266.

The four always expresses the coming into being of what is essentially human, the *emergence of human consciousness*. Thus, the alchemical process also begins with such a division into the four elements, by which the body is put back into its primordial state and so can undergo transformation.

Children's Dreams: Notes from the Seminar Given in 1936–1940,
p. 367.

Alchemy represents the projection of a drama both cosmic and spiritual in laboratory terms. The *opus magnum* [the great work] had two aims: the rescue of the human soul and the salvation of the cosmos. What the alchemists called "matter" was in reality the [unconscious] self. The "soul of the world," the *anima mundi*, which was identified with the *spiritus mercurius* [the Mercurial spirit], was imprisoned in matter. It is for this reason that the alchemists believed in the *truth* of "matter," because "matter" was actually their own psychic life. But it was a question of freeing this "matter," of saving it—in a word, of finding the philosopher's stone, the *corpus glorificationis* [the glorified body].

"Eliade's Interview for *Combat*" (1952), *C. G. Jung Speaking*, p. 228.

The real nature of matter was unknown to the alchemist: he knew it only in hints. Inasmuch as he tried to explore it he projected the unconscious into the darkness of matter in order to illuminate it. In order to explain the mystery of matter he projected yet another mystery—namely his unknown psychic background—into what was to be explained.

Psychology and Alchemy (1944), CW 12, § 345.

This remarkable capacity of the human psyche for change, expressed in the transcendent function, is the principal object of late medieval alchemistic philosophy, where it was expressed in terms of alchemical symbolism.

The Relations between the Ego and the Unconscious (1916/1928),

CW 7, § 360.

Alchemy, with its wealth of symbols, gives us an insight into an endeavour of the human mind which could be compared with a religious rite, an *opus divinum* [divine task]. The difference between them is that the alchemical opus was not a collective activity rigorously defined as to its form and content, but rather, despite the similarity of their fundamental principles, an individual undertaking on which the adept staked his whole soul for the transcendental purpose of producing a unity. It was a work of reconciliation between apparently incompatible opposites, which, characteristically, were understood not merely as the natural hostility of the physical elements but at the same time as a moral conflict. Since the object of this endeavour was seen outside as well as inside, as both physical and psychic, the work extended as it were through the whole of nature, and its goal consisted in a symbol which had an empirical and at the same time a transcendental aspect.

Mysterium Coniunctionis (1955–56), CW 14, § 790.

In general, the alchemists strove for a *total* union of opposites in symbolic form, and this they regarded as the indispensable condition for the healing of all ills. Hence they sought to find ways and means to produce that substance in which all opposites were united. It had to be material as well as spiritual, living as well as inert, masculine as well as feminine, old as well as young, and—presumably—morally neutral. It had to be created by man, and at the same time, since it was an "increatum" [a transcendent creation], by God himself, the *Deus terrestris* [the earthly God].

Mysterium Coniunctionis (1955–56), CW 14, § 676.

First I had to find evidence for the historical prefiguration of my inner experiences. That is to say, I had to ask myself, "Where have my particular premises already occurred in history?" If I had not succeeded in finding such evidence, I would never have been able to substantiate my ideas. Therefore, my encounter with alchemy was decisive for me, as it provided me with the historical basis which I hitherto lacked.

Memories, Dreams, Reflections (1962), p. 200.

[N]obody has ever know what this primal matter is. The alchemists did not know, and nobody has found out what is really meant by it, because it is a substance in the unconscious which is needed for the incarnation of the god.

Nietzsche's Zarathustra: Notes of the Seminar Given in 1934–1939,
Vol. II (4 March 1936), p. 886.

The only certain thing is that for all the alchemists matter had a divine aspect.

Mysterium Coniunctionis (1955–56), CW 14, § 766.

All, from the very earliest times, are agreed that their art is sacred and divine, and likewise that their work can be completed only with the help of God. This science of theirs is given only to the few, and none understands it unless God or a master has opened his understanding. The knowledge acquired may not be passed on to others unless they are worthy of it. Since all the essentials are expressed in metaphors they can be communicated only to the intelligent, who possess the gift of comprehension.

Psychology and Alchemy (1944), CW 12, § 423.

Alchemists are, in fact, decided solitaries; each has his say in his own way. They rarely have pupils, and of direct tradition there seems to have been very little, nor is there much evidence of any secret societies or the like. Each worked in the laboratory for himself and suffered from loneliness. On the other hand, quarrels were rare.

Psychology and Alchemy (1944), CW 12, § 422.

["T]rue" alchemy was never a business or a career, but a genuine *opus* to be achieved by quiet, self-sacrificing work. One has the impression that each individual tried to express his own particular experiences, quoting the dicta of the masters only when they seemed to offer analogies.

Psychology and Alchemy (1944), CW 12, § 422.

For the alchemist, the one primarily in need of redemption is not man, but the deity who is lost and sleeping in matter.

Psychology and Alchemy (1944), CW 12, § 420.

Light on the nature of alchemy began to come to me only after I had read the text of the *Golden Flower*, that specimen of Chinese alchemy which Richard Wilhelm sent me in 1928. I was stirred by the desire to become more closely acquainted with the alchemical texts. I commissioned a Munich bookseller to notify me of any alchemical books that might fall into his hands. Soon afterward I received the first of them, the *Artis Auriferae Volumina Duo* (1593), a comprehensive collection of Latin treatises among which are a number of the "classics" of alchemy.

I let this book lie almost untouched for nearly two years. Occasionally I would look at the pictures, and each time I would think, "Good Lord, what nonsense! This stuff is impossible to understand." But it persistently intrigued me, and I made up my mind to go into it more thoroughly. The next winter I began, and soon found it provocative and exciting. To be sure, the texts still seemed to be blatant nonsense, but here and there would be passages that seemed significant to me, and occasionally I even found a few sentences which I thought I could understand. Finally I realized that the alchemists were talking in symbols—those old acquaintances of mine. "Why, this is fantastic," I thought. "I simply must learn to decipher all this." By now I was completely fascinated, and buried myself in the texts as often as I had the time. One night, while I was studying them, I suddenly recalled the dream that I was caught in the seventeenth century. At last I grasped its meaning. "So that's it! Now I am condemned to study alchemy from the very beginning."

Memories, Dreams, Reflections (1962), pp. 204–5.

I worked on this book for 16 years. My acquaintance with alchemy in 1930 took me away from it. The beginning of the end came in 1928, when Wilhelm sent me the text of the "Golden Flower," an alchemical treatise. There the contents of this book found their way into actuality and I could no longer continue working on it. To the superficial observer, it will appear like madness. It would also have developed into one, had I not been able to absorb the overpowering force of the original experiences. With the help of alchemy, I could finally arrange them into a whole. I always knew that these experiences contained something precious, and therefore I knew of nothing better than to write them down in a "precious," that is to say costly, book and to paint the images that emerged through reliving it all—as well as I could. I knew how frightfully inadequate this undertaking was, but despite much work and many distractions I remained true to it, even if another possibility never . . . [the manuscript dated 1959 breaks off here]

"Epilogue," *The Red Book* (1917/2009), p. 360.

16
On Life

The years when I was pursuing my inner images were the most important in my life—in them everything essential was decided. It all began then; the later details are only supplements and clarifications of the material that burst forth from the unconscious, and at first swamped me. It was the *prima materia* [original matter] for a life's work.

Memories, Dreams, Reflections (1962), p. 199.

"My soul, where are you? Do you hear me? I speak, I call you—are you there? I have returned, I am here again. I have shaken the dust of all the lands from my feet, and I have come to you, I am with you. After long years of long wandering, I have come to you again. Should I tell you everything I have seen, experienced, and drunk in? Or do you not want to hear about all the noise of life and the world? But one thing you must know: the one thing I have learned is that one must live this life.

"The life is the way, the long sought-after way to the unfathomable, which we call divine. There is no other way, all other ways are false paths. I found the right way, it led me to you, to my soul. I return, tempered and purified. Do you still know me? How long the separation lasted! Everything has become so different. And how did I find you? How strange my journey was! What words shall I use to tell you on what twisted paths a good star has guided me to you? Give me your hand, my almost forgotten soul. How warm the joy at seeing you again, you long disavowed soul. Life has led me back to you. Let us thank the life I have lived for all the happy and all the sad hours, for every joy, for every sadness. My soul, my journey should continue with you. I will wander with you and ascend to my solitude."

The Red Book (1915/2009), p. 232.

There is no morality, no moral decision, without freedom. There is only morality when you can choose, and you cannot chose if you are forced.

Nietzsche's Zarathustra: Notes of the Seminar Given in 1934–1939,

Vol. I (21 November 1934), p. 262.

For what is more precious than life to a living creature? If one lives only a half or a third of life, what is the use of living? Life only has meaning when it is really lived. Otherwise it is like a pear tree that blossoms every spring and never brings forth a pear; you remember Christ himself condemned that which bears no fruit, when he cursed the barren fig tree. People who live sterile lives are like that fig tree, they do not fulfill the will of the Lord. If they want to live, they must live with the whole of their being.

Visions: Notes of the Seminar Given in 1930–1934, Vol. I (18 February 1931), p. 232.

The utterances of the heart—unlike those of the discriminating intellect—always relate to the whole. The heartstrings sing like an Aeolian harp only under the gentle breath of a mood, an intuition, which does not drown the song but listens. What the heart hears are the great, all-embracing things of life, the experiences which we do not arrange ourselves but which happen to us.

"On the Tale of the Otter" (1932), CW 18, § 1719.

Man needs difficulties, they are necessary for health.

"The Transcendent Function" ([1916]/1958), CW 8, § 143.

Everything psychic is pregnant with the future.

Mysterium Coniunctionis (1955–56), CW 14, § 53.

There are plenty of people who are not yet born. They all seem to be here, they walk about—but as a matter of fact, they are not yet born, because they are behind a glass wall, they are in the womb. They are in the world only on parole and are soon to be returned to the pleroma [fullness] where they started originally. They have not formed a connection with this world; they are suspended in the air; they are neurotic, living the provisional life.

The Psychology of Kundalini Yoga: Notes of the Seminar Given in 1932, p. 28.

In psychology one possesses nothing unless one has experienced it in reality. Hence a purely intellectual insight is not enough, because one knows only the words and not the substance of the thing from inside.

Aion (1951), CW 9ii, § 61.

The word created the world and came before the world. It lit up like a light in the darkness, and the darkness did not comprehend it.

And thus the word should become what the darkness can comprehend, since what use is the light if the darkness does not comprehend it? But your darkness should grasp the light.

The Red Book (1915/2009), p. 270.

Nobody touches the unconscious without leaving something of himself there. You may forget or repress it, but then you are no longer whole. When you have learned that two times two makes four, it will be so in all eternity—it will never be five.

The Psychology of Kundalini Yoga: Notes of the Seminar Given in 1932 (26 October, 1932), p. 58.

We must do what Christ did. We must make mistakes. We must live out our own vision of life. And there will be no error. If you avoid error you do not live; in a sense even it may be said that every life is a mistake, for no one has found the truth. When we live like this we know Christ as a brother, and God indeed becomes man. This sounds like a terrible blasphemy, but not so. For then only can we understand Christ as he would want to be understood, as a fellow man; then only does God become man in ourselves.

"Is Analytical Psychology a Religion?" (1937), *C. G. Jung Speaking,* p. 98.

Only what is really oneself has the power to heal.

The Relations between the Ego and the Unconscious (1928), CW 7, § 258.

Out of the unconscious flows the well of life, and what you don't accept in yourself naturally falls back into that well and poisons it; when you don't recognize certain facts, they form a layer in the unconscious through which the water of life must come up, and it will be poisoned by all those things you have left down below. If they are accepted in your conscious life, then they are mixed with other more valuable and cleaner substances, and the odious qualities of the lower functions disappear more or less. They only form little shadows here and there, sort of spice for the good things. But by excluding them, you cause them to heap up and they become entirely evil substances; for a thing to become poisonous, you only need to repress it.

Nietzsche's Zarathustra: Notes of the Seminar Given in 1934–1939,
Vol. II (12 May 1937), p. 1058.

[I]t is most important that you should be born; you ought to come into this world—otherwise you cannot realize the self, and the purpose of this world has been missed. Then you must simply be thrown back into the melting pot and be born again.

The Psychology of Kundalini Yoga: Notes of the Seminar Given in 1932
(19 October, 1932), pp. 28–29.

What sets one man free is another man's prison.

The Tavistock Lectures: On the Theory and Practice of Analytical
Psychology (1935), CW 18, § 163.

Tears, sorrow, and disappointment are bitter, but wisdom is the comforter in all psychic suffering.

Mysterium Coniunctionis (1955–56), CW 14, § 330.

For me life was something that had to be lived and not talked about.

Letter to Kurt Wolff, 17 June 1958, *Letters, Vol. II*, p. 452.

[W]isdom begins only when one takes things as they are; otherwise we get nowhere, we simply become inflated balloons with no feet on the earth. So it is a healing attitude when one can agree with the facts as they are; only then can we live in our body on this earth, only then can we thrive.

Visions: Notes of the Seminar Given in 1930–1934, Vol. I (27 January
1932), p. 545.

No field could thrive if we assumed that the oats we sowed were wheat, nor could our dog thrive if we took it to be a camel, and so it is unfair to our friends and unfair to ourselves to assume that we can be supermen.

Visions: Notes of the Seminar Given in 1930–1934, Vol. I (27 January 1932), p. 545.

When you come to that loneliness with yourself—when you are eternally alone—you are forced in upon yourself and are bound to become aware of your background. And the more there is of the personal unconscious, the more the collective unconscious forces itself upon you. If the personal unconscious is cleared up, there is no particular pressure, and you will not be terrorized; you stay alone, read, walk, smoke, and nothing happens, all is "just so," you are right with the world.

Dream Analysis: Notes of the Seminar Given in 1928–1930 (12 December 1928), p. 75.

At Bollingen, I am in the midst of my true life, I am most deeply myself.

Memories, Dreams, Reflections (1962), p. 225.

Knowledge of processes in the background early shaped my relationship to the world. Basically, that relationship was the same in my childhood as it is to this day. As a child I felt myself to be alone, and I am still, because I know things and must hint at things which others apparently know nothing of, and for the most part do not want to know. Loneliness does not come from having no people about one, but from being unable to communicate the things that seem important to oneself, or from holding certain views which others find inadmissible. The loneliness began with the experiences of my early dreams, and reached its climax at the time I was working on the unconscious. If a man knows more than others, he becomes lonely. But loneliness is not necessarily inimical to companionship, for no one is more sensitive to companionship than the lonely man, and companionship thrives only when each individual remembers his individuality and does not identify himself with others.

Memories, Dreams, Reflections (1962), p. 356.

Whether his fate comes to him from without or from within, the experiences and happenings on the way remain the same.

"Commentary on *The Secret of the Golden Flower*" (1929), CW 13,

§ 26.

Just where we don't expect life, there it will be, because the life that we know is almost exhausted. The new life always comes from an unexpected corner.

Visions: Notes of the Seminar Given in 1930–1934, Vol. I (27 May

1931), p. 377.

A man likes to believe that he is master of his soul. But as long as he is unable to control his moods and emotions, or to be conscious of the myriad secret ways in which unconscious factors insinuate themselves into his arrangements and decisions, he is certainly not his own master. These unconscious factors owe their existence to the autonomy of the archetypes. Modern man protects himself against seeing his own split state by a system of compartments. Certain areas of outer life and of his own behaviour are kept, as it were, in separate drawers and are never confronted with one another.

"Approaching the Unconscious" (1966), *Man and His Symbols*, p. 83.

How often in the critical moments of life everything hangs on what appears to be a mere nothing!

"The Phenomenology of the Spirit in Fairytales" (1945/1948), CW 9i,

§ 408.

It is important to have a secret, a premonition of things unknown. It fills life with something impersonal, a *numinosum*. A man who has never experienced that has missed something important. He must sense that he lives in a world which in some respects is mysterious; that things happen and can be experienced which remain inexplicable; that not everything which happens can be anticipated. The unexpected and the incredible belong in this world. Only then is life whole. For me the world has from the beginning been infinite and ungraspable.

Memories, Dreams, Reflections (1962), p. 356.

Doubt is the crown of life because truth and error come together. Doubt is living, truth is sometimes death and stagnation. When you are in doubt you have the greatest opportunity to unite the dark and light sides of life.

Dream Analysis: Notes of the Seminar Given in 1928–1930 (23 January 1929), p. 89.

A civilization does not decay, it regenerates.

"The Meaning of Psychology for Modern Man" (1933/1934), CW 10, § 299.

[I]t seems as if all the personal entanglements and dramatic changes of fortune that make up the intensity of life were nothing but hesitations, timid shrinking, almost like petty complications and meticulous excuses for not facing the finality of this strange and uncanny process of crystallization. Often one has the impression that the personal psyche is running around this central point like a shy animal, at once fascinated and frightened, always in flight, and yet steadily drawing nearer.

Psychology and Alchemy (1944), CW 12, § 326.

So long as he knows that he is the carrier of life and that it is therefore important for him to live, then the mystery of his soul lives also—no matter whether he is conscious of it or not. But if he no longer sees the meaning of his life in its fulfilment, and no longer believes in man's eternal right to this fulfilment, then he has betrayed and lost his soul, substituting for it a madness which leads to destruction, as our time demonstrates all too clearly.

Mysterium Coniunctionis (1955–56), CW 14, § 201.

I am an orphan, alone; nevertheless I am found everywhere. I am one, but opposed to myself. I am youth and old man at one and the same time. I have known neither father nor mother, because I have had to be fetched out of the deep like a fish, or fell like a white stone from heaven. In woods and mountains I roam, but I am hidden in the innermost soul of man. I am mortal for everyone, yet I am not touched by the cycle of aeons.

Memories, Dreams, Reflections (1962), p. 227.

I was driven to ask myself in all seriousness: "What is the myth you are living?" I found no answer to this question, and had to admit that I was not living with a myth, or even in a myth, but rather in an uncertain cloud of theoretical possibilities which I was beginning to regard with increasing distrust. I did not know that I was living a myth, and even if I had known it, I would not have known what sort of myth was ordering my life without my knowledge. So, in the most natural way, I took it upon myself to get to know "my" myth, and I regarded this as the task of tasks, for—so I told myself—how could I, when treating my patients, make due allowance for the personal factor, for my personal equation, which is yet so necessary for a knowledge of the other person, if I was unconscious of it? I simply had to know what unconscious or preconscious myth was forming me, from what rhizome I sprang. This resolve led me to devote many years of my life to investigating the subjective contents which are the products of unconscious processes, and to work out methods which would enable us, or at any rate help us, to explore the manifestations of the unconscious.

Symbols of Transformation (1912/1952), CW 5, pp. xxiv–xxv.

What had led me astray during the crisis was my passion for being alone, my delight in solitude. Nature seemed to me full of wonders, and I wanted to steep myself in them. Every stone, every plant, every single thing seemed alive and indescribably marvellous. I immersed myself in nature, crawled, as it were, into the very essence of nature and away from the whole human world.

Memories, Dreams, Reflections (1962), p. 32.

[W]hat are words? Be tentative with words, value them well, take safe words, words without catches, do not spin them with one another so that no webs arise, for you are the first who is ensnared in them. For words have meanings. With words you pull up the underworld. Word, the paltriest and the mightiest. In words the emptiness and the fullness flow together. Hence the word is an image of God. The word is the greatest and the smallest that man created, just as what is created through man is the greatest and the smallest.

The Red Book (1915/2009), p. 299.

Try to tell the truth. You would like to tell the truth, I am sure. Nobody likes to lie if he is not forced to. But just tell the truth for twenty-four hours and see what happens! In the end you can't stand yourself any more.

"Questions and Answers at Oxford" (1938), *C. G. Jung Speaking*,
p. 109.

"Be yourself," as the Americans say.

"Man's Immortal Mind" (1935), *C. G. Jung Speaking*, p. 87.

[Y]ou always become the thing you fight the most.

"Diagnosing the Dictators" (1938), *C. G. Jung Speaking*, p. 129.

[N]othing is more thrilling than trying to understand. One comes to see that life is great and beautiful, that nonsense and stupidity do not always triumph.

"A Wartime Interview" (1942), *C. G. Jung Speaking*, p. 145.

Nature can help you only if you manage to get time for yourself. You need to be able to relax in the garden, completely at peace, or to walk. From time to time I need to stop, to just stand there. If someone were to ask me: What are you thinking of just now?—I wouldn't know. I think unconsciously.

"On Creative Achievement" (1946), *C. G. Jung Speaking*, p. 166.

The life of most ideas consists in their controversial nature, i.e., that you can disagree with them, even if you recognize their importance for a majority. If you would fully agree with them, you could replace yourself just as well by a gramophone record. Moreover, if you don't disagree, you are not good as a *directeur de conscience*, since there are many other people suffering from the same difficulty and being badly in need of your understanding.

Letter to Victor White, 10 April 1954, *The Jung-White Letters*, p. 238.

Nothing but unexpected things kept happening to me. Much might have been different if I myself had been different. But it was as it had to be; for all came about because I am as I am. Many things worked out as I planned them to, but that did not always prove of benefit to me. But almost everything developed naturally and by destiny.

Memories, Dreams, Reflections (1962), p. 358.

Not as my sorrow, but as the sorrow of the world; not a personal isolating pain, but a pain without bitterness that unites all humanity.

"The Structure of the Psyche" (1927/1931), CW 8, § 316.

If you discover what you call a truth, you should test it, try to eat it. If it feeds you it is good, but if you cannot live by it and only assume it ought to feed other people, then it is bad. The real test is that your truth should be good for yourself. Not one dog is coming to sniff at it if it doesn't feed yourself. If you are not satisfied with it, if you cannot enjoy it for twenty, fifty years, or a whole lifetime, it is no good. If you are hungry, if you think your companions must be redeemed, and that they must be grateful to you on top of all, then you make a mistake: you may know the idea is no good. So don't play the missionary. Don't try to eat the goods of others. Let other people belong to themselves and look after their own improvement: let them eat themselves. If they are really satisfied, then nobody should disturb them. If they are not satisfied with what they possess, they will probably seek something better; and if you are the one who has the better thing, they will surely come and get it from you.

Nietzsche's Zarathustra: Notes of the Seminar Given in 1934–1939,
Vol. I (31 October 1934), pp. 213–14.

[T]he way of nature will bring you quite naturally wherever you have to go.

Visions: Notes of the Seminar Given in 1930–1934, Vol. I (10 June 1931), pp. 402–3.

It is often tragic to see how blatantly a man bungles his own life and the lives of others yet remains totally incapable of seeing how much the whole tragedy originates in himself, and how he continually feeds it and keeps it going. Not *consciously*, of course—for consciously he is engaged in bewailing and cursing a faithless world that recedes further and further into the distance. Rather, it is an unconscious factor which spins the illusions that veil his world. And what is being spun is a cocoon, which in the end will completely envelop him.

Aion (1951), CW 9ii, § 18.

A visible enemy is always better than an invisible one.

The Psychology of the Transference (1946), CW 16, § 420.

[N]ietzsche began to write *Zarathustra*, which is his outstanding work, quite different from everything he did before and after, when he was between 37 and 38. That is the critical time. In the second part of life you begin to question yourself. Or rather, you don't; you avoid such questions, but something in yourself asks them, and you do not like to hear that voice asking "What is the goal?" And next, "Where are you going now?" When you are young you think, when you get to a certain position, "This is the thing I want." The goal seems to be quite visible. People think, "I am going to marry, and then I shall get into such and such a position, and then I shall make a lot of money, and then I don't know what." Suppose they have reached it; then comes another question: "And now what? Are we really interested in going on like this forever, for ever doing the same thing, or are we looking for a goal as splendid or as fascinating as we had it before?" Then the answer is: "Well, there is nothing ahead. What is there ahead? Death is ahead." That is disagreeable, you see; that is most disagreeable. So it looks as if the second part of life has no goal whatever. Now you know the answer to that. From time immemorial man has had the answer: "Well, death is a goal; we are looking forward, we are working forward to a definite end." The religions, you see, the great religions, are systems for preparing the second half of life for the end, the goal, of the second part of life.

"Questions and Answers at Oxford" (1938), *C. G. Jung Speaking*, pp. 106–7.

Meaninglessness inhibits fullness of life and is therefore equivalent to illness. Meaning makes a great many things endurable—perhaps everything. No science will ever replace a myth, and a myth cannot be made out of any science. For it is not that "God" is a myth, but that myth is the revelation of a divine life in man. It is not we who invent myth, rather it speaks to us as a Word of God. The Word of God comes to us, and we have no way of distinguishing whether and to what extent it is different from God.

Memories, Dreams, Reflections (1962), p. 340.

Unlived life is a destructive, irresistible force that works softly but inexorably.

"Woman in Europe" (1927), CW 10, § 252.

In my medical experience as well as in my own life I have again and again been faced with the mystery of love, and have never been able to explain what it is.

Memories, Dreams, Reflections (1962), p. 353.

Human imperfection is always a discord in the harmony of our ideals. Unfortunately, no one lives in the world as we desire it, but in the world of actuality where good and evil clash and destroy one another, where no creating or building can be done without dirtying one's hands.

"Woman in Europe" (1927), CW 10, § 263.

People do fall in reality; they might even break a leg, as a sort of symbolic action. Accidents may happen, particularly when there is great unwillingness to go down consciously and intentionally. Then the unconscious simply takes people by the neck and forces them down, which, of course, may lead to disaster. It does not necessarily lead to disaster, but it may if one doesn't help the thing along, if one doesn't follow the intimations of fate willingly and consciously. So it is perfectly justifiable that the situation should arouse some fear, particularly the fear that the brakes are perhaps not strong enough; for there is some acceleration in going down that path to the unconscious—the speed has a tendency to increase. One finds when one takes the downward way that after a while it is almost too easy. Therefore we say that if you give the little finger to the devil, he takes the whole arm, and finally the whole body.

Visions: Notes of the Seminar Given in 1930–1934, Vol. I (19 November 1930), pp. 93–94.

It is death to the soul to become unconscious. People die before there is death of the body, because there is death in the soul. They are mask-like leeches, walking about like spectres, dead but sucking. It is a sort of death. I have seen a man who has converted his mind into a pulp. You can succeed in going away from your problems, you need only to look away from them long enough. You may escape, but it is the death of the soul.

Dream Analysis: Notes of the Seminar Given in 1938–1940 (23 January 1929), p. 90.

No one can know what the ultimate things are. We must therefore take them as we experience them. And if such experience helps to make life healthier, more beautiful, more complete and more satisfactory to yourself and to those you love, you may safely say: "This was the grace of God."

Psychology and Religion (1938/1940), CW 11, § 167.

One must never look to the things that ought to change. The main question is how we change ourselves.

Letter to Eugen Diesel, 10 April 1942, *Letters, Vol. I*, p. 314.

Never say no or yes on principle. Say it only when you *feel* it is really *yes*. If it is really *no*, it is no. If you say yes for any outer reason, you are sunk.

"A Talk with Students at the Institute" (1958), *C. G. Jung Speaking*, p. 361.

It does not matter whether you do a thing or whether it happens to you; whether it reaches you from without or happens within, fate moves through yourself and outside circumstances equally. It is as if outside circumstances were simply projections of your own psychological structure. Of course subjectively it matters a lot, but psychologically it does not matter whether you are the cause of the misfortune or whether the misfortune comes to you. In either case you are miserable and that is all that counts; you are the victim whether it is a self-inflicted misery or whether the world has inflicted it upon you.

Nietzsche's Zarathustra: Notes of the Seminar Given in 1934–1939, Vol. II (6 May 1936), p. 896.

If you are completely destroyed by the world, then the world which destroyed you must be completely transformed, because you looked upon it with the eye that transforms, the eye that contains the germ of what is new.

Visions: Notes of the Seminar Given in 1930–1934, Vol. I (21 May 1931), p. 361.

[L]ove is nothing in itself. It is always a special human being who loves and the love is worth just as much as the individual.

Nietzsche's Zarathustra: Notes of the Seminar Given in 1934–1939,
Vol. II (10 June 1936), p. 997.

No one can make history who is not willing to risk everything for it, to carry the experiment with his own life through to the bitter end, and to declare that his life is not a continuation of the past, but a new beginning. Mere continuation can be left to the animals, but inauguration is the prerogative of man, the one thing he can boast of that lifts him above the beasts.

"Woman in Europe" (1927), CW 10, § 268.

[O]nly those individuals can attain to a higher degree of consciousness who are destined to it and called to it from the beginning, i.e., who have a capacity and an urge for higher differentiation. In this matter men differ extremely, as also do the animal species, among whom there are conservatives and progressives. Nature is aristocratic, but not in the sense of having reserved the possibility of differentiation exclusively for species high in the scale. So too with the possibility of psychic development: it is not reserved for specially gifted individuals. In other words, in order to undergo a far-reaching psychological development, neither outstanding intelligence nor any other talent is necessary, since in this development moral qualities can make up for intellectual shortcomings.

On the Psychology of the Unconscious (1917/1926/1943), CW 7, § 198.

The great thing to know is that the important things are not so important, and the unimportant things are not so unimportant.

Visions: Notes of the Seminar Given in 1930–1934, Vol. I (3 June 1931), p. 390.

[J]ust as evening gives birth to morning, so from the darkness arises a new light, the *stella matutina*, which is at once the evening and the morning star—Lucifer, the light-bringer.

"The Spirit Mercurius" (1943/1948), CW 13, § 299.

What happens outside also happens in him, and what happens in him also happens outside.

"The Structure of the Psyche" (1927/1931), CW 8, § 329.

There is nothing I am quite sure about. I have no definite convictions—not about anything, really. I know only that I was born and exist, and it seems to me that I have been carried along. I exist on the foundation of something I do not know. In spite of all uncertainties, I feel a solidity underlying all existence and a continuity in my mode of being.

Memories, Dreams, Reflections (1962), p. 358.

This is how you must live—without reservation, whether in giving or withholding, according to what the circumstances require. Then you will get through. After all, if you should still get stuck, there is always the enantiodromia from the unconscious, which opens new avenues when conscious will and vision are failing.

"Four 'Contacts with Jung,'" *C. G. Jung Speaking*, pp. 158–59.

The goal of life is the realization of the self. If you kill yourself you abolish that will of the self that guides you through life to that eventual goal. An attempt at suicide doesn't affect the intention of the self to become real, but it may arrest your personal development inasmuch as it is not explained. You ought to realize that suicide is murder, since after suicide there remains a corpse exactly as with any ordinary murder.

Letter to Mrs. N., 13 October 1951, *Letters, Vol. II*, p. 25.

Even if the whole world were to fall to pieces, the unity of the psyche would never be shattered.

"The Meaning of Psychology for Modern Man" (1933/1934), CW 10, § 306.

People will do anything, no matter how absurd, in order to avoid facing their own souls.

Psychology and Alchemy (1944), CW 12, § 126.

A man who has not passed through the inferno of his passions has never overcome them. They then dwell in the house next door, and at any moment a flame may dart out and set fire to his own house. Whenever we give up, leave behind, and forget too much, there is always the danger that the things we have neglected will return with added force.

Memories, Dreams, Reflections (1962), p. 277.

One should never think that man can reach perfection, he can only aim at completion—not to be perfect but to be complete. That would be the necessity and the indispensable condition if there were any question of perfection at all. For how can you perfect a thing if it is not complete? Make it complete first and see what it is then. But to make it complete is already a mountain of a task, and by the time you arrive at absolute completion, you find that you are already dead, so you never reach that preliminary condition for perfecting yourself. Completion is not perfection; to make a building perfect one must first construct it, and a thing which is not even half finished cannot be perfected. First make it complete; then polish it up if you have time and breath left. But usually one's whole life is eaten up in the effort at completion.

Visions: Notes of the Seminar Given in 1930–1934, Vol. I (17 February 1932), p. 590.

Your questions are unanswerable because you want to know how one *ought* to live. One lives as one *can*. There is no single, definite way for the individual which is prescribed for him or would be the proper one. If that's what you want you had best join the Catholic Church, where they tell you what's what. Moreover this way fits in with the average way of mankind in general. But if you want to go your individual way, it is the way you make for yourself, which is never prescribed, which you do not know in advance, and which simply comes into being of itself when you put one foot in front of the other. If you always do the next thing that needs to be done, you will go most safely and sure-footedly along the path prescribed by your unconscious. Then it is naturally no help at all to speculate about how you ought to live. And then you know, too, that you cannot know it, but quietly do the next and most necessary thing. So long as you think you don't yet know what this is, you still have too much money to spend in useless speculation. But if you do with conviction the next and most necessary thing, you are always doing something meaningful and intended by fate.

Letter to Frau N., 15 December 1933, *Letters, Vol. I*, pp. 132–33.

Ultimate truth, if there be such a thing, demands the concert of many voices.

"Foreword to Neumann: *The Origins and History of Consciousness*"
(1949), CW 18, § 1236.

Wisdom is not and never has been something for the many, because foolishness forever will be the main thing the world craves for.

Letter to Mr. N., 25 October 1935, *Letters, Vol. I*, p. 200.

It is a general truth that one can only understand anything in as much as one understands oneself.

Nietzsche's Zarathustra: Notes of the Seminar Given in 1934–1939,
Vol. I (4 December 1935), p. 742.

If you are in yourself, you become aware of your incapacity. You will see how little capable you are of imitating the heroes and of being a hero yourself. So you will also no longer force others to become heroes. Like you, they suffer from incapacity. Incapacity, too, wants to live, but it will overthrow your Gods.

The Red Book (1915/2009), p. 245.

It is no small matter to acknowledge one's yearning. For this many need to make a particular effort at honesty. All too many do not want to know where their yearning is, because it would seem to them impossible or too distressing. And yet yearning is the way of life. If you do not acknowledge your yearning, then you do not follow yourself, but go on foreign ways that others have indicated to you. So you do not live your life but an alien one. But who should live your life if you do not live it? It is not only stupid to exchange your own life for an alien one, but also a hypocritical game, because you can never really live the life of others, you can only pretend to do it, deceiving the other and yourself, since you can only live your own life.

The Red Book (1915/2009), p. 249.

Fulfill that which comes to you.

The Red Book (1915/2009), p. 300.

Be the man through whom you wish to influence others.

"Problems of Modern Psychotherapy" (1929), CW 16, § 167.

The knowledge of your heart is how your heart is.

The Red Book (1915/2009), p. 234.

No one can or should halt sacrifice. Sacrifice is not destruction, sacrifice is the foundation stone of what is to come. Have you not had monasteries? Have not countless thousands gone into the desert? You should carry the monastery in yourself. The desert is within you. The desert calls you and draws you back, and if you were fettered to the world of this time with iron, the call of the desert would break all chains. Truly, I prepare you for solitude.

The Red Book (1915/2009), p. 230.

[A] lonely man like yourself will perhaps find companions. But these companions are all in yourself, and the more you find outside the less you are sure of your own truth. Find them first in yourself, integrate the people in yourself. There are figures, existences, in your unconscious that will come to you, that will integrate in you, so that you may perhaps come into a condition in which you don't know yourself. You will say, I am this, I am that, I am practically everywhere, I am exactly like a whole people—and when doubt arises you are whole.

Nietzsche's Zarathustra: Notes of the Seminar Given in 1934–1939,
Vol. II (12 February 1936), p. 831.

One can speak in beautiful words about love, but about life? And life stands above love. But love is the inescapable mother of life. Life should never be forced into love, but love into life. May love be subject to torment, but not life. As long as love goes pregnant with life, it should be respected; but if it has given birth to life from itself, it has turned into an empty sheath and expires into transience.

The Red Book (1915/2009), p. 327.

The serious problems in life, however, are never fully solved. If ever they should appear to be so it is a sure sign that something has been lost. The meaning and purpose of a problem seem to lie not in its solution but in our working at it incessantly. This alone preserves us from stultification and petrification.

"The Stages of Life" (1930–31), CW 8, § 771.

To live oneself means: to be one's own task. Never say it is a pleasure to live oneself. It will be no joy but a long suffering, since you must become your own creator. If you want to create yourself, then you do not begin with the best and the highest, but with the worst and the deepest. Therefore say that you are reluctant to live yourself. The flowing together of the stream of life is not joy but pain, since it is power against power, guilt, and shatters the sanctified.

The Red Book (1915/2009), pp. 249–50.

We imagine ourselves to be sort of supermen, like Nietzsche's superman who said, God is dead. But if God is dead, *he* must be God, and so naturally a superman, lifted up beyond the human level. For a while that may give one a wonderful feeling of elation and grandeur, but before long one will be left high and dry because one is separated from the sources of life.

Visions: Notes of the Seminar Given in 1930–1934, Vol. I (18 February 1931), p. 225.

Mankind feels that life has a meaning when one lives and there are relatively few exceptions to that rule.

Visions: Notes of the Seminar Given in 1930–1934. Vol. I (3 December 1930), p. 138.

[L]et no day pass without humbly remembering that everything still has to be learned.

The Psychology of the Transference (1946), CW 16, § 464.

The tension of the future is unbearable in us. It must break through narrow cracks, it must force new ways. You want to cast off the burden, you want to escape the inescapable. Running away is deception and detour. Shut your eyes so that you do not see the manifold, the outwardly plural, the tearing away and the tempting. There is only one way and that is your way; there is only one salvation and that is your salvation. Why are you looking around for help? Do you believe that help will come from outside? What is to come is created in you and from you. Hence look into yourself. Do not compare, do not measure. No other way is like yours. All other ways deceive and tempt you. You must fulfil the way that is in you.

The Red Book (1915/2009), p. 308.

So long as he knows that he is the carrier of life and that it is therefore important for him to live, then, the mystery of his soul lives also—no matter whether he is conscious of it or not. But if he no longer sees the meaning of his life in its fulfilment, and no longer believes in man's eternal right to this fulfilment, then he has betrayed and lost his soul, substituting for it a madness which leads to destruction, as our time demonstrates all too clearly.

Mysterium Coniunctionis (1955–56), CW 14, § 201.

A truth is only a truth when it lives, otherwise it is perfectly non-sensical; it must be able to change into its own opposite, to even become an untruth at times. So we cannot really identify with such a conviction or truth; we know that it moves under our feet and it doesn't matter, or it should not matter, whether its aspect is positive or negative. But it is exceedingly difficult to think paradoxically, I admit.

Visions: Notes of the Seminar Given in 1930–1934. Vol. II (21 February 1934), p. 1311.

Anyone who falls so low has depth.

"The Post-War Psychic Problems of the Germans" (1945), *C. G. Jung Speaking*, p. 153.

My life as I had lived it had often seemed to me like a story that has no beginning and no end. I had the feeling that I was a historical fragment, an excerpt for which the preceding and succeeding text was missing. My life seemed to have been snipped out of a long chain of events, and many questions had remained unanswered. Why had it taken this course? Why had I brought these particular assumptions with me? What had I made of them? What will follow? I felt sure that I would receive an answer to all these questions as soon as I entered the rock temple. There I would learn why everything had been thus and not otherwise. There I would meet the people who knew the answer to my question about what had been before and what would come after.

Memories, Dreams, Reflections (1962), p. 291.

You will realize what that means for a man who thinks he is the only one who suffers from his particular ailment and feels responsible for it. When he hears that it is a general problem, he is comforted, at once it puts him back into the lap of humanity; he knows that many people are having the same experience, and he can talk to them and is not isolated. Before, he didn't dare speak about it; now he knows that everyone understands.

> *Dream Analysis: Notes of the Seminar Given in 1928–1930* (5 December 1928), p. 65.

I observe myself in the stillness of Bollingen and with all my experience of nearly eight decades must admit that I have found no rounded answer to myself. I am just as much in doubt about myself as before, the more so the more I try to say something definite. It is as though familiarity with oneself alienated one from oneself still further.

> Letter to Aniela Jaffé, Bollingen, 6 April 1954, *Letters, Vol. II*, p. 163.

When thinking leads to the unthinkable, it is time to return to simple life. What thinking cannot solve, life solves, and what action never decides is reserved for thinking.

> *The Red Book* (1915/2009), p. 293.

Happy is he who can be a hermit in his own desert. He survives.

> *The Red Book* (1915/2009), p. 327.

The touchstone is being alone with oneself.

> This is the way.

> *The Red Book* (1915/2009), p. 330.

[I]f one loves life then surely something should come from it. You see, life wants to be real; if you love life you want to live really, not as a mere promise hovering above things. Life inevitably leads down into reality. Life is of the nature of water: it always seeks the deepest place, which is always below in the darkness and heaviness of the earth.

> *Nietzsche's Zarathustra: Notes of the Seminar Given in 1934–1939, Vol. I* (29 May 1935), p. 508.

17
The Individuation Process

The task consists in integrating the unconscious, in bringing together "conscious" and "unconscious." I have called this the individuation process, and for further details must refer the reader to my later works.

Symbols of Transformation (1912/1952), CW 5, § 459.

[Y]ou cannot be redeemed without having undergone the transformation in the initiation process.

Nietzsche's Zarathustra: Notes of the Seminar Given in 1934–1939,
Vol. I (22 May 1935), p. 502.

Conscious and unconscious do not make a whole when one of them is suppressed and injured by the other. If they must contend, let it at least be a fair fight with equal rights on both sides. Both are aspects of life. Consciousness should defend its reason and protect itself, and the chaotic life of the unconscious should be given the chance of having its way too—as much of it as we can stand. This means open conflict and open collaboration at once. That, evidently, is the way human life should be. It is the old game of hammer and anvil: between them the patient iron is forged into an indestructible whole, an "individual."

This, roughly, is what I mean by the individuation process. As the name shows, it is a process or course of development arising out of the conflict between the two fundamental psychic facts.

"Conscious, Unconscious, and Individuation" (1939), CW 9i,
§§ 522–23.

[I]ndividuation is not an intensification of consciousness, it is very much more. For you must have the consciousness of something before it can be intensified, and that means experience, life lived. You can only be really conscious of things which you have experienced, so individuation must be understood as life. Only life integrates, only life and what we do in life makes the individual appear. You cannot individuate, for instance, by locking yourself up in a cell, you can only individuate in your concrete life, you appear in your deed; there you can individuate and nowhere else. Real consciousness can only be based upon life; upon things experienced, but talking about these things is just air. It is a sort of conscious understanding, but it is not individuation. Individuation is the accomplishment through life. For instance, say a cell begins to divide itself and to differentiate and develop into a certain plant or a certain animal; that is the process of individuation. It is that one becomes what one is, that one accomplishes one's destiny, all the determinations that are given in the form of the germ; it is the unfolding of the germ and becoming the primitive pattern that one was born with.

Visions: Notes of the Seminar Given in 1930–1934, Vol. II (22 June, 1932), pp. 757–58.

It was only after the illness that I understood how important it is to affirm one's destiny. In this way we forge an ego that does not break down when incomprehensible things happen; an ego that endures, that endures the truth, and that is capable of coping with the world and with fate. Then, to experience defeat is also to experience victory. Nothing is disturbed—neither inwardly nor outwardly—for one's own continuity has withstood the current of life and of time. But that can come to pass only when one does not meddle inquisitively with the workings of fate.

Memories, Dreams, Reflections (1962), p. 297.

Human beings have one faculty which, though it is of the greatest utility for collective purposes, is most pernicious for individuation, and that is the faculty of imitation. Collective psychology cannot dispense with imitation, for without it all mass organizations, the State and the social order, are impossible. Society is organized, indeed, less by law than by the propensity to imitation, implying equally suggestibility, suggestion, and mental contagion. But we see every day how people use, or rather abuse, the mechanism of imitation for the purpose of personal differentiation: they are content to ape some eminent personality, some striking characteristic or mode of behaviour, thereby achieving an outward distinction from the circle in which they move. We could almost say that as a punishment for this the uniformity of their minds with those of their neighbours, already real enough, is intensified into an unconscious, compulsive bondage to the environment. As a rule these specious attempts at individual differentiation stiffen into a pose, and the imitator remains at the same level as he always was, only several degrees more sterile than before. To find out what is truly individual in ourselves, profound reflection is needed; and suddenly we realize how uncommonly difficult the discovery of individuality is.

The Relations between the Ego and the Unconscious (1916/1928),
CW 7, § 242.

[I]t is utterly important that one should be in this world, that one really fulfills one's *entelechia*, the germ of life which one is. Otherwise you can never start Kundalini; you can never detach. You simply are thrown back, and nothing has happened; it is an absolutely valueless experience. You must believe in this world, make roots, do the best you can, even if you have to believe in the most absurd things—to believe, for instance, that this world is very definite, that it matters absolutely whether such-and-such a treaty is made or not. It may be completely futile, but you have to believe in it, have to make it almost a religious conviction, merely for the purpose of putting your signature under the treaty, so that trace is left of you. For you should leave some trace in this world which notifies that you have been here, that something has happened. If nothing happens of this kind you have not realized yourself; the germ of life has fallen, say, into a thick layer of air that kept it suspended. It never touched the ground, and so never could produce the plant. But if you touch the reality in which you live, and stay for several decades if you leave your trace, then the impersonal process can begin. You see, the shoot must come out of the ground, and if the personal spark has never gotten into the ground, nothing will come out of it; no *linga* [creative core] or Kundalini will be there, because you are still staying in the infinity that was before.

The Psychology of Kundalini Yoga: Notes of the Seminar Given in 1932
(19 October, 1932), p. 29.

If you fulfil the pattern that is peculiar to yourself, you have loved yourself, you have accumulated and have abundance; you bestow virtue then because you have luster. You radiate; from your abundance something overflows. But if you hate and despise yourself—if you have not accepted your pattern—then there are hungry animals (prowling cats and other beasts and vermin) in your constitution which get at your neighbours like flies in order to satisfy the appetites which you have failed to satisfy. Therefore, Nietzsche says to those people who have not fulfilled their individual pattern that the bestowing soul is lacking. There is no radiation, no real warmth; there is hunger and secret stealing.

Nietzsche's Zarathustra: Notes of the Seminar Given in 1934–1939,
Vol. II (29 January 1936), p. 801.

[I]f your soul is detachable, as in the primitive condition, you are simply hypnotized into a sort of somnambulistic state or trance, and whatever you experience in that condition is not felt because it has not been experienced in the body; you were not there when it happened. Only if you first return to the body, to your earth, can individuation take place, only then does the thing become true.

Visions: Notes of the Seminar Given in 1930–1934, Vol. II (21
February 1934), p. 1314.

[I]t is part of the message of Zarathustra to preach the importance of the body, otherwise his message would have no basis; the idea of individuation, as he preaches it in that chapter, implies the body.

You cannot individuate if you are a spirit; moreover, you don't even know how spirit feels because you are in the body. So if you speak of individuation at all, it necessarily means the individuation of beings who are in the flesh, in the living body. It is of course meant to become a reality, or it would remain only a good idea in the mind— one would be individuated because one had such an idea in one's head. People ordinarily think that a right thought must be throughout, not realizing that it is only a very small noise in the attic, and the rest of the house is as it always was, nothing having happened at all. It is just an illusion when you think the right thought in your head means a reality; it is a reality as far as a thought reality reaches; the thought itself is real, but it has not become a reality in space. It has not been expressed by the whole of you. So Zarathustra has the right idea no doubt; he includes the body in the process of individuation, and he emphasizes it because without the body there would only be a disincarnated spirit.

Nietzsche's Zarathustra: Notes of the Seminar Given in 1934–1939,
Vol. I (31 October 1934), p. 202.

The aim of individuation is nothing less than to divest the self of the false wrappings of the persona on the one hand, and of the suggestive power of primordial images on the other.

The Relations between the Ego and the Unconscious (1916/1928),
CW 7, § 269.

[O]ne cannot individuate as long as one is playing a role to oneself; the convictions one has about oneself are the most subtle form of persona and the most subtle obstacle against any true individuation. One can admit practically anything, yet somewhere one retains the idea that one is nevertheless so-and-so, and this is always a sort of final argument which counts apparently as a plus; yet it functions as an influence against true individuation. It is a most painful procedure to tear off those veils, but each step forward in psychological development means just that, the tearing off of a new veil. We are like onions with many skins, and we have to peel ourselves again and again in order to get at the real core.

Visions: Notes of the Seminar Given in 1930–1934, Vol. II (23 November 1932), p. 821.

In general, it [individuation] is the process by which individual beings are formed and differentiated; in particular, it is the development of the psychological individual as a being distinct from the general, collective psychology.

Psychological Types (1921), CW 6, § 757.

Even if you don't become a complete realization of yourself, you become at least a person; you have a certain conscious form. Of course, it is not a totality; it is only a part, perhaps, and your true individuality is still behind the screen—yet what is manifested on the surface is surely a unit. One is not necessarily conscious of the totality, and perhaps other people see more clearly who you are than you do yourself. So individuality is always. It is everywhere. Everything that has life is individual—a dog, a plant, everything living—but of course it is far from being conscious of its individuality. A dog has probably an exceedingly limited idea of himself as compared with the sum total of his individuality. As most people, no matter how much they think of themselves, are egos, yet at the same time they are individuals, almost as if they were individuated. For they are in a way individuated from the very beginning of their lives, yet they are not conscious of it. Individuation only takes place when you are conscious of it, but individuation is always there from the beginning of your existence.

The Psychology of Kundalini Yoga: Notes of the Seminar Given in 1932 (12 October, 1932), p. 5.

A plant that is meant to produce a flower is not individuated if it does not produce a flower, it must fulfill the cycle; and the man that does not develop consciousness is not individuated, because consciousness is his flower, it is his life, it belongs to our process of individuation that we shall become conscious. You see, all that a man does, whatever he attempts, means his individuation, it is an accomplishment, a fulfillment of his possibilities; and one of his foremost possibilities is the attainment of consciousness. That really makes him man: to man, life should be conscious.

Visions: Notes of the Seminar Given in 1930–1934, Vol. II (22 June 1932), p. 759.

Animals generally signify the instinctive forces of the unconscious, which are brought into unity within the mandala. This integration of the instincts is a prerequisite for individuation.

"Concerning Mandala Symbolism" (1950), CW 9i, § 660.

It is obvious that a social group consisting of stunted individuals cannot be a healthy and viable institution; only a society that can preserve its internal cohesion and collective values, while at the same time granting the individual the greatest possible freedom, has any prospect of enduring vitality. As the individual is not just a single, separate being, but by his very existence presupposes a collective relationship, it follows that the process of individuation must lead to more intense and broader collective relationships and not to isolation.

Psychological Types (1921), CW 6, § 758.

In the last analysis every life is the realization of a whole, that is, of a self, for which reason this realization can also be called "individuation." All life is bound to individual carriers who realize it, and it is simply inconceivable without them. But every carrier is charged with an individual destiny and destination, and the realization of these alone makes sense of life.

Psychology and Alchemy (1944), CW 12, § 330.

[I]f the individuation process is made conscious, consciousness must confront the unconscious and a balance between the opposites must be found. As this is not possible through logic, one is dependent on *symbols* which make the irrational union of opposites possible. They are produced spontaneously by the unconscious and are amplified by the conscious mind. The central symbols of this process describe the self, which is man's totality, consisting on the one hand of that which is conscious to him, and on the other hand of the contents of the unconscious.

Answer to Job (1952), CW 11, § 755.

Individuation appears, on the one hand, as the synthesis of a new unity which previously consisted of scattered particles, and on the other hand, as the revelation of something which existed before the ego and is in fact its father or creator and also its totality.

"Transformation Symbolism in the Mass" (1942/1954), CW 11, § 400.

Individuation has two principal aspects: in the first place it is an internal and subjective process of integration, and in the second it is an equally indispensable process of objective relationship. Neither can exist without the other, although sometimes the one and sometimes the other predominates.

The Psychology of the Transference (1946), CW 16, § 448.

[I]ndividuation is an expression of that biological process—simple or complicated as the case may be—by which every living thing becomes what it was destined to become from the beginning. This process naturally expresses itself in man as much psychically as somatically.

"Foreword to White's *God and the Unconscious*" (1952), CW 11,

§ 460.

One of the most important and difficult tasks in the individuation process is to bridge the distance between people. There is always a danger that the distance will be broken down by one party only, and this invariably gives rise to a feeling of violation followed by resentment. Every relationship has its optimal distance, which of course has to be found by trial and error.

Letter to Oskar A. H. Schmitz, 20 September 1928, *Letters, Vol. I*,

pp. 53–54.

[Y]ou can never get to yourself without loving your neighbour—
that is indispensable; you would never arrive at yourself if you were
isolated on top of Mt. Everest, because you never would have a
chance to know yourself. You would have no means of comparison
and could only make a difference between yourself and the wind
and the clouds, the sun and the stars, the ice and the moon. And if
you lose yourself in the crowd, in the whole of humanity, you also
never arrive at yourself; just as you can get lost in your isolation,
you can also get lost in utter abandonment to the crowd. So whoever insists upon loving his neighbour cannot do it without loving
himself to a certain extent.

Nietzsche's Zarathustra: Notes of the Seminar Given in 1934–1939,
Vol. II (24 June 1936), pp. 1019–20.

Individuation does not shut one out from the world, but gathers
the world to oneself.

"On the Nature of the Psyche" (1947/1954), CW 8, § 432.

[L]ife makes no sense if completely detached, we are only complete in a community or in a relationship. There is no possibility
of individuation on the top of Mount Everest where you are sure
that nobody will ever bother you. Individuation always means
relationship.

Visions: Notes of the Seminar Given in 1930–1934, Vol. II (21 March
1934), p. 1367.

[I]t may be that for sufficient reasons a man feels he must set out on
his own feet along the road to wider realms. It may be that in all the
garbs, shapes, forms, modes, and manners of life offered to him he
does not find what is peculiarly necessary for him. He will go alone
and be his own company. He will serve as his own group, consisting
of a variety of opinions and tendencies—which need not necessarily be marching in the same direction. In fact, he will be at odds
with himself, and will find great difficulty in uniting his own multiplicity for purposes of common action. Even if he is outwardly

protected by the social forms of the intermediary stage, he will have no defence against his inner multiplicity. The disunion with himself may cause him to give up, to lapse into identity with his surroundings.

Memories, Dreams, Reflections (1962), pp. 343–44.

As a rule people are simply forced through the logical development of analysis to take up their individual fate, their particular situation with all its advantages and shortcomings. You could call it individuation.

Visions: Notes of the Seminar Given in 1930–1934, Vol. I (5 November 1930), p. 58.

The individual is the only reality.

"Approaching the Unconscious" (1966), *Man and His Symbols*, p. 58.

The instinct of individuation is found everywhere in life, for there is no life on earth that is not individual. Each form of life is manifested in a differentiated being naturally, otherwise life could not exist. An innate urge of life is to produce an individual as complete as possible.

The Psychology of Kundalini Yoga: Notes of the Seminar Given in 1932 (12 October, 1932), p. 4.

Every advance in culture is, psychologically, an extension of consciousness, a coming to consciousness that can take place only through discrimination. Therefore an advance always begins with individuation, that is to say with the individual, conscious of his isolation, cutting a new path through hitherto untrodden territory.

"On Psychic Energy" (1928), CW 8, § 111.

One cannot individuate without being with other human beings. One cannot individuate on top of Mount Everest or in a cave somewhere where one doesn't see people for seventy years: one can only individuate with or against something or somebody. Being an individual is always a link in the chain; it is not an absolutely detached situation, in itself only, with no connection outside.

Nietzsche's Zarathustra: Notes of the Seminar Given in 1934–1939,
Vol. I (13 June 1934), p. 102.

Individuation is becoming the thing which is not the ego, and that is very strange.

The Psychology of Kundalini Yoga: Notes of the Seminar Given in 1932
(19 October, 1932), p. 39.

The goal of psychological, as of biological, development is self-realization, or individuation. But since man knows himself only as an ego, and the self, as a totality, is indescribable and indistinguishable from a God-image, self-realization—to put it in religious or metaphysical terms—amounts to God's incarnation. That is already expressed in the fact that Christ is the son of God.

"A Psychological Approach to the Dogma of the Trinity"
(1942/1948), CW 11, § 233.

The goal is important only as an idea; the essential thing is the *opus* which leads to the goal: *that* is the goal of a lifetime.

The Psychology of the Transference (1946), CW 16, § 400.

The concept of individuation plays a large role in our psychology. In general, it is the process by which individual beings are formed and differentiated; in particular, it is the development of the psychological *individual* as a being distinct from the general, collective psychology. Individuation, therefore, is a process of *differentiation*, having for its goal the development of the individual personality.

Psychological Types (1921), CW 6, § 757.

[W]e must not understand the individual as turned in only upon himself; otherwise individuation would lead to the complete disappearance of the sane individual. He must reappear again. In the case of the really creative artist, he goes on being the creative artist because that is the means by which he links himself up and communicates with the outside world. There is no point in turning in—disappearing—if you are not coming back with a message to the people outside.

Nietzsche's Zarathustra: Notes of the Seminar Given in 1934–1939,
Vol. I (6 November 1935), p. 668.

[W]hen you get into a disagreeable situation where you see no opening, no direct path, you assume that you are quite alone with yourself. In a way it is a very good thing that you think so; otherwise you would never make up your mind, you would remain merely a child. You must believe that you are practically alone. But you may find yourself in a really tight place where you can't get out, where you are helpless. Then you recognize that you are not alone, because such an absolute impasse is an archetypal situation, and an archetypal figure becomes constellated, a fact in your psychology, a potential, and so you are up to the situation. This has repeated itself innumerable times in history, man has again and again passed through such situations and has a psychological method of adapting, the thing to do in such a case. For by his consciousness alone, particularly the dim consciousness of early ages, man was quite unable to invent such a thing; to primitive man everything was revealed, he invented absolutely nothing, he could not think, *it* thought. So it is the totality of the psyche that functions in that way; the psyche produces a double, it brings up another figure; that is a psychological fact. The *psychopompos* is this second figure; you can call it the daimon [divine manifestation], or the shadow, or a god, or an ancestor spirit; it does not matter what name you give it, it is simply a figure; it might even be an animal. For in such a predicament we are *dépossédés* [dispossessed], we lose the power of our ego, we lose our self-confidence. Until that moment, we were willful or arbitrary, we had made our own choice, we had found out a way, we had proceeded as far as this particular place. Then suddenly we are in an impasse, we lose faith in ourselves, and it is just as if all of our energy became regressive. And then our psyche reacts by constellating that double, which has the effect of leading us out of the situation.

Visions: Notes of the Seminar Given in 1930–1934, Vol. I (3 June
1931), p. 385.

Individuation means becoming an "in-dividual," and, in so far as "individuality" embraces our innermost, last, and incomparable uniqueness, it also implies becoming one's own self. We could therefore translate individuation as "coming to selfhood" or "self-realization."

The Relations between the Ego and the Unconscious (1916/1928),
CW 7, § 266.

The metaphysical process is known to the psychology of the unconscious as the individuation process. In so far as this process, as a rule, runs its course unconsciously as it has from time immemorial, it means no more than the acorn becomes an oak, the calf a cow, and the child an adult. But if the individuation process is made conscious, consciousness must confront the unconscious and a balance between the opposites must be found. As this is not possible through logic, one is dependent on *symbols* which make the irrational union of opposites possible. They are produced spontaneously by the unconscious and are amplified by the conscious mind.

Answer to Job (1952), CW 11, § 755.

Have your congregation understood that they must close their ears to the traditional teachings and go through the darknesses of their own souls and set aside everything in order to become that which every individual bears in himself as his individual task, and that no one can take this burden from him?

Letter to Dorothee Hoch, 3 July 1952, *Letters, Vol. II*, p. 76.

The transcendent function does not proceed without aim and purpose, but leads to the revelation of the essential man. It is in the first place a purely natural process, which may in some cases pursue its course without the knowledge or assistance of the individual, and can sometimes forcibly accomplish itself in the face of op-position. The meaning and purpose of the process is the realization, in all its aspects, of the personality originally hidden away in the embryonic germ-plasm; the production and unfolding of the original, potential wholeness. The symbols used by the unconscious to this end are the same as those which mankind has always used to express wholeness, completeness, and perfection: symbols, as a rule, of the quaternity and the circle. For these reasons I have termed this the *individuation process*.

This natural process of individuation served me both as a model and guiding principle for my method of treatment.

On the Psychology of the Unconscious (1917/1926), CW 7, §§ 186–87.

[I]ndividuation is an ineluctable psychological necessity.

The Relations between the Ego and the Unconscious (1916/1928),

CW 7, § 241.

The more you cling to that which all the world desires, the more you are Everyman, who has not yet discovered himself and stumbles through the world like a blind mind leading the blind with somnambulistic certainty into the ditch. Everyman is always a multitude. Cleanse your interest of that collective sulphur which clings to all like a leprosy. For desire only burns in order to burn itself out, and in and from this fire arises the true living spirit which generates life according to its own laws, and is not blinded by the short-sightedness of our intentions or the crude presumption of our superstitious belief in the will.

Mysterium Coniunctionis (1955–56), CW 14, § 192.

One often finds that motif, the hidden treasure, or the blossoming of the treasure or the flower in mythology or folklore. It is supposed to blossom after a certain period, say nine years, nine months, nine days. On the ninth night, the treasure comes up to the surface and whoever happens to be on the spot on the ninth can take it, but the next night it goes down to the depths, and then it takes nine years and nine months and nine days before it blossoms again. That is the demonstration in folklore of the difficulty of psychological realization.

Dream Analysis: Notes of the Seminar Given in 1928–1930 (4 June 1930), p. 653.

We can see today that the entire alchemical procedure for uniting the opposites, which I have described in the foregoing, could just as well represent the individuation process of a single individual, though with the not unimportant difference that no single individual ever attains to the richness and scope of the alchemical symbolism. This has the advantage of having been built up through the centuries, whereas the individual in his short life has at his disposal only a limited amount of experience and limited powers of portrayal.

Mysterium Coniunctionis (1955–56), CW 14, § 792.

[I]ndividuation is a natural phenomenon, and in a way an inescapable goal, which we have reason to call *good for us*, because it liberates us from the otherwise insoluble conflict of opposites (at least to a noticeable degree). It is not invented by man, but Nature herself produces its archetypal image.

"Jung and Religious Belief" (1958), CW 18, § 1641.

[I]f one is allowed to speak of complete individuation at all, I should say that it would be conscious experience of the totality of nature. But such a thing is only possible if the individual in every moment of existence fulfills his complete being, lives the primitive pattern, fulfills all the expectations that he was originally born with. Naturally one would be abstracted from that universal consciousness through any attempt at a provisional life, for the moment one looks ahead one neglects what is here. The provisional life is a mutilated existence, it is only half a life, giving absolutely no chance of fulfillment, which is the only guarantee for a consciousness that is in harmony with the totality of nature. Only when you behave exactly as you are meant to behave are you the friend and the brother of all living things; then you are right in your place, and then you suddenly understand that everything else is in its place. That is the experience which old China called Tao, but that is a very mystical concept. One realizes how rare, how almost impossible such an experience is, because it is linked up with the completeness of experience in every stage of life.

Visions: Notes of the Seminar Given in 1930–1934, Vol. II (22 June 1932), pp. 760–61.

The difference between the "natural" individuation process, which runs its course unconsciously, and the one which is consciously realized, is tremendous. In the first case consciousness nowhere intervenes; the end remains as dark as the beginning. In the second case so much darkness comes to light that the personality is permeated with light, and consciousness necessarily gains in scope and insight. The encounter between conscious and unconscious has to ensure that the light which shines in the darkness is not only comprehended by the darkness, but comprehends it.

Answer to Job (1952), CW 11, § 756.

The conscious realization of what is hidden and kept secret certainly confronts us with an insoluble conflict; at least this is how it appears to the conscious mind. But the symbols that rise up out of the unconscious in dreams show it rather as a confrontation of opposites, and the images of the goal represent their successful reconciliation. Something empirically demonstrable comes to our aid from the depths of our unconscious nature. It is the task of the conscious mind to understand these hints. If this does not happen, the process of individuation will nevertheless continue. The only difference is that we become its victims and are dragged along by fate towards that inescapable goal which we might have reached walking upright, if only we had taken the trouble and had been patient enough to understand in time the meaning of the numina that cross our path.

Answer to Job (1952), CW 11, § 746.

When a summit of life is reached, when the bud unfolds and from the lesser the greater emerges, then, as Nietzsche says, "One becomes Two," and the greater figure, which one always was but which remained invisible, appears to the lesser personality with the force of revelation.

"Concerning Rebirth" (1940/1950), CW 9i, § 217.

When Lao-tzu says: "All are clear, I alone am clouded," he is expressing what I now feel in advanced old age. Lao-tzu is the example of a man with superior insight who has seen and experienced worth and worthlessness, and who at the end of his life desires to return into his own being, into the eternal unknowable meaning. The archetype of the old man who has seen enough is eternally true. At every level of intelligence this type appears, and its lineaments are always the same, whether it be an old peasant or a great philosopher like Lao-tzu. This is old age, and a limitation. Yet there is so much life that fills me: plants, animals, clouds, day and night, and the eternal in man. The more uncertain I have felt about myself, the more there has grown up in me a feeling of kinship with all things. In fact it seems to me as if that alienation which so long separated me from the world has become transferred into my own inner world, and has revealed to me an unexpected unfamiliarity with myself.

Memories, Dreams, Reflections (1962), p. 359.

18
Death, Afterlife, and Rebirth

Death has laid its hand upon our friend. The darkness out of which his soul had risen has come again and has undone the life of his earthly body, and has left us alone in pain and sorrow.

To many death seems to be a brutal and meaningless end to a short and meaningless existence. So it looks, if seen from the surface and from the darkness. But when we penetrate the depths of the soul and when we try to understand its mysterious life, we shall discern that death is not a meaningless end, the mere vanishing into nothingness—it is an accomplishment, a ripe fruit on the tree of life. Nor is death an abrupt extinction, but a goal that has been unconsciously lived and worked for during half a lifetime.

In the youthful expansion of our life we think of it as an ever-increasing river, and this conviction accompanies us often far beyond the noonday of our existence. But if we listen to the quieter voices of our deeper nature we become aware of the fact that soon after the middle of our life the soul begins its secret work, getting ready for the departure. Out of the turmoil and error of our life the one precious flower of the spirit begins to unfold, the four-petaled flower of the immortal light, and even if our mortal consciousness should not be aware of its secret operation, it nevertheless does its secret work of purification.

"Memorial to J. S." (1927), CW 18, §§ 1705–7.

I have often been asked what I believe about death, that unproblematical ending of individual existence. Death is known to us simply as the end. It is the period, often placed before the close of the sentence and followed only by memories or after-effects in others. For the person concerned, however, the sand has run out of the glass; the rolling stone has come to rest. When death confronts us, life always seems like a downward flow or like a clock that has been wound up and whose eventual "running down" is taken for granted. We are never more convinced of this "running down" than when a human life comes to its end and before our eyes, and the question of the meaning and worth of life never becomes more urgent or more agonizing than when we see the final breath leave a body which a moment before was living. How different does the meaning of life seem to us when we see a young person striving for distant goals and shaping the future, and compare this with an incurable invalid, or with an old man who is sinking reluctantly and impotently into the grave!

"The Soul and Death" (1934), CW 8, § 796.

We must give nature a chance to fulfill itself. Then only can we detach, and then it comes about quite naturally. One could say: Live your life to the full and then you can die. This idea was expressed by Cicero, the idea that the fullness of life brings about the fullness of time and the moment which is ripe for death. That was the antique standpoint and in a way it is true; when nothing remains, it is the end; everything has been said and done, it is perfectly natural, even logical, that one vanishes. If one has done one's duty, fulfilled one's task, one can then die, one can say goodbye and disappear.

Visions: Notes of the Seminar Given in 1930–1934, Vol. I (10 June 1931), p. 402.

Since the unconscious gives us the feeling that it is something alien, a non-ego, it is quite natural that it should be symbolized by an alien figure. Thus, on the one hand, it is the most insignificant of things, while on the other, so far as it potentially contains that "round" wholeness which consciousness lacks, it is the most significant of all. This "round" thing is the great treasure that lies hidden in the cave of the unconscious, and its personification is this personal being who represents the higher unity of conscious and unconscious. It is a figure comparable to Hiranyagarbha, Purusha, Atman, and the mystic Buddha. For this reason I have elected to call it the "self," by which I understand a psychic totality and at the same time a centre, neither of which coincides with the ego but includes it, just as a larger circle encloses a smaller one.

The intuition of immortality which makes itself felt during the transformation is connected with the peculiar nature of the unconscious. It is, in a sense, non-spatial and non-temporal. The empirical proof of this is the occurrence of so-called telepathic phenomena, which are still denied by hypersceptical critics, although in reality they are much more common than is generally supposed. The feeling of immortality, it seems to me, has its origin in a peculiar feeling of extension in space and time, and I am inclined to regard the deification rites in the mysteries as a projection of this same psychic phenomenon.

"Concerning Rebirth" (1940/1950), CW 9i, §§ 248–49.

It is sufficiently obvious that life, like any other process, has a beginning and an end and that every beginning is also the beginning of the end.

On the Psychology of the Unconscious (1917/1926), CW 7, § 34.

[I]n addition to the spirit of this time there is still another spirit at work, namely that which rules the depths of everything contemporary. The spirit of this time would like to hear of use and value. I also thought this way, and my humanity still thinks in this way. But that other spirit forces me nevertheless to speak, beyond justification, use, and meaning. But I did not consider that the spirit of the depths from time immemorial and for all the future possesses a greater power than the spirit of this time, who changes with the generations. The spirit of the depths has subjugated all pride and arrogance to the power of judgment. He took away my belief in science, he robbed me of the joy of explaining and ordering things, and he let devotion to the ideals of this time die out in me. He forced me down to the last and simplest things.

The spirit of the depths took my understanding and all my knowledge and placed them at the service of the inexplicable and the paradoxical. He robbed me of speech and writing for everything that was not in his service, namely the melting together of sense and nonsense, which produces the supreme meaning.

The Red Book (1915/2009), p. 229.

The spirit of the time whispered to me: "This supreme meaning, this image of God, this melting together of the hot and the cold, that is you and only you." But the spirit of the depths spoke to me:

"You are an image of the unending world, all the last mysteries of becoming and passing away live in you. If you did not possess all this, how could you know?"

The Red Book (1915/2009), p. 230.

Life has always seemed to me like a plant that lives on its rhizome. Its true life is invisible, hidden in the rhizome. That part that appears above ground lasts only a single summer. Then it withers away—an ephemeral apparition. When we think of the unending growth and decay of life and civilizations, we cannot escape the impression of absolute nullity. Yet I have never lost a sense of something that lives and endures underneath the eternal flux. What we see is the blossom, which passes. The rhizome remains.

Memories, Dreams, Reflections (1962), p. 4.

As a doctor, I make every effort to strengthen the belief in immortality, especially with older patients when such questions come threateningly close. For, seen in correct psychological perspective, death is not an end but a goal, and life's inclination towards death begins as soon as the meridian is passed.

"Commentary on *The Secret of the Golden Flower*" (1929), CW 13, § 68.

Above all, we know desperately little about the possibilities of continued existence of the individual soul after death, so little that we cannot even conceive how anyone could prove anything at all in this respect. Moreover, we know only too well, on epistemological grounds, that such a proof would be just as impossible as the proof of God. Hence we may cautiously accept the idea of karma only if we understand it as *psychic heredity* in the very widest sense of the word. Psychic heredity does exist—that is to say, there is inheritance of psychic characteristics such as predisposition to disease, traits of character, special gifts, and so forth.

"Psychological Commentary on *The Tibetan Book of the Dead*" (1935/1953), CW 11, § 845.

[F]or when the soul vanished at death, it was not lost; in that other world it formed the living counterpole to the state of death in this world.

The Psychology of the Transference (1946), CW 16, § 493.

There was the idea that the spirits of the ancestors were still living in the vessels used in the household, in pots, amphoras, etc., an idea which probably comes from the fact that in old civilizations the dead were buried in the great wine jars or amphoras such as were used to hold grain. In Peru, as well as in the Near East, the dead were buried in such vessels, or when they were burned, the ashes were put in the amphoras. Perhaps that is the rational origin of this idea, but besides, we have a much better psychological explanation in the peculiar fact that, according to legend, the dwarfs did the housework. For instance, when a woman was kind and put something aside for them—a drop of milk perhaps—and particularly if she was not curious about them, then in the night they cleaned up the house with brush and water. When she got up the next morning, the whole house was clean, all done by the brownies, the dwarfs.

Visions: Notes of the Seminar Given in 1930–1934, Vol. I (18 November 1931), pp. 449–50.

We grow up, we blossom and we wilt, and death is ultimate quietude—or so it seems.

Letter to Miguel Serrano, 14 September 1960, *Letters, Vol. II*, p. 596.

In my rather long psychological experiences I have observed a great many people whose unconscious psychic activity I was able to follow into the immediate presence of death. As a rule the approaching end was indicated by those symbols which, in normal life also, proclaim changes of psychological condition—rebirth symbols such as changes of locality, journeys, and the like. I have frequently been able to trace back for over a year, in a dream-series, the indications of approaching death, even in cases where such thoughts were not prompted by the outward situation. Death, therefore, has its onset long before death. Moreover, this often shows itself in peculiar changes of personality which may precede death by quite a long time. On the whole, I was astonished to see how little ado the unconscious psyche makes of death. It would seem as though death were relatively unimportant, or perhaps our psyche does not bother about what happens to the individual. But it seems that the unconscious is all the more interested in *how* one dies; that is, whether the attitude of consciousness is adjusted to dying or not.

"The Soul and Death" (1934), CW 8, § 809.

If we still want to overcome death, then we must enliven it.

The Red Book (1915/2009), p. 244.

[T]he dead have become ever more distinct for me as the voices of the Unanswered, Unresolved, and Unredeemed; for since the questions and demands which my destiny required me to answer did not come to me from outside, they must have come from the inner world. These conversations with the dead formed a kind of prelude to what I had to communicate to the world about the unconscious; a kind of pattern of order and interpretation of its general contents.

Memories, Dreams, Reflections (1962), pp. 191–92.

Life is never so beautiful as when surrounded by death.

Introduction to Jungian Psychology: Notes of the Seminar on Analytical Psychology Given in 1925, p. 85.

We lack concrete proof that anything of us is preserved for eternity. At most we can say that there is some probability that something of our psyche continues beyond physical death. Whether what continues to exist is conscious of itself, we do not know either. If we feel the need to form some opinion on this question, we might possibly consider what has been learned from the phenomena of psychic dissociation. In most cases where a split-off complex manifests itself it does so in the form of a personality, as if the complex had a consciousness of itself. Thus the voices heard by the insane are personified.

Memories, Dreams, Reflections (1962), p. 322.

[T]he spirits of those who die before their time will live, for the sake of our present incompleteness, in dark hordes in the rafters of our houses and besiege our ears with urgent laments, until we grant them redemption through restoring what has existed since ancient times under the rule of love.

The Red Book (1915/2009), p. 297.

I also think of the possibility that through the achievement of an individual a question enters the world, to which he must provide some kind of answer. For example, my way of posing the question as well as my answer may be unsatisfactory. That being so, someone who has my karma—or I myself—would have to be reborn in order to give a more complete answer. It might happen that I would not be reborn again so long as the world needed no such answer, and that I would be entitled to several hundred years of peace until someone was once more needed who took an interest in these matters and could profitably tackle the task anew. I imagine that for a while a period of rest could ensue, until the stint I had done in my lifetime needed to be taken up again.

Memories, Dreams, Reflections (1962), pp. 318–19.

[I]n the redemption of the individual, the whole past will be redeemed, and that includes all the inferior things as well, the animals, and all the ancestral souls, everything that has not been completed; all creation will be redeemed in the *apokatástasis* [at the time of the Last Judgement], there will be a complete restoration of things as they have been. Primitives express that quite plainly; they say that when the hero steps out of the belly of the monster, not only he comes out but his dead parents who have also been swallowed by the time dragon, and not only his parents but all the people of the tribe who have disappeared in time, and even rivers and mountains and woods, whole countries come out of the whale-dragon. All the vanished memories of former situations will be restored, everything will be brought back to its original condition.

Visions: Notes of the Seminar Given in 1930–1934, Vol. II (7 February 1934), p. 1280.

[O]nce again it was the dead who addressed crucial questions to me. They came—so they said—"back from Jerusalem, where they found not what they sought." This had surprised me greatly at the time, for according to the traditional views the dead are the possessors of great knowledge. People have the idea that the dead know far more than we, for Christian doctrine teaches that in the hereafter we shall "see face to face." Apparently, however, the souls of the dead "know" only what they knew at the moment of death, and nothing beyond that. Hence their endeavour to penetrate into life in order to share in the knowledge of men. I frequently have a feeling that they are standing directly behind us, waiting to hear what answer we will give to them, and what answer to destiny. It seems to me as if they were dependent on the living for receiving answers to their questions, that is, on those who have survived them and exist in a world of change: as if omniscience or, as I might put it, omniconsciousness, were not at their disposal, but could flow only into the psyche of the living, into a soul bound to a body. The mind of the living appears, therefore, to hold an advantage over that of the dead in at least one point: in the capacity for attaining clear and decisive cognitions.

Memories, Dreams, Reflections (1962), p. 308.

If there were to be a conscious existence after death, it would, so it seems to me, have to continue on the level of consciousness attained by humanity, which in any age has an upper though variable limit. There are many human beings who throughout their lives and at the moment of death lag behind their own potentialities, and—even more important—behind the knowledge which has been brought to consciousness by other human beings during their own lifetimes. Hence their demand to attain in death that share of awareness which they had failed to win in life.

Memories, Dreams, Reflections (1962), pp. 308–9.

[D]eath is the more enduring of all things, that which can never be canceled out. Death gives me durability and solidity.

The Red Book (1915/2009), p. 323.

The libido of man contains the two opposite urges or instincts: the instinct to live and the instinct to die. In youth the instinct toward life is stronger, and that is why young people don't cling to life— they have it. The libido as an energetic phenomenon contains the pairs of opposites, otherwise there would be no movement of the libido.

Introduction to Jungian Psychology: Notes of the Seminar on Analytical Psychology Given in 1925, p. 77

Beginning and end are unavoidable aspects of all processes. Yet on closer examination it is extremely difficult to see where one process ends and another begins, since events and processes, beginnings and endings, merge into each other and form, strictly speaking, an indivisible continuum.

"The Soul and Death" (1934), CW 8, § 812.

And so it is—death is indeed a fearful piece of brutality; there is no sense pretending otherwise. It is brutal not only as a physical event, but far more so psychically: a human being is torn away from us, and what remains is the icy stillness of death. There no longer exists any hope of a relationship, for all the bridges have been smashed at one blow. Those who deserve a long life are cut off in the prime of their years, and good-for-nothings live to a ripe old age. This is a cruel reality which we have no right to sidestep. The actual experience of the cruelty and wantonness of death can so embitter us that we conclude there is no merciful God, no justice, and no kindness.

Memories, Dreams, Reflections (1962), p. 314.

Around five o'clock in the afternoon on Sunday the front doorbell began ringing frantically. It was a bright summer day; the two maids were in the kitchen, from which the open square outside the front door could be seen. Everyone immediately looked to see who was there, but there was no one in sight. I was sitting near the doorbell, and not only heard it but saw it moving. We all simply stared at one another. The atmosphere was thick, believe me! Then I knew that something had to happen! The whole house was filled as if there were a crowd present, crammed full of spirits. They were packed deep right up to the door, and the air was so thick it was scarcely possible to breathe. As for myself, I was all a-quiver with the question, "For God's sake, what in the world is this?" Then they cried out in chorus, "We have come back from Jerusalem where we found not what we sought." That is the beginning of the *Septem Sermones* [*Seven Sermons to the Dead*].

Memories, Dreams, Reflections (1962), pp. 190–91.

Community with the dead is what both you and the dead need. Do not commingle with any of the dead, but stand apart from them and give to each his due. The dead demand your expiatory prayers.

The Red Book (1915/2009), p. 342.

The maximum awareness which has been attained anywhere forms, so it seems to me, the upper limit of knowledge to which the dead can attain. That is probably why earthly life is of such great significance, and why it is that what a human being "brings over" at the time of his death is so important. Only here, in life on earth, where the opposites clash together, can the general level of consciousness be raised.

Memories, Dreams, Reflections (1962), p. 311.

There is one necessary but hidden and strange work—a major work—which you must do in secret, for the sake of the dead. He who cannot attain his own visible field and vineyard is held fast by the dead, who demand the work of atonement from him. And until he has fulfilled this, he cannot get to his outer work, since the dead do not let him. He shall have to search his soul and act in stillness at their behest and complete the mystery, so that the dead will not let him. Do not look forward so much, but back and into yourself, so that you will not fail to hear the dead.

The Red Book (1915/2009), p. 297.

In general, the conception people form of the hereafter is largely made up of wishful thinking and prejudices. Thus in most conceptions the hereafter is pictured as a pleasant place. That does not seem so obvious to me. I hardly think that after death we shall be spirited to some lovely flowering meadow. If everything were pleasant and good in the hereafter, surely there would be some friendly communication between us and the blessed spirits, and an outpouring upon us of goodness and beauty from the prenatal state. But there is nothing of the sort. Why is there this insurmountable barrier between the departed and the living? At least half the reports of encounters with the dead tell of terrifying experiences with dark spirits; and it is the rule that the land of the dead observes icy silence, unperturbed by the grief of the bereaved.

Memories, Dreams, Reflections (1962), pp. 320–21.

The souls or spirits of the dead are identical with the psychic activity of the living; they merely continue it. The view that the psyche is a spirit is implicit in this. When therefore something psychic happens in the individual which he feels as belonging to himself, that something is his own spirit. But if anything psychic happens which seems to him strange, then it is somebody else's spirit, and it may be causing a possession. The spirit in the first case corresponds to the subjective attitude, in the latter case to public opinion, to the time-spirit, or to the original, not yet human, anthropoid disposition which we also call the *unconscious*.

"The Phenomenology of the Spirit in Fairytales" (1945/1948), CW 9i, § 388.

Myths are the earliest forms of science. When I speak of things after death, I am speaking out of inner prompting, and can go no further than to tell you dreams and myths that relate to the subject.

Memories, Dreams, Reflections (1962), p. 304.

The cult of the soul seems to be a later extension of the belief in spirits. The souls of the dead are honored as spirits. After death, at least one soul of the dead man continues to exist. In magic, the fact that the soul can be brought under the sway of a foreign influence is of great importance. The souls of dead ancestors are especially significant. Thus, for example, any important new events must be immediately reported to them.

Nietzsche's Zarathustra: Notes of a Seminar Given in 1934–1939, Vol. I (12 December 1934), p. 303.

[W]hile the man who despairs marches toward nothingness, the one who has placed his faith in the archetype follows the tracks of life and lives right into his death. Both, to be sure, remain in uncertainty, but the one lives against his instincts, the other with them.

Memories, Dreams, Reflections (1962), p. 306.

We are so convinced that death is simply the end of a process that it does not ordinarily occur to us to conceive of death as a goal and a fulfilment, as we do without hesitation the aims and purposes of youthful life in its ascendance.

"The Soul and Death" (1934), CW 8, § 797.

Well, you see, I have treated many old people and it's quite interesting to watch what the unconscious is doing with the fact that it is apparently threatened with a complete end. It disregards it. Life behaves as if it were going on, and so I think it is better for an old person to live on, to look forward to the next day, as if he had to spend centuries, and then he lives properly. But when he is afraid, when he doesn't look forward, he looks back, he petrifies, he gets stiff and he dies before his time. But when he's living and looking forward to the great adventure that is ahead, then he lives, and that is about what the unconscious is intending to do. Of course, it's quite obvious that we're all going to die, and this is the sad finale of everything; but nevertheless, there is something in us that doesn't believe it apparently. But this is merely a fact, a psychological fact— it doesn't mean to me that it proves something. It simply is so. For instance, I may not know why we need salt, but we prefer to eat salt, because we feel better. And so when you think in a certain way you may feel considerably better, and I think if you think along the lines of nature then you think properly.

"The 'Face to Face' Interview" (1959), *C. G. Jung Speaking*, p. 438.

One shouldn't attach the dead to the living, otherwise they both get estranged from their proper spheres and are thrown into a state of suffering.

Letter to Count Hermann Keyserling, 25 August 1928, *Letters, Vol. I*, p. 53.

[T]he world, I feel, is far too unitary for there to be a hereafter in which the rule of opposites is completely absent. There, too, is nature, which after its fashion is also God's. The world into which we enter after death will be grand and terrible, like God and like all of nature that we know. Nor can I conceive that suffering should entirely cease.

Memories, Dreams, Reflections (1962), p. 321.

When the vital forces fail, when participating in life is an effort, and the great tiredness settles over everything, death brings the boon of sleep. Once the world has sunk down, there is no desire to see it rise up again. It is only we, the living, who have lost something, and lament this loss. All things pass away, graves are the milestones of existence. For the young, the death of the parents opens a new chapter of life. They are now the carriers of life and the present, and nothing hangs over them any more except an as yet unfulfilled destiny. May you go towards it with all the courage it needs.

Letter to Regula Rohland-Oeri, 23 December 1950, *Letters, Vol. I*,
p. 569.

A man should be able to say he has done his best to form a conception of life after death, or to create some image of it—even if he must confess his failure. Not to have done so is a vital loss. For the question that is posed to him is the age-old heritage of humanity: an archetype, rich in secret life, which seeks to add itself to our own individual life in order to make it whole. Reason sets the boundaries far too narrowly for us, and would have us accept only the known—and that too with limitations—and live in a known framework, just as if we were sure how far life actually extends. As a matter of fact, day after day we live far beyond the bounds of our consciousness; without our knowledge, the life of the unconscious is also going on within us. The more the critical reason dominates, the more impoverished life becomes; but the more of the unconscious, and the more of myth we are capable of making conscious, the more of life we integrate. Overvalued reason has this in common with political absolutism: under its dominion the individual is pauperized.

Memories, Dreams, Reflections (1962), p. 302.

Eleanor Bertine has already given me the news of your illness in a letter I received a few days ago. I wish I could talk to you personally, but one is so far from each other and it is such a long time we are separated from the rest of the world that one feels quite hopeless about a communication. We don't trust even our letters to be capable of jumping over the abyss which yawns between us and the wide world. Still I hope that a good star conveys my letter to you.

As you know, the angel of death has struck me down too and almost succeeded in wiping me off the slate. I have been practically an invalid ever since, recovering very slowly from all the arrows that have pierced me on all sides. Fortunately enough my head has not suffered and I could forget myself in my scientific work. On the whole my illness proved to be a most valuable experience, which gave me the inestimable opportunity of a glimpse behind the veil. The only difficulty is to get rid of the body, to get quite naked and void of the world and the ego-will. When you can give up the crazy will to live and when you seemingly fall into a bottomless mist, then the truly *real* life begins with everything which you were meant to be and never reached. It is something ineffably grand. I was free, completely free and whole, as I never felt before. I found myself 15,000 km. from the earth and I saw it as an immense globe resplendent in an inexpressibly beautiful blue light. I was on a point exactly above the southern end of India, which shone in a bluish silvery light with Ceylon like a shimmering opal in the deep blue sea. I was in the universe, where there was a big solitary rock containing a temple. I saw its entrance illuminated by a thousand small flames of coconut oil. I knew I was to enter the temple and I would reach full knowledge. But at this moment a messenger from the world (which by then was a very insignificant corner of the universe) arrived and said that I was not allowed to depart and at this moment the whole vision collapsed completely. But from then on for three weeks I slept, and was wakeful each night in the universe and experienced the complete vision. Not I was united with somebody or something—*it* was united, it was the *hierosgamos* [the sacred marriage], the mystic Agnus [lamb]. It was a silent invisible festival permeated by an incomparable, indescribable feeling of eternal bliss, such as I never could have imagined as being within reach of human experience. Death is the hardest thing from the outside and as long as we are outside of it. But once inside you taste of such completeness and peace and fulfillment that you don't want to return. As a matter of fact, during the first month after my first vision I suffered from black depressions because I felt that I was recovering. It was like dying. I did not want to live and to return into this fragmentary, restricted, narrow, almost mechanical life, where you were subject to the laws of gravity and cohesion, imprisoned in a system of 3 dimensions and whirled along with other bodies in the turbulent stream of time. There was fullness, meaning fulfillment, *eternal* movement (not movement in time).

Letter to Kristine Mann, 1 February 1945, *Letters, Vol. I*, pp. 357–58.

[O]ne does not receive spiritual rebirth in vain, but for quite a definite purpose. And it is not that you are lifted up into heaven where it would not make any difference, because the whole of heaven consists of twice—or thrice-born ones, and if you are received into the assembly of light and are a little candle, you are nothing. If you are reborn as a candle, you will be sent into the darkness; no sooner is your rebirth rite over than you are sent right down to hell with the just and the unjust.

Visions: Notes of the Seminar Given in 1930–1934, Vol. II (25 January 1933), p. 887.

[W]hen we obtain a complete realization of the self, there comes with it the feeling of immortality. Even in analysis such a moment may come. It is the goal of individuation to reach the sense of the continuation of one's life through the ages. It gives one a feeling of eternity on this earth.

Introduction to Jungian Psychology: Notes of the Seminar on Analytical Psychology Given in 1925, p. 154.

What happens after death is so unspeakably glorious that our imagination and our feelings do not suffice to form even an approximate conception of it. A few days before my sister died her face wore an expression of such inhuman sublimity that I was profoundly frightened.

A child, too, enters into this sublimity, and there detaches himself from this world and his manifold individuations more quickly than the aged. So easily does he become what *you* also are that he apparently vanishes. Sooner or later all the dead become what we also are. But in this reality we know little or nothing about that mode of being, and what shall we still know of this earth after death? The dissolution of our time-bound form in eternity brings no loss of meaning. Rather does the little finger know itself a member of the hand.

Letter to Frau N., 11 July 1944, *Letters, Vol. I*, p. 343.

We shy away from the word "eternal," but I can describe the experience only as the ecstasy of a non-temporal state in which present, past, and future are one. Everything that happens in time had been brought together into a concrete whole. Nothing was distributed over time, nothing could be measured by temporal concepts. The experience may be defined as a state of feeling, but one which cannot be produced by imagination. How can I imagine that I exist simultaneously the day before yesterday, today, and the day after tomorrow? There would be things which would not yet have begun, other things which would be indubitably present, and others again which would already be finished—and yet all this would be one. The only thing that feeling could grasp would be a sum, an iridescent whole, containing all at once expectation of a beginning, surprise at what is now happening, and satisfaction or disappointment with the result of what has happened. One is interwoven into an indescribable whole and yet observes it with complete objectivity.

Memories, Dreams, Reflections (1962), pp. 295–96.

We need the coldness of death to see clearly. Life wants to live and to die, to begin and to end. You are not forced to live eternally, but you can also die, since there is a will in you for both. Life and death must strike a balance in your existence. Today's men need a large slice of death, since too much incorrectness lives in them, and too much correctness died in them. What stays in balance is correct, what disturbs balance is incorrect. But if balance has been attained, then that which preserves it is incorrect and that which disturbs it is correct. Balance is at once life and death. For the completion of life a balance with death is fitting. If I accept death, then my tree greens, since dying increases life. If I plunge into the death encompassing the world, then my buds break open. How much our life needs death!

Joy at the smallest things comes to you only when you have accepted death. But if you look out greedily for all that you could still live, then nothing is great enough for your pleasure, and the smallest things that continue to surround you are no longer a joy. Therefore I behold death, since it teaches me how to live.

If you accept death, it is altogether like a frosty night and an anxious misgiving, but a frosty night in a vineyard full of sweet grapes. You will soon take pleasure in your wealth. Death ripens. One needs death to be able to harvest the fruit. Without death, life would be meaningless, since the long-lasting rises again and denies its own meaning. To be, and to enjoy your being, you need death, and limitation enables you to fulfill your being.

The Red Book (1915/2009), pp. 274–75.

This star is the God and the goal of man.

This is his one guiding God,

in him man goes to his rest,

toward him goes the long journey of the soul after death,

in him everything that man withdraws from the greater world shines
    resplendently.

To this one God man shall pray.

Prayer increases the light of the star,

it throws a bridge across death,

it prepares life for the smaller world, and assuages the hopeless desires
    of the greater.

When the greater world turns cold, the star shines.

The Red Book (1917/2009), p. 354.

Suggested Further Reading

The Archive for Research in Archetypal Symbolism. *The Book of Symbols.* Editor-in-Chief, Ami Ronnberg, Editor, Kathleen Martin. Cologne: Taschen, 2010.

Bennet, E. A. *What Jung Really Said.* New York: Schocken, 1983.

———. *C. G. Jung.* Asheville, NC: Chiron, 2006.

Bishop, Paul. *Carl Jung (Brief Lives).* London: Reaktion Books, 2014.

Campbell, Joseph, ed. *The Portable Jung.* New York: Penguin Books, 1976.

Dourley, John P. *The Illness That We Are: A Jungian Critique of Christianity.* Toronto: Inner City, 1984.

———. *A Strategy for a Loss of Faith: Jung's Proposal.* Toronto: Inner City, 1992.

———. *On Behalf of the Mystical Fool: Jung on the Religious Situation.* London and New York: Routledge, 2010.

Edinger, Edward. *The Creation of Consciousness: Jung's Myth for Modern Man.* Toronto: Inner City, 1984.

Hannah, Barbara. *Jung: His Life and Work. A Biographical Memoir.* New York: Putnam's, 1976

———. *The Inner Journey: Lectures and Essays on Jungian Psychology.* Toronto: Inner City, 2000.

Harding, M. Esther. *The Parental Image: Its Injury and Reconstruction.* Toronto: Inner City, 2003.

Hillman, James, *The Soul's Code: In Search of Character and Calling.* New York: Random House, 1996.

Hollis, James. *The Middle Passage: From Misery to Meaning in Midlife.* Toronto: Inner City, 1993.

Humbert, Elie. *C. G. Jung: The Fundamentals of Theory and Practice.* Ashville, NC: Chiron, 1988.

Jacobi, Jolande. *Complex, Archetype, Symbol in the Psychology of C. G. Jung.* Princeton: Princeton University Press, 1971.

Jaffé, Aniela. *Jung's Last Years.* Dallas: Spring, 1984.

———. *The Myth of Meaning in the Work of C. G. Jung.* Zürich: Daimon, 1984.

Johnson, Robert A. *He: Understanding Masculine Psychology.* New York: Harper and Row, 1977.

———. *She: Understanding Feminine Psychology.* New York: Harper and Row, 1977.

———. *We: Understanding the Psychology of Romantic Love.* New York: Harper and Row, 1983.

———. *Balancing Heaven and Earth: A Memoir.* New York: HarperCollins, 1998.

Jung, C. G. *Modern Man in Search of a Soul*. New York: Harcourt, Brace, 1933.

———. *Word and Image*. Edited by Aniela Jaffé. Princeton: Princeton University Press, 1979.

Jung, Emma. *Animus and Anima. Two Papers*. Putnam, Connecticut: Spring, 2008.

Samuels, Andrew, Shorter, Bani, and Plaut, Fred. *A Critical Dictionary of Jungian Analysis*. London: Routledge, 1986.

Shamdasani, Sonu. *Jung and the Making of Modern Psychology: The Dream of a Science*. Cambridge: Cambridge University Press, 2003.

———. *C. G. Jung: A Biography in Books*. New York and London: W. W. Norton, 2012.

Sharp, Daryl. *C. G. Jung Lexicon: A Primer of Terms and Concepts*. Toronto: Inner City, 1991.

———. *Jung Uncorked: Rare Vintages from the Cellar of Analytical Psychology*. Four Volumes. Toronto: Inner City, 2008–2013.

Sherry, Jay. *Carl Gustav Jung: Avant-Garde Conservative*. New York: Pagrave-Macmillan, 2010.

Stein, Murray, ed. *Jungian Analysis*. Boston: Shambala, 1984.

———. *Jung's Map of the Soul: An Introduction*. Chicago: Open Court, 1998.

———. *Minding the Self: Jungian Meditations on Contemporary Spirituality*. London and New York: Routledge, 2014.

Stevens, Anthony, ed. *The Essential Jung*. Princeton: Princeton University Press, 1983.

———. *Jung: A Very Short Introduction*. Oxford: Oxford University Press, 1994.

———. *The Talking Cure*. Three Volumes: 1 *The Founding Fathers— Sigmund Freud and C. G. Jung*, 2 *Warring Egos, Object Relations and Attachment Theory*, 3 *The Way Ahead—Jung and Evolutionary Psychotherapy*. Toronto: Inner City, 2013.

Storr, Anthony: *On Jung*. Princeton: Princeton University Press, 1999.

Tacey, David. *How to Read Jung*. London: Granta Books, 2006.

———, ed. *The Jung Reader*. New York and London: Routledge, 2012.

von Franz, Marie-Louise. *The Way of the Dream. Dr. Marie-Louise von Franz in Conversation with Fraser Boa*. Toronto: Windrose Films, 1988.

———. *Psychotherapy*. Boston: Shambala, 1993.

———. *Creation Myths*. Boston: Shambala, 1995.

———. *C. G. Jung: His Myth in Our Time*. Toronto: Inner City, 1998.

———. *The Classic Jungian and The Classic Jungian Tradition*. Edited by James A. Hall and Daryl Sharp. Toronto: Inner City, 2008.

Wilhelm, Richard. *The Secret of the Golden Flower: A Chinese Book of Life*.

Translated and explained by Richard Wilhelm. With a commentary by C. G. Jung. New York: Harcourt, Brace, 1962.

Wilhelm, Richard, and Baynes, Cary F., trans.. *The I Ching or Book of Changes*. Foreword by C. G. Jung. Princeton: Princeton University Press, 1967.

Works Cited

Collected Works (*CW*) in 20 Volumes. Edited by Sir Herbert Read, Michael Fordham, Gerhard Adler, and William McGuire as executive editor. Translated by R.F.C. Hull. Twenty volumes, Bollingen Series 20. Princeton: Princeton University Press, 1953–1979.

Collected Works 1, *Psychiatric Studies*, 1970.

Collected Works 2, *Experimental Researches*.Translated by Leopold Stein in collaboration with Diana Riviere, 1973.

Collected Works 3, *The Psychogenesis of Mental Disease*, 1960.

Collected Works 4, *Freud and Psychoanalysis*, 1961.

Collected Works 5, *Symbols of Transformation. An Analysis of the Prelude to a Case of Schizophrenia.* 2nd ed., 1967.

Collected Works 6, *Psychological Types.* A revision by R.F.C. Hull of the translation by H. G. Baynes, 1971.

Collected Works 7, *Two Essays on Analytical Psychology.* 2nd ed., 1966.

Collected Works 8, *The Structure and Dynamics of the Psyche.* 2nd ed., 1969.

Collected Works 9i, *The Archetypes and the Collective Unconscious.* 2nd ed., 1969.

Collected Works 9ii, *Aion. Researches in to the Phenomenology of the Self.* 2nd ed., 1968.

Collected Works 10, *Civilization in Transition.* 2nd ed., 1970.

Collected Works 11, *Psychology and Religion: East and West.* 2nd ed., 1969.

Collected Works 12, *Psychology and Alchemy.* 2nd ed., 1968.

Collected Works 13, *Alchemical Studies*, 1967.

Collected Works 14, *Mysterium Coniunctionis. An Inquiry into the Separation and Synthesis of Psychic Opposites in Alchemy.* 2nd ed., 1970.

Collected Works 15, *The Spirit in Man, Art, and Literature*, 1966.

Collected Works 16, *The Practice of Psychotherapy. Essays on the Psychology of the Transference and Other Subjects.* 2nd., 1966.

Collected Works 17, *The Development of Personality*, 1954.

Collected Works 18, *The Symbolic Life. Miscellaneous Writings*, 1954.

Collected Works 19, *General Bibliography of C. G. Jungs Writings.* Compiled by Lisa Ress with collaborators, 1979.

Collected Works 20, *General Index to the Collected Works of C. G. Jung.* Compiled by Barbara Foryan and Janet M. Glover, 1979.

The Red Book. Liber Novus. Edited and introduced by Sonu Shamdasani. Translated by Mark Kyburz, John Peck, and Sonu Shamdasani. Philemon Series. New York and London: W. W. Norton, 2009.

The Question of Psychological Types. The Correspondence of C. G. Jung and

Hans Schmid-Guisan, 1915–1916. Edited by John Beebe and Ernst Falzeder. Translated by Ernst Falzeder with the collaboration of Tony Woolfson. Philemon Series. Princeton and Oxford: Princeton University Press, 2013.

Introduction to Jungian Psychology. Notes of the Seminar on Analytical Psychology Given in 1925. Revised with a new introduction and updates by Sonu Shamdasani. Philemon Series. Princeton: Princeton University Press, 2012.

Dream Analysis. Notes of the Seminar Given in 1928–1930 by C. G. Jung. Edited by William McGuire. Princeton: Princeton University Press, 1984.

Visions. Notes of the Seminar Given in 1930–1934 by C. G. Jung. Edited by Claire Douglas. Two Volumes. Princeton: Princeton University Press: 1997.

The Psychology of Kundalini Yoga. Notes of the Seminar Given in 1932 by C. G. Jung. Edited and introduced by Sonu Shamdasani. Princeton: Princeton University Press, 1996.

Nietzsches Zarathustra. Notes of the Seminar Given in 1934–1939 by C. G. Jung. Edited by James L. Jarrett. Two Volumes. Princeton: Princeton University Press, 1988.

Children's Dreams. Notes from the Seminar Given in 1936–1940 by C. G. Jung. Edited by Lorenz Jung and Maria Meyer-Grass. Translated by Ernst Falzeder with the collaboration of Tony Woolfson. Philemon Series. Princeton: Princeton University Press, 2008.

The Jung-White Letters. Edited by Ann Conrad Lammers and Adrian Cunningham. Consulting Editor Murray Stein. Philemon Series. Hove, East Sussex, and New York: Routledge, 2007.

C. G. Jung Letters. Selected and edited by Gerhard Adler in collaboration with Aniela Jaffe. Translated by R. F. C. Hull. Two Volumes, Vol. 1, 1906–1950, Vol. 2, 1951–1961. Princeton: Princeton University Press, 1973 and 1976.

Memories, Dreams, Reflections. Recorded and edited by Aniela Jaffe. Translated by Richard and Clara Winston. New York: Pantheon Books, 1963.

Meetings with Jung. Conversations recorded during the years 1946–1961 by E. A. Bennet. Zurich: Daimon, 1985.

C. G. Jung Speaking. Interviews and Encounters. Edited by William McGuire and R.F.C. Hull. Princeton: Princeton University Press, 1977.

Man and His Symbols. Conceived and edited by Carl G. Jung. New York: Doubleday, 1964.

C. G. Jung. Psychological Reflections. A New Anthology of His Writings 1905–1961. Edited by Jolande Jacobi in collaboration with R.F.C. Hull. Princeton: Princeton University Press. Second edition, 1970.

Index

A page number which appears more than once indicates multiple quotes on that page.

totality of man. *See* self

touching the unconscious, 10

traditional teachings, 295

"Transcendent Function, The," CW 8, 23–24, 26, 77, 86–88, 90, 225, 226, 234, 261

transcendent function, 26, 27, 46, 47, 77, 154, 255, 295–296. *See also* mediatory product; union of opposites

transference, 89, 91, 95. *See also* projection; psychic infection

transform/transformation, 273, 283; in alchemy, 248; imperfect, 248; psychological, 83, 97, 193

"Transformation Symbolism in the Mass," CW 11, 3, 51, 112–113, 193, 254, 290

transformer, symbol as, 62

treasure, motif of hidden, 296

treatment vs. development in analysis, 94

tree, cosmic, 247. *See also* alchemy

truth, 57, 58, 100, 266, 268, 269–270, 277, 281; religious, 197; in symbols, 58

two-handed God, 180

"2,000-Year Old Man, The," *C.G. Jung Speaking,* 29

type/typology, 124–125, 125, 126, 158; classes of, 126; functions of, 126, 127

unconscious/unconsciousness, 4–7, 32, 35, 39, 49, 54, 62, 70, 81, 85, 119, 131, 148, 149–150, 174, 177, 180, 187, 190, 202, 206, 209, 211, 213, 233, 239, 240, 250, 254, 262, 265, 310, 313; and alchemy, 250; alien figure as, 301; and animus, 44, 136; and art, 146, 229; assimilation of, 4; attitudes and, 13; autonomy of, 9–10; collective, 3, 9, 12–13, 29, 82, 153, 229, 232, 264; compensations, 38; complexes in, 31; confrontation with, 235–236; and conscious, 22, 23, 59, 106, 113,116–117, 128, 143, 234, 235, 241, 242, 283, 289–290;

content(s) of, 8, 24, 25; and creativity, 227, 229; danger of, 10–11; darkness as, 254; and death, 305; disalliance with, 6; and dreams, 80; experience of, 12; Freud on, 85; function of, 19; and God, 173, 192; harmony with, 11; images from, 246; independence of, 71; individuation, 298; interference of, 24; of man, 133; mask of, 10; and memory, 7; as mother, 7; movements, 225; mutual, 90; nature and, 11, 14; in old age, 311–312; opposite in the, 10, 149; path to, 272; people, 13–14; personal, 11, 12, 13, 45, 47, 149, 264; in personality, 116–117, 236; personification of, 238; as primal mother, 7; projection of, 25; purposes, 7; relation to, 158; and religion, 13, 179, 187, 192; role of, 10; and shadow, 34; symbols from, 298; time in, 24; touching, 10; union with conscious, 59, 301; undeveloped personality, 120; of woman, 133

understanding, 268, 277

Undiscovered Self, The, CW 10, 13, 21–22, 34, 142, 179, 179, 194–195, 195, 199–200, 200

unity of the psyche, 275

unlived life, 103, 109, 110, 271; of parents, 103, 109, 110

union, of conscious and unconscious, 59, 301; of rational and irrational, 58; of opposites, 27, 49, 147, 153, 154, 155, 166, 184, 247, 248, 256, 289, 297

vessels, spirits in, 304

victory and defeat, 284

virtues, and evil, 213

vision(s), 67; during illness, 313–315

Visions, Vol. I, 11, 11, 22, 35, 35–36, 38, 40, 44, 45–46, 50, 52, 70, 71, 72, 95, 107, 107–108, 121–122, 122, 128, 129, 136, 136, 137, 139, 143–144, 147–148, 151, 153, 154–155, 158,

The Collected Works of C. G. Jung

Editors: Sir Herbert Read, Michael Fordham, and Gerhard Adler; executive editor, William McGuire. Translated by R.F.C. Hull, except where noted.

The Collected Works of C. G. Jung is now available in a complete digital edition that is full-text searchable. The Complete Digital Edition includes volumes 1–18 and volume 19, the Complete Bibliography of C. G. Jung's Writings. Volumes 1–18 of The Complete Digital Edition are also available for individual purchase. For ordering information, please go to http://press.princeton.edu/titles/10294.html.

1. PSYCHIATRIC STUDIES (1957; 2d ed., 1970)
　　On the Psychology and Pathology of So-Called Occult
　　　　Phenomena (1902)
　　On Hysterical Misreading (1904)
　　Cryptomnesia (1905)
　　On Manic Mood Disorder (1903)
　　A Case of Hysterical Stupor in a Prisoner in Detention (1902)
　　On Simulated Insanity (1903)
　　A Medical Opinion on a Case of Simulated Insanity (1904)
　　A Third and Final Opinion on Two Contradictory Psychiatric
　　　　Diagnoses (1906)
　　On the Psychological Diagnosis of Facts (1905)

2. EXPERIMENTAL RESEARCHES (1973)
　　Translated by Leopold Stein in collaboration with Diana Riviere
　　STUDIES IN WORD ASSOCIATION (1904–7, 1910)
　　The Associations of Normal Subjects (by Jung and F. Riklin)
　　　　An Analysis of the Associations of an Epileptic
　　The Reaction-Time Ratio in the Association Experiment
　　Experimental Observations on the Faculty of Memory
　　Psychoanalysis and Association Experiments
　　The Psychological Diagnosis of Evidence
　　Association, Dream, and Hysterical Symptom
　　The Psychopathological Significance of the Association Experiment
　　Disturbances in Reproduction in the Association Experiment
　　The Association Method
　　The Family Constellation
　　PSYCHOPHYSICAL RESEARCHES (1907–08)

(continued)

On the Psychophysical Relations of the Association Experiment
Psychophysical Investigations with the Galvanometer and
    Pneumograph in Normal and Insane Individuals (by F. Peterson
    and Jung)
Further Investigations on the Galvanic Phenomenon and Respiration
    in Normal and Insane Individuals (by C. Ricksher and Jung)
Appendix: Statistical Details of Enlistment (1906); New Aspects
    of Criminal Psychology (1908); The Psychological Methods of
    Investiga- tion Used in the Psychiatric Clinic of the University of
    Zurich (1910); On the Doctrine Complexes ([1911] 1913); On the
    Psychological Di- agnosis of Evidence (1937)

3. THE PSYCHOGENESIS OF MENTAL DISEASE (1960)
    The Psychology of Dementia Praecox (1907)
    The Content of the Psychoses (1908/1914)
    On Psychological Understanding (1914)
    A Criticism of Bleuler's Theory of Schizophrenic Negativism (1911)
    On the Importance of the Unconscious in Psychology
        (1914)
    On the Problem of Psychogenesis in Mental Disease (1919)
    Mental Disease and the Psyche (1928)
    On the Psychogenesis of Schizophrenia (1939)
    Recent Thoughts on Schizophrenia (1957)
    Schizophrenia (1958)

4. FREUD AND PSYCHOANALYSIS (1967)
    Freud's Theory of Hysteria: A Reply to Aschaffenburg (1906)
    The Freudian Theory of Hysteria (1908)
    The Analysis of Dreams (1909)
    A Contribution to the Psychology of Rumour (1910–11)
    On the Significance of Number Dreams (1910–11)
    Morton Prince, "The Mechanism and Interpretation of Dreams":
        A Critical Review (1911)
    On the Criticism of Psychoanalysis (1910)
    Concerning Psychoanalysis (1912)
    The Theory of Psychoanalysis (1913)
    General Aspects of Psychoanalysis (1913)
    Psychoanalysis and Neurosis (1916)
    Some Crucial Points in Psychoanalysis: A Correspondence between
        Dr. Jung and Dr. Loÿ (1914)
    Prefaces to "Collected Papers on Analytical Psychology" (1916, 1917)
    The Significance of the Father in the Destiny of the Individual
        (1909/1949)

Introduction to Kranefeldt's "Secret Ways of the Mind" (1930)
Freud and Jung: Contrasts (1929)

5. SYMBOLS OF TRANSFORMATION ([1911–12/1952] 1956; 2d ed., 1967)

   PART I

   Introduction
   Two Kinds of Thinking
   The Miller Fantasies: Anamnesis
   The Hymn of Creation
   The Song of the Moth

   PART II

   Introduction
   The Concept of Libido
   The Transformation of Libido
   The Origin of the Hero
   Symbols of the Mother and Rebirth
   The Battle for Deliverance from the Mother
   The Dual Mother
   The Sacrifice
   Epilogue
   Appendix: The Miller Fantasies

6. PSYCHOLOGICAL TYPES ([1921] 1971)
   A revision by R.F.C. Hull of the translation by H. G. Baynes
   Introduction
   The Problem of Types in the History of Classical and Medieval
      Thought
   Schiller's Idea on the Type Problem
   The Apollonian and the Dionysian
   The Type Problem in Human Character
   The Type Problem in Poetry
   The Type Problem in Psychopathology
   The Type Problem in Aesthetics
   The Type Problem in Modern Philosophy
   The Type Problem in Biography
   General Description of the Types
   Definitions
   Epilogue
   Four Papers on the Psychological Typology (1913, 1925, 1931, 1936)

7. TWO ESSAYS ON ANALYTICAL PSYCHOLOGY (1953;
   2d ed., 1966)
   On the Psychology of the Unconscious (1917/1926/1943)

(continued)

(continued)

(continued)

18. THE SYMBOLIC LIFE (1954)
    Translated by R.F.C. Hull and others
    Miscellaneous Writings

19. COMPLETE BIBLIOGRAPHY OF C. G. JUNG'S WRITINGS
    (1976; 2d ed., 1992)

20. GENERAL INDEX OF THE COLLECTED WORKS (1979)

THE ZOFINGIA LECTURES (1983)
    Supplementary Volume A to the Collected Works.
    Edited by William McGuire, translated by
    Jan van Heurck, introduction by
    Marie-Louise von Franz

PSYCHOLOGY OF THE UNCONSCIOUS ([1912] 1992)
    A STUDY OF THE TRANSFORMATIONS AND SYMBOLISMS OF THE
    LIBIDO. A CONTRIBUTION TO THE HISTORY OF THE EVOLUTION
    OF THOUGHT
    Supplementary Volume B to the Collected Works.
    Translated by Beatrice M. Hinkle,
    introduction by William McGuire

Notes to C. G. Jung's Seminars

DREAM ANALYSIS ([1928–30] 1984)
    Edited by William McGuire

NIETZSCHE'S *ZARATHUSTRA* ([1934–39] 1988)
    Edited by James L. Jarrett (2 vols.)

ANALYTICAL PSYCHOLOGY ([1925] 1989)
    Edited by William McGuire

THE PSYCHOLOGY OF KUNDALINI YOGA ([1932] 1996)
    Edited by Sonu Shamdasani

INTERPRETATION OF VISIONS ([1930–34] 1997)
    Edited by Claire Douglas

CHILDREN'S DREAMS ([1936–40] 2008)
    Edited by Lorenz Jung and Maria Meyer-Grass, translated by Ernst
    Falzeder with the collaboration of Tony Woolfson